THE WAGNERS OF BRIGHTON

THE
WAGNERS
OF
BRIGHTON

Anthony Wagner
and
Antony Dale

PHILLIMORE

1983

Published by
PHILLIMORE & CO. LTD.
London and Chichester

Head Office: Shopwyke Hall,
Chichester, Sussex, England

ISBN 0 85033 445 4

Typeset in the United Kingdom by:
Fidelity Processes - Selsey - Sussex

Printed and bound in Great Britain by
THE CAMELOT PRESS LTD.
Southampton, Hants.

'Tote rien se torne en declin,
Tot chiet, tot muert, tot vait a fain

.   .   .   .   .   .

Se par cler ne est mise en livre
                Robert Wace
                        (1135-1174)

CONTENTS

*Chapters I, II, VI and VII are the work of Sir Anthony Wagner;
Chapters III, IV and V are that of Antony Dale.*

LIST OF ILLUSTRATIONS

(*between pages 86 and 87*)

WAGNERS OF GOLDBERG, COBURG AND LONDON

HENRY MICHELL WAGNER, who became Vicar of Brighton in 1824, was the great-grandson of Melchior Wagner of Pall Mall. Melchior came to England from Germany about 1709 and ended up as hatter by appointment to Kings George I, II and III, and founder of a prosperous family business. H. M. Wagner's mother's father, Henry Michell, of Sussex yeoman stock, had been Vicar of Brighton from 1744 to 1789. These two elements of wealth and a clerical tradition, which were thus a part of the nineteenth century Brighton Wagners' inheritance, had been enhanced by Melchior Wagner's marriage to the daughter of a French Huguenot refugee and his son's marriage to the granddaughter of another. In the Michell family moreover there were classical scholars of distinction.

The Wagner line can be taken back in Germany three generations beyond Melchior to one Michael Wagner, a tailor of Goldberg in Silesia, who was dead by October 1629 when his son Caspar, also a tailor, married Ursula, daughter of Georg Kirsch of the Wolfgasse in that town. Goldberg which owes its origin and name to a gold mine, is a small ancient town (population 6,804 in 1905, given civic rights in 1211) formerly in the Duchy of Liegnitz, whose protestant ducal family (of the Piast line, whose branches divided Silesia among them) expired in 1675, when the duchy came into the possession of the Holy Roman Emperor and so under Catholic dominance. Silesia, lying on the frontier of East and West, of German, Pole and Bohemian, has seen such alternations through the centuries and is now once more in Poland.

Presumably it was this political and religious change that caused Hans Heinrich Wagner (1650–1724), Caspar's son, to remove himself in 1677 some 250 miles westward from Goldberg to Coburg, where partitions and transfers among the Saxe-Altenburg and Saxe-Gotha branches of the Saxon house of Wettin had not affected the Lutheran faith of the rulers of the population. It has always been known from the family bible entry made by George Wagner (1722–1796) that his father, Melchior, was born at Coburg on the 7th July 1685. But it was not, probably, until Henry Wagner (1840–1926), the first genealogist of the family, made enquiries in Coburg in 1862 or a little before, that the earlier generations came to light. Numerous entries of Wagner baptisms, marriages and burials were then found in the registers of the ancient church of St. Moritz there and from these a pedigree of the Coburg Wagners was easily constructed. From this it appeared that Melchior, son of Hans Heinrich Wagner, hatmaker, was born and was baptised there on the 7th July 1685, his godfather being Melchior Wille, hatter and vintner.

The remarkably full and complete archives of the town of Coburg contain also a far rarer type of record, namely a series of complete census returns (*Seelen-register*) of all its inhabitants, house by house, at successive dates. In the earliest of these, dated 1678, the Wagner family has not been found. But two households of them appear in the census of 1721; that of Melchior's father Johann (or Hans) Heinrich Wagner, and that of Melchior's elder brother, another Johann Heinrich.

1

The father was living in the street called the Steinweg, was a hat maker, aged 71, had lived in Coburg 44 years and had been born in 'Golberg' (that is, Goldberg). Living also in the house were his 48-year-old second wife, an unmarried daughter of 18, a 16-year-old apprentice, a clothworker of 42 with an 18-year-old wife and two children, and another 44-year-old man of unstated occupation. From the *Proclamationsbuch* we learn that on 21 June 1678 Hans Heinrich Wagner, citizen and hatmaker, son of the late Caspar Wagner, citizen and tailor of Goldberg in Silesia, and Anna Catharina, daughter of the late Wolff Bauer and stepdaughter of Hans Müller, the younger, hatter, had announced their intention to marry— as they duly did at St. Moritz on 8 July.

These entries took Henry Wagner to Goldberg, where in 1863 he duly obtained a certificate of the baptism on 16 October 1650 of Hans Heinrich, son of Caspar Wagner, tailor, and then and later certificates of a number of other Wagner entries. The ground was gone over again for A. R. Wagner in 1934 by Professor Leopold Oelenheinz of Coburg—the Coburg records personally and those of Goldberg by correspondence—when some further points came to light. In particular the house in the Steinweg, Coburg, which Hans Heinrich Wagner purchased for 500 florins on 18 April 1688, was identified (by tracing successive ownerships) as the present Number 26, and A.R.W. saw it when he visited Coburg for the second time in 1973. Further Coburg records of the family were at that time brought to light by Dr. Freiherr von Andrian-Werburg, Oberregierungsarchivrat of the Coburg Staatsarchiv, by Herr Backhaus, Stadtoberinspektor of the Coburg Stadtarchiv, and by Herr Herbert Appeltshauser of Coburg, to all of whom due gratitude is recorded.

The record of the first marriage of Caspar Wagner on 28 October 1629 shows that his father was Michael Wagner, tailor of Goldberg, then deceased. The earliest Wagner entry found at Goldberg is the baptism on 14 December 1622 of Melchior, son of Georg Wagner, serving man, while on 12 September 1635, Balthasar, son of Baltzer Wagner, day labourer (*taglöhner*) was baptized. Thus in the space of a few years the names attributed to the three magi or kings, whose relics were brought to Cologne by Barbarossa in 1162, Caspar, Melchior and Balthazar, occur as those of Wagners in Goldberg.

The names and occupations of godparents are given in the baptismal records and the occupations indicate the social position of the Wagners. At Goldberg we have a girdler, a deacon, a butcher, a hatter, a head miller (*Obermüller*), a court juror (*Hofe-Schöppe*), a senator (or the like, being styled *Herr*), a baker, a revenue clerk, clothiers, a town-juror (*Stadt-Schöppe*) and a millowner. At Coburg the occupations of godparents and marriage connections include hatmakers, a labourer in a vineyard, a woolcomber, a shoemaker, a miller, a pewterer, a gold and silver smith, a stocking weaver, a rooter, a farrier, a waistband maker, a baker, a saddler, a ropemaker, a journeyman carpenter and a potter.

One recorded incident brings Hans Heinrich Wagner briefly to life. On 3 June 1690 one Valtin Hähnlein brought a charge that when they two, with Hans Schmitt, a saddler, and Christoph Aumüller had been playing bowls together, Wagner had thrown the bowl away and, as they came to words with each other, struck the complainant in the face with his fist, so that his nose and mouth bled. On 27 June it was noted that Hans Heinrich Wagner was sentenced to pay two florins for this and had done so.[1]

By his first wife Anna Catharina, daughter of Wolfgang Bauer (then dead, who had been at different dates a soldier, day labourer and vineyard worker), whom he married at Coburg, two years after he arrived there, in 1679, Hans Heinrich Wagner had four sons and two daughters. All the sons were hatters and Johann Heinrich, the eldest, is described in the burial entry of his third wife at Coburg in 1751 as 'Hof huthmacher', so presumably held an appointment as hatter to the ducal court. Melchior, the second son, came to England in 1708 or 1709. The other two sons, Johann Georg (1688–1760) and Johann Thomas (1691–1764), remained in Coburg. Johann Georg's son Johann Andreas (b. 1722), likewise a hatter, moved to Hanover and left descendants traceable to the present day in Peru, Mexico and the United States of America.

The family bible tells us that Melchior Wagner came to England in the latter part of the reign of Queen Anne, and as the second half of that reign began in 1708, while Melchior was naturalized on 13 July 1709,[2] we have a close dating for his arrival. On 18 May 1714 he was married (by licence) at Greenwich to Mary Anne, daughter and eldest child of Antoine or Anthony Teulon, a French protestant refugee from Valleraugue in the Cévennes, who had established himself at Greenwich as a feltmaker and hatter by 8 January 1691 when this daughter was born there. It has been possible in recent years to establish the Teulon male line ancestry in Valleraugue for six generations before the refugee and back to the early sixteenth century. The name has been found there much earlier still and female lines of ancestry have been traced back further again, through families of minor nobility (d'Algrefeuille, d'Assas, de Montgros, de Peyregrosse). In two instances descents back to the twelfth century can be claimed. The research was carried out for A.R.W. between 1967 and 1971 by M. Yves Chassin du Guerny of the Archives Départementales du Gard at Nîmes and the results were embodied in a paper contributed to the Proceedings of the Huguenot Society of London (Vol. XXI, part 6, 1971, pp. 569–608, Sir Anthony Wagner, 'The Teulon Ancestry in France').

The Teulons were small proprietors at the Mas de Malet (now Mallet), high up in the Hérault valley, above Valleraugue, between the mountains of l'Espérou and l'Aigoual. Guillaume Teulon of the Mas de Malet is mentioned in 1346. The line is traced continuously from a Jean Teulon, deceased in 1533. In the 16th and 17th centuries the family occupations include a priest, three notaries, a merchant, a tailor, three woolcarders, a shoemaker, a hatter, a carpenter, a merchant in Catalonia, and a captain in the army, whose son acquired a fief and became Seigneur de Birenque. The refugee's great-great-grandfather was a protestant by 1603 and his line continued protestant until the Revocation of the Edict of Nantes in 1685. On 23 October in that year Jean Teulon of Malet abjured the protestant faith. When he came to make his will on 3 April 1716, he named his elder son Jean as deceased and left to his younger son Antoine 'quy est hors du Royaume cinq sols pour luy estre payé'. This Antoine was the protestant refugee, who probably went first to Jersey and then to England. His wife Anne, daughter of Pierre Desfaux of Meyrueis near Valleraugue, was described in her burial entry of 1730 at Lee in Kent as 'Mrs. Ann Toolin from Lewisham of the Island of Jersey' and a portrait of her in the possession of her descendant Mrs. Donald Barker has long been known as 'Anne of Jersey'. Antoine's subsequent settlement in Greenwich must have been as one of the Huguenot colony there led

3

by Henry de Massue, Marquis de Ruvigny, who came to England in 1686 aged about 80 and died at Greenwich in 1689. His son and namesake was in 1697 made Earl of Galway. John Evelyn records that on 24 April 1687 at Greenwich 'I staied to heare the French sermon, which succeded (in the same place, & after use of the English liturgie translated into French) the congregation consisting of about 100 French Protestants refugiés from the Persecution of which Monsieur de Rouvigny (present) was the chiefe, & had obtain'd the use of the Church after the Parish had ended their owne Service'. Evelyn went on other occasions to French services in Ruvigny's private chapel in a room of the Queen's house.[3] The Marquis later built the Huguenots a chapel of their own in London Street, Greenwich.

Antoine or Anthony Teulon, hatmaker of Greenwich, had letters of denization 11 March 1699/1700 and was naturalized by Act of Parliament 1 April 1708.* He was buried at Lee, near by, in 1740 (see p. 172). His wife's brother, John Desfaux, likewise a hatter of Greenwich, was naturalized in 1709 and died in 1727. Besides Mary Anne Wagner, Anthony Teulon had two other daughters and two sons. The elder son John (baptized at Greenwich in 1698) settled in Scotland where in 1746 he was appointed Ross Herald—the first of my family known to me to have been linked with the heraldic profession. He died in 1765 and was buried in the Greyfriars Burial Ground in Edinburgh. Anthony Teulon's younger son and namesake was, like his father, a feltmaker and hatter of Greenwich, where he died in 1776. His son, who will be mentioned later, Melchior Seymour Teulon (1734-1806) was apprenticed in 1748 to his uncle Melchior Wagner. The sisters, Anne and Elizabeth, were both married to Huguenots from the Cévennes; Anne in 1728 to John Deshons from Ganges; Elizabeth in 1719 to John Liron from Meyrueis.

It may be that Melchior Wagner, arriving from Germany about 1709 to pursue the hatter's trade, found his first footing here among these French protestant hatters already established in Greenwich. His own great opportunity came, however, less than three months after his marriage, when in August 1714 a German prince from Hanover succeeded to the throne of Great Britain as King George I. Melchior seems at this time to have been living in Soho, a great settlement of highly skilled foreign craftsmen, for it was at St. Anne's, Soho, between 1715 and 1720 that his first five children were christened or buried. On 11 July 1717, however, he received a warrant of appointment as hatter to King George I[4] and at some date between 1717 and 1719 he moved into a house belonging to the Crown on the south side of Pall Mall. Dr. F. H. W. Sheppard, General Editor of the Survey of London, gave this information from the rate books of the parish

His younger son and namesake Anthony Teulon (1700-1776) is shown in the Church Rate book as living in 1744 in a house on the site of the present Manor House, Old Road, Lee, now the repository for the Archives and Local History Department of the Borough of Lewisham. This was originally a large farmhouse built about 1700 and added to at different dates. By about 1707 it had been divided into two separate residences and the records appear to indicate that pairs of tenants occupied it together. Other Huguenots lived near by. From 1742 to 1744 the house is shown as vacant, so that it is not clear whether Anthony the elder lived and died here or elsewhere in Lee.

Daniel Jamineau lived in the house next to the east in the early 18th century, where Sir George Champion followed him. M. Grimani lived next to the west and beyond him the Papillon family so that of the seven large houses in Lee four had Huguenot associations.

*Information from Mrs. Edwyn Birchenough of Lee.

of St. James, Piccadilly and added that this house must have been further east than No. 93 (later renumbered 89), to which the Wagners had moved by 1738 and where they remained for about a century. In Pall Mall Melchior's youngest son George was born on 4 December 1722 and at his baptism the sponsors were King George I and Dorothy, Viscountess Townshend (1686-1726), the sister of Sir Robert Walpole. The King's christening presents were a jewelled watch stolen from the house of Malcolm Wagner (1856-1933), and a silver-mounted tortoise shell snuff box.

It is tantalizing that the qualities of skill, enterprise and personality which, before he was forty, had brought Melchior Wagner to the head of his trade in the country of his adoption, can only be conjectured. That a German should commend himself to a German king may seem natural, but one would like to know the means and stages by which it was done. Two—or perhaps three—portraits of him survive. The first and best is a miniature, a small oval, set in gold and enamel, with his hair at the back, stated on a parchment label, which was attached to it, to have been painted by De Loutherbourg.[5] This was probably the elder Philipp Jakob de Loutherbourg (B. at Basel, c. 1698; D. at Paris 1768) the father of Philip James the Royal Academician. The second is a small oil painting on paper, possibly from the miniature. The third, a large silhouette in a black oval frame, relieved by a gold moulding, may be of Melchior, or perhaps, of his elder son Anthony.

That Melchior maintained contact and friendship with his family in Germany is shown by his standing sponsor to Johann Melchior, son of his brother Johann Heinrich, who was baptized at St. Moritz, Coburg, on 21 November 1738. Melchior is described in the register as *Hutmacher zu London*. One supposes that the godson was the 'Mr. Melchior Wagner, jun^r', who was buried at Putney, Surrey, on 16 October 1761. Perhaps he died when on a visit to his uncle and godfather, having come to learn from him or to settle in England.

A document preserved in the archives at Coburg[6] appears to record another act of benevolence on Melchior's part to his relations there. It is a petition presented at Coburg on the 13th of September 1755 to the Lords of the Privy Council and Council of Justice of Saxony by Anna Barbara Jaschin (feminine of Jasch), a widow, setting out that her late mother's brother, Johann Wagner, 'at present citizen and hatter in England, had during the past unusually cold weather two years ago sent as a present to each of his brothers and sisters of this country and their children a hundred Thalers for their sustentation, *ex nudo amore*, of which fourth hundred Thalers due to us three children my brother and I have received forty French florins (Gulden fränkisch) each, while the forty florins due to my sister, who is confined to the lunatic asylum at Hildburghausen have been withheld and retained by our honourable town council'. The petition concerns the responsibility for the insane sister and the right to her property. There can be little doubt (and the Coburg archivist agrees) that the generous English Uncle Johann was in fact Melchior, whose Coburg brothers were named Johann Heinrich, Johann Georg and Johann Thomas. The petitioner was presumably a daughter of their sister Anna Catharina, who was aged 18 at the census of 2 April 1721.

Melchior Wagner was sworn a liveryman of the Feltmakers' Company of London which controlled the hat industry on 13 December 1773, became Middle

Warden in 1736, Renter Warden in 1744, Upper Warden in 1746, but paid a fine of £20 to avoid becoming Master in 1747. A receipt dated 20 October 1742 preserved among the Household Accounts of Frederick Prince of Wales (Vol. XXI, fo. 93) in the archives of the Duchy of Cornwall casts a gleam of light on the more splendid part of Melchior's trade. (See below for Accounts).

Payments to him by Lord Fitzwalter in 1734 are recorded in *English History from Essex Sources*, 1550–1750, Essex Record Office Publications, No. 17, 1952, p. 161, from the Mildmay Archives. It may, however, be surmised that the contracts for army cap-making were even more profitable than the fashionable trade. Frank Whitbourn in *Mr. Lock of St. James's Street His Continuing Life and Changing Times*, Heinemann, London, 1971, quotes (p. 25) from *A General*

Made for the Use of His Royal Highness Prince of Wales By Melchior Wagner

		£	s.	d.
	A fine Beavor Hatt	1	10	0
1740/1	a fine White Ostrich feather	1	8	0
January 8	silver button and double chain loop		2	0
	a Cockade and box		3	0
	A fine Beavor Hatt	1	10	0
1741	a Rich Gold Lace	1	0	0
April 30	button and a double chain Loop		2	6
	Lacing box and a Cockade		3	6
May 1	a gold Girdle & Silver buckle Gilt		18	0
	A fine Beavor Hatt	1	10	0
	a Rich Silver Lace		18	0
the 9	button and a double chain Loop		2	0
	a silver Girdle and buckle		14	0
	Lacing box & a Cockade		3	0
	A fine Beavor Hatt	1	10	0
	a rich Silver Lace		18	0
1741	button & a double chain loop		2	0
May 29	Silver Girdle and silver buckle		14	0
	Lacing box and Cockade		3	6
	A fine Beavor Hatt	1	10	0
A[r] 29	A Silver Girdle and buckle		14	0
	silver button and a double chain loop		2	0
	Lacing box and Cockade		3	0
	A fine Beavor Hatt	1	10	0
Nov. 17	a gold Girdle and Silver buckle Gilt		18	0
	Lacing box and Cockade		3	6
		£18	13	0

October 20th 1742.

£18 13 0   Received of the Right Honourable Thomas Earl of Scarborough, Treasurer and Receiver Gen[l.] to His Royal Highness Frederick Prince of Wales the sum of eighteen pounds thirteen shillings In full of the Bill I say received by warrant.

Melchior Wagner.

Description of All Trades, 1747, an account of the distinction between Cap-Makers, Felt-Makers, Hat-banders and Milliners to the effect that 'there were divers kinds of caps worn . . . for different uses, and made by as many different sets of people. Those for the Army is one brand, and the most profitable, of which there are not above two or three principal undertakers, who employ a number of *Hands*, chiefly women and girls, who seldom take Apprentices', adding that the Hatter was concerned only with the finishing and styling of the hat for individual use, while the 'felt: or 'hood' on which he worked was manufactured 'across the water' in Bermondsey, where the smell of the tanneries and leather manufacturies was tolerated as it was not in St. James's. Mr. Whitbourn (pp. 26–32) describes the processes in further detail, including that use of nitrate of mercury whose effect on the brain proverbially made hatters mad.

Melchior Seymour Teulon (1734–1806), as already mentioned a nephew of Mrs. Melchior Wagner (son of her brother Anthony Teulon, 1700–1776, hatter of Greenwich), was on 5 September 1748 'at the age of fourteen . . . sent to London and put apprentice to his uncle', Melchior Wagner of Pall Mall. He came from a religious home and 'was naturally of a thoughtful serious turn of mind'. In his uncle's house, however, we are told, 'he entered upon a new scene of life, being introduced into a gay family of young people, who spent their evenings in all the fashionable amusements of the times, in which (when business allowed), he was induced to take his part, and became particularly fond of Music and Dancing, and frequently attended theatrical performances. He, however', says his Methodist biographer, 'never gave in to the vicious courses, to which such pursuits too often lead'. The family were constant attendants at St. James's Church, and at the monthly Sacrament, and required all their young people to attend with them. About the year 1752–3 the Rev. Dr. Secker, then Rector of St. James's, began a Sunday evening lecture;[7] taking occasion to improve the event of several shocks of an Earthquake, which happened about that time, and gave great alarm to many, and produced a temporary reform in his uncle's family. Plays and cards were for a while suspended, and family prayers begun, which continued till the pious doctor was promoted to the Archbishopric of Canterbury;[8] when with his faithful warnings, all fears of the Earthquake vanished: and with them the practice of this round of duties, and they gradually resumed their usual pleasures'.[9] However, the relapse of the Wagners did not, it seems, engulf Melchior Teulon, who later became a Methodist and a friend of John Wesley, near whom he lies buried in Bunhill Fields.

The architect brothers, Samuel Sanders Teulon (1812–1873), whose Victorian fame has now revived, and the less well known William Milford Teulon (1823–1900) were grandsons of Edward Teulon (1742–1795), Melchior Seymour Teulon's younger brother.

The Huguenot connection, which, I suppose, engendered both the piety and the business habits, was reinforced in the generation of Melchior Wagner's children. Huguenot refugees who were farmers or farm labourers for the most part settled in countries where land was to be had more readily than in England. Those who came here were ministers, lawyers, physicians, merchants, tradesmen and skilled craftsmen, these last being the majority. In London Soho was a main centre of their settlement. Melchior's eldest son Anthony Wagner (1718–1761) married first at St. Helen's Bishopsgate on 21 Feb. 1744–5 Leah daughter of Peter

Debonnaire, merchant, of Stratford le Bow, son of a refugee from St. Quentin by a Parisian mother. After her death in the same year he married secondly on 4 December 1749 Anna daughter of Abraham Dupuis of Pall Mall, a court milliner to the Dowager Princess of Wales and son of a refugee said to be from Bordeaux. Melchior's younger son George (1722-1796), the ancestor of the later Wagners, married at St. John's Hampstead in 1748 Mary Wilhelmina, daughter of Henry Godde (1702-1764) sometime of Newman Street, Marylebone, and grand-daughter of Peter Godde, a refugee from an unidentified Bussy in Burgundy. The Hampstead register describes her as of the parish of St. Martin in the Fields. Her father Henry Godde, died in 1764 at Clewer. Anne Wagner (1716-1768), Melchior's daughter, married Clement Paillet (1706-1758) of Deptford son of Clements Paillet (of a family from Goze in Poitou) by Leah le Keux of a family of the old Canterbury Huguenot settlement. One of their granddaughters, Harriet Paillet (D. 1814) married Sir Lewis Versturme, K.H. (D. 1833), said to be a natural son of George III. A great-grandson of Anne Paillet was Dr. Thomas Charles Byde Rooke, F.R.C.S. (D. 1806) of Honolulu, who adopted his wife's niece Emma (1836-1885). She in 1856 married Kaméhaméha II, King of the Sandwich Islands (D. 1863). As a widow Queen Emma visited London in 1865, staying with Lady Franklin, at whose house Henry Wagner met her.[10]

In the first two generations of their settlement in England (though not there-after) the refugee families intermarried extensively, so that through the Huguenot links thus established the Wagners have indirect marriage connections with many more of the families who figure in the great Huguenot genealogical corpus on which Henry Wagner, as we shall see, spent much of his life. The Teulon family had links with those of Desfaux, Liron, Laroque, Fargues, Rocher, Cazalet and Deshons: the Debonnaire family with St. Amant, L'Epine, Milon, Le Keux, Didier, Lernault and Mariette; the Dupuis family with Pullain and Boucher; and that of Paillet with Pinaud, Le Keux (again), Morisseau, Roberdan and Loiseau.

After two generations (except among the Spitalfields weavers) such families were Anglicized and made English marriages—often indeed sooner. These marriages too were often of interest. Among the English links of the Wagners' Huguenot connections three in particular had influence on the family history. Anna (née Dupuis), the widow of Anthony Wagner, married secondly Captain Francis Cooke (D. 1816 aged 93) of the Second Regiment of Dragoon Guards, who was a younger brother of William Cooke (1711-1797), Head Master of Eton from 1743 to 1745, Fellow of Eton from 1747 to 1772, Provost of King's College, Cambridge, from 1722 till his death and Dean of Ely from 1780. Doubtless through this connection Anna's nephew George Dupuis (1757-1839) was at Eton from 1771 to 1776 and became the progenitor of a dynasty of Eton fellows and masters.[11] In 1805, as we shall see, Henry Michell Wagner was sent to Eton and was followed there by seven more of the Wagner family.

The second link was through the marriage of Mrs. George Wagner's first cousin, Anna Jackson (1738-1789) in 1764 to the Rev. Samuel Smith, LL.D. (1731-1808), Head Master of Westminster School from 1764 to 1788. During those years two, if not three, of George Wagner's sons were at Westminster, George (1764-1831) from 1773 to 1781 and Anthony (1770-1847) from 1779 to 1786. Their elder brother Melchior Henry (1749-1811) was also thought by his grand-son to have been there, though the school records do not show him.[12]

8

The third link is through Frances Godde (1695-1749), 'tire-woman to the Queen' (i.e., Caroline, Queen of George II), Mrs. George Wagner's aunt. By her first marriage to Richard Pigot (D. 1729) of Peploe, Shropshire, Frances Godde had three remarkable sons. George Pigot (1719-1777) entered the service of the East India Company in Madras in 1737 and rose to be Governor and Commander in Chief there in 1755. He was made a Baronet in 1764 and a Peer of Ireland as Baron Pigot of Patshull in 1766. He gave an Indian Cheetah to King George III and about 1765 commissioned George Stubbs to paint it with two Indian attendants. This picture the Pigot family sold at Sotheby's in 1970 for £220,000. Lord Pigot died while under arrest at the hands of his Council. The Pigot diamond, which he left behind him, was sold by lottery under Act of Parliament for £23,998. It passed to Ali Pasha by whose order it was at his death crushed to powder. Lord Pigot was unmarried but has many descendants through two illegitimate daughters who married well and had large families.

The second son, a lieutenant-general, succeeded to Lord Pigot's baronetcy under a special remainder. The third rose from able seaman to be Admiral of the Blue and became a Lord of the Admiralty and Commander in Chief in the West Indies. Two of Lord Pigot's nieces married into the aristocracy. Their descendants (among whom was Daisy, Countess of Warwick) have included in our day a Duchess, a Countess and five Earls.

After Richard Pigot's death in 1729 his widow Frances (Godde) married secondly a Colonel in the Guards, John Wyvill of Walton on Thames (D. 1740). She and her son George, the future Lord Pigot, were in 1764 godparents to her great-nephew George Wagner (1764–1846. See page 13 below). Pigot descendants were still conscious of the family connection in 1814, when Mrs. Vernon, Lord Pigot's niece, on a tour in Derbyshire identified Mrs. M. H. Wagner and her daughters in an inn at Matlock in Derbyshire, where they all chanced to be staying and renewed old links.

The Goddes, like the Teulons, had also Methodist links, very different from their connections on the Pigot side. Mrs. George Wagner's brother, Henry Godde (1739–1809) married a wife who had been companion to Selina, Countess of Huntingdon, the foundress of Lady Huntingdon's connexion; while another of Henry's sisters, Frances Godde (1734–1805), and her husband James Ireland (1724–1814) of Brislington Hall near Bristol, where he was a merchant and banker, were intimates of the Wesleys, of William Romaine (another Huguenot), of J. W. Fletcher of Madeley and of other leaders of the revival. They entertained them at Brislington constantly in the summer months, James Ireland's 'delicate health compelling them to winter abroad, mostly at Montpellier', a régime which prolonged his life to ninety years.

We must picture this largely but not solely religious and mercantile Wagner family against the special and fascinating background of eighteenth century Pall Mall. The street had been laid out on crown land in 1661 and the houses were built during the next decades. The great *Survey of London* volumes on the parish of St. James Westminster[13] enable us to picture them in some detail. By 1700 it was 'the ordinary residence of all strangers because of its Vicinity to the Queen's Palace, the Park, the Parliament House, the Theatres, and the Choclate and Coffee Houses, where the best Company frequents'. In 1720 it was 'a fine long Street', 'The Houses on the South side', where the Wagners lived, 'have a Pleasant Prospect into the King's Garden, and besides they have small Gardens behind them, which reach to the Wall' of St. James's Park 'and to many of them are raised Mounts, which give them the Prospect of the said Garden, and the Park'. By 1764, however, its beauty was 'greatly disfigured by several mean houses of the lowest mechanicks being interspersed in it in many places, and many of them joining to the most sumptuous edifices'. In the early nineteenth century, though 'a stately aristocratic-looking street' with 'private mansions fit for the residence of the wealthy and noble', it was at its east end 'bordered with filthy alleys; inhabited by abandoned characters'.[14] At its west end were the notorious brothels of King's Place, now Pall Mall Place.

No. 93 (later 89) was a broad, solid looking house, three windows wide, probably of the early or middle eighteenth century, but restored by M. H. Wagner in 1810. It stood between two houses of similar size, of which No. 90, to the east, was occupied in 1801 by Lord Temple, and No. 88, to the West, from 1775 to 1780 by Nathaniel Hone, the portrait painter. Beyond these, however, were on each side great mansions or palaces; to the east Buckingham House, the town mansion of the Grenvilles of Stowe, Earls Temple and Marquesses (later Dukes) of Buckingham, for whom it was rebuilt by Soane in the 1790's; and to the west York House, later Cumberland House, built for the Duke of York by Matthew Brettingham in 1761–3 and altered for the Duke of Cumberland between 1771 and 1790; The Board of Ordnance took it over from 1806 and in 1855 the Board was absorbed by the War Office, which at the same time took over Buckingham House and in 1859 Nos. 88 to 90 including the Wagner house: there remaining till 1908, when the War Office removed to Whitehall and all the houses were demolished to make way for the Royal Automobile Club.

Across the road at No. 25 lived Andrew Millar (d. 1768), the publisher of Johnson's Dictionary and Robertson's and Hume's Histories. In 1826 Sir Walter Scott stayed in this house with its then occupant, his son in law J. G. Lockhart. Farther east on the south side was the house (from 1787 to 1823), of John Julius Angerstein, whose collection of pictures became the nucleus of the National Gallery, which was first housed here; beyond this the great palace of Carlton House; and east again, from 1768 to 1778, the first home of the Royal Academy. To the west, between Cumberland House, and St. James's Palace, were No. 84, the house (from 1768 to 1809) of James Christie the Auctioneer; Schomberg House: the house (no. 79) which Charles II gave to Nell Gwynne (thus still the only non-Crown freehold) where the two Dr. William Heberdens, father and son, who attended the Wagners, lived from 1771 to 1814: Sir Edward Walpole's house (No. 71); and No. 68, the house of the Vulliamy family of clockmakers from 1765 to 1854.

Further east on the north side was the Cocoa Tree Club, first heard of as a chocolate house in Pall Mall in 1698 in a house on part of the later site of Cumberland House, mentioned in the Spectator, thence moving before 1757 to the north side, then further along, and in 1799 to St. James's Street, where it stayed till it closed its doors in 1932. Three doors to the east on the north side at No. 49, William Almack took over in 1759 a house recently built by Henry Holland of Fulham, the father of the architect, for an 'alehouse or victualling house'. East of this Almack acquired further houses and by 1761 was known for dinners organised with his partner Edward Boodle (third son of John Boodle of the Three Tuns, Oswestry) who took over No. 50 in 1768 and died there in 1772. In 1783 what had by then become the gaming club known as Boodle's removed to St. James's Street. In 1764, with another partner or assistant William Brooks, Almack was concerned in the foundation of another gaming club at No. 49 which also in 1778 moved to St. James's Street and continues as Brooks's Club.

Further east still was No. 52 built in 1726-7 by William Pickering (d. 1734), herald painter and eponym of Pickering Place, and man of many trades, one of them ancestral to a wine merchant's in St. James's Street, now Berry Brothers (of whom is A.R.W.'s Vintner colleague and friend Anthony Berry). From 1738 to 1787 No. 52 was occupied by the great booksellers and publishers Robert and James Dodsley, trading under the sign of Tully's Head and, even more than Andrew Millar, bringing Samuel Johnson to Pall Mall. Next in this house lived Benjamin Vandergucht, painter and picture dealer, who, however, in 1788 assigned his lease to the printsellers of Cheapside, Alderman John Boydell (1719-1804) and his brother Josiah. With the younger George Dance as architect they rebuilt the house as the Shakespeare Gallery opened in 1790, and Alderman Boydell conducted it as 'the most ambitious scheme of art patronage of the day', though Gillray caricatured him as 'worshipping the Genius of Avarice and mutilating pictures in the galley in order to attract public attention'.[15]

What more fascinating street can there have been in eighteenth century London for an intelligent tradesman to live in, or what better pitch to trade in than Pall Mall?

Melchior's sons Anthony and George were apprenticed to him in the Feltmakers' Company in 1732-3 and 1736 respectively and both were made free of the Company and admitted Masters in 1743. In 1744 Melchior was, as we have seen, elected Renter Warden. 'Mr. Wagner being at Bath for his health at the time of his being elected Upper Warden' on 2 October 1746, appeared on 2 Feb. 1746-7 'at Court and was sworn into his office of upper warden'. On 1 October 1747 he was elected Master, but paid a fine of £20 to be excused and £3 to be excused a public dinner. Directories show that by 1749 (or earlier) he had taken Anthony and George into partnership and by 1758 had retired in their favour. His residence in later years was at Putney (though Pall Mall was still his place of business) and there he died on 31 December 1764. He was buried in the family vault at Lee in Kent, as his wife had been in 1742 and his son Anthony's first wife in 1745. This vault was doubtless acquired through the Teulons at adjoining Greenwich and in it nine of the Wagners were buried between 1742 and 1811. The substantial table tomb still stands there in the old St. Margaret's churchyard.

The St. James's Chronicle recorded that 'On Sunday Morning', 28 June 1761, 'as Mr. [Anthony] Wagner, an eminent Hatter in Pall-Mall, was riding out of Town, his Horse fell in St. James's Street, by which Accident he had the Misfortune to break his Arms, and put his other Shoulder out, and was otherwise bruised.' Lloyd's Evening Post, and British Chronicle added that 'Mr. Wagner, Hatter to his Majesty, had the misfortune of being flung from his horse facing St. James's gate, by which accident he dislocated his shoulders, and broke one of his arms'. The next issue records his death 'July 2. Mr. Anthony Wagner, Hatter to his Majesty, of the bruise he received on Tuesday last by a fall from his horse.' The London Chronicle adds that he died 'at his house in Pall Mall'. He was buried in the vault in Fulham churchyard belonging to the family of his second wife Anna Dupuis. She and his nephews, George and Anthony Wagner, were later buried there also in 1836 and 1847.

Anthony Wagner's widow married secondly Captain Francis Cooke of the 2nd Dragoon guards, brother of Dr. William Cooke (1711-1797), Head Master of Eton (1743-5), Provost of King's College, Cambridge (1772-97) and Dean of Ely (1780-97). From 1748 Dr. Cooke was also Rector of Denham, Buckinghamshire, where his daughter Elizabeth Anne (d. 1825) married Benjamin Way (1740-1808) of Denham Place. Their Way descendants recalled among Dr. Cooke's visitors only one 'who was not a dignitary of the Church'. This was Dr. Cooke's brother, Francis, who was a Colonel in the army and had fought at Minden; about whose lady the younger generation used to whisper a merry tale. She had been the widow of a Mr. Wagner of Pall Mall; and possibly at her instigation, Mr. Wagner had suggested to His Majesty, King George II, that he would like to be made a Baronet, a request that blunt King George refused testily. 'No, no, Wagner', pronounced His Majesty, 'I *can't* make you a gentleman.'[16]

Similar stories have been told of others. Sir James Laurence, *On the Nobility of the British Gentry*, 4th ed. 1840, p. 38, 'Ferri de Constant, in his "Londres et les Anglais", published 1814, says: ... The nurse of James the First, who had followed him to London, entreated him to make her son a gentleman: "My good woman", said the King, "a gentleman I could never make him, though I could make him a Lord." '

Selden, *Table Talk*, says that God Almighty cannot make a gentleman.

John Casswell, *The South Sea Bubble*, 1960, p. 5n. 'George I is reported to have said he could make Bateman a peer but not a gentleman'. This was Sir James Bateman (d. 1718), father of the first Lord Bateman.

When Melchior died at Putney on 31 December 1764, the London Chronicle, describing him as 'Hatter to his late Majesty', added 'which business has been carried on for several years past by his son, now his present Majesty's Hatter'. This was George Wagner (1722-1796), the godson of George I, who had sole control of the business from his brother's death in 1761 until 1772 when he took his own eldest son Melchior Henry Wagner (1749-1811) into partnership. George's career was evidently very prosperous, but he refused opportunities of civic advancement which came his way. A record in his own hand in the family bible tells us that 'the 7th day of June 1768 he was nominated (by the Rt. Honble. Thomas Harley Esquire Lord Mayor) for the Office of Sheriff of this City, and County of Middlesex. January 2d. 1769 was invited to put up for Alderman of Farringdon without, but declined it, on account of Jn⁰· Wilkes Esqʳ· standing, was a second time invited to the same honor for the Ward of Candlewick and Elected Sheriff both of which he also declined in the year 1777'.

In 1772 George took his eldest son Melchior Henry (1749-1811) into partnership. It was in 1780 that William Hickey on his return to England from India wrote 'My next calls were at Rymer's for boots, Wagners for hats, and Williams of Bond Street for leather breeches'.[17] In 1784 Melchior Henry married and Directories of 1785 show that his father had moved to 13 Duke Street, Westminster, leaving the young couple in residence at the Pall Mall shop. In 1788 he retired from the business, leaving it to his son. Duke Street backed on the east side of St. James's Park as Queen Anne's Gate does on the south side and was something like it in character. Duke Street was later absorbed into neighbouring Delahay Street and the part of it where George Wagner lived was pulled down in 1862 to make room for the New Public Offices. George Wagner, according to his great-grandson Henry, 'was fond of the arts, and filled his house with pictures which at his death were put up at Christie's, but fetched very little'.[18] His own portrait, a crayon, and his wife's, in oil, have both been attributed[19] to Thomas Frye (1710–1762), who might have painted them in London in 1759 or 1760. There are also miniature oval pencil drawings of them, perhaps done at the time of their marriage in 1748. George is also said to have owned a Claude. Apart from family portraits only one of George Wagner's pictures remained in the family. This was a good contemporary painting on panel of King Edward VI, which George (erroneously) called his Holbein. Melchior Henry gave it to his brother in law John Henry Michell (1759–1844) from whom it was bought back by Melchior Henry's son, George Henry Malcolm Wagner. A.R.W. bought it at the sale in 1933 of the effects of the latter's grandson Malcolm Wagner.

By his will of 29 May 1788[20] George Wagner gave £500 each immediately to his wife, and his son Melchior Henry. To her he left his jewels, pictures, furniture and other chattels in Duke Street and to his son the premises in Pall Mall, for what remainder of time the lease had to run, on condition that within three months he sign a bond to give his mother £100 a year. To her he left also the interest of £16,000 in the Reduced 3 per cents, but if during her lifetime her sons Anthony and George attain 21 years or her daughters marry, they are each to receive £1,000. He appoints executors his wife, Dr. Samuel Smith, Head Master of Westminster School (1764–1788) and Prebendary of Westminster Abbey, the Rev. Sackville Stephens Bale, Rector of Withyham, Sussex, and Thomas Walley Partington, Esquire, of Brook Street, in the parish of St. George, Hanover Square.[21]

Samuel Smith, LL.D. (1731–1808), as mentioned earlier, was Mrs. Wagner's uncle by marriage, having in 1764 married Anna Jackson, her mother's sister.[22] Sackville Stephens Bale (1753–1836) was Mrs. Wagner's nephew, the son of her sister, Louisa Godde (1735) by the Rev. Sackville Spencer Bale, Rector of Withyham. The youngest son of Sackville Stephens Bale was Charles Sackville Bale (1793–1880), a well known art collector. Waagen's *Art Treasures* II, 329–32 and IV, 116–121 gives some account of his collection, the dispersal of which took up 13 afternoons at Christie's between 13 and 31 May 1881.

Between her husband's death in 1796 and her own in 1808 Mrs. George Wagner lived at a house in Elysium Row, Fulham, whose Georgian houses, with the date 1738, still stand at the western end of the New King's Road.[23] They looked at this date towards the river across nursery gardens and were not far from the large Dupuis family house Purser's Cross. Mrs. Wagner's was probably Northumberland House, whose handsome brick front was rendered a few years ago. After her death in 1808 her eldest son M. H. Wagner bought a neighbouring house, 11 Elysium Row, now 130 New King's Road, for his brother the Rev. George Wagner (1764–1836) who had been inducted in 1790 as Rector of Mursley, Buckinghamshire, on the presentation of Sampson (Gideon), Lord Eardley, the son in law of Sir John Eardley Wilmot, an old friend of the Rev. Henry Michell (see page 14).

Chapter II

LONDON AND SUSSEX: THE MICHELLS

MELCHIOR HENRY WAGNER (1749-1811) was taken into partnership in the Pall Mall business by his father, as we have seen, in 1772. On the 27th of May 1784 he married at St. Nicholas' Church, Brighthelmston (now called Brighton), Sussex, Anne Elizabeth (1757-1841), daughter of the Rev. Henry Michell (1715-1789), Vicar of that parish. How they met is unknown, but the Prince of Wales had paid his first visit to Brighton in 1783 and the number of its visitors was growing fast. The admission register of St. John's College, Cambridge, records that Melchior Henry's younger brother George Wagner (1764-1831) was at school at Brighthelmston and this was probably between 1781, when he left Westminster, and 1786, when he went up to Cambridge. Perhaps he was a pupil of Henry Michell, who is known to have taken pupils, among them the future Duke of Wellington. Henry Wagner records[1] that at the end of a visit to Brighton M. H. Wagner was told by his bride elect, 'that now she did not wish to see him again until her wedding day', adding that their union was singularly happy.

The Michells were substantial yeomen of Shipley near Horsham. Henry's father, John (1682-1735) was an attorney of Lewes. Henry was born there in 1715 and entered Clare Hall, Cambridge, as a sizar in 1732, graduating Bachelor of Arts in 1735, M.A. 1739 and Fellow from 1738 to 1740. In 1739 he was instituted Rector of Maresfield and in 1744 Vicar of Brighthelmston and Rector of Bletchingdon. These preferments he held till his death in 1789, 'enjoying ample means, the friendship of many men of note, and the reputation of an accomplished Greek and Latin scholar'.[2] 'The most distinguished personages that visited Brighthelmston courted his acquaintance, and not unfrequently gave him considerable proofs of their munificence and esteem.' His son James Charles Michell (1767-1841) averred that his father 'first raised the consequence of that now Royal and populous town, and at the time the Nobility, who visited it, were content with the huts of fishermen, "the Rooms" were nightly the resort of all, and there the Company assembled to drink tea, and play a pool of quadrille, departing at eleven o'clock'. 'I remember', he adds, 'when, except the Inns, my Father's house contained the largest room in the town, 20 feet square, the dormitory of the Priory of St. Bartholomew: the kitchen had been the Refectory. In the former I have seen Garrick, Foote and Dr. Johnson. He occasionally received pupils into his house, with whom he educated his sons, and at a late period of his life, the Hero of Waterloo for a short time was placed under his tuition, and became a resident within the Vicarage-house of Brighthelmston. This house upon my Father's death was taken down, and a modern edifice erected upon its site, by the Rev. Mr. Hudson, his successor.'[3]

When this house was in turn vacated by the Rev. H. M. Wagner in 1835, his uncle the Rev. John Henry Michell (1759-1844) wrote to his sister Anne Elizabeth Wagner, 'I could not but sympathise, my dearest sister, with you on your last farewell to the site of the Old Vicarage. There is something in the recollections of local scenery in our earliest days, that must excite melancholy feelings, and as to myself the reminiscences of such spots are more vivid as I advance in weakness of mind and body. Had I a talent for delineating with a pencil, what is now before my imagination, I could sketch the back garden with its then apparently large but now very small dimensions, and all its walks and our several plots, and our cages for jackdaws and hutches for rabbits with dear Mamma's sacred gooseberry tree, and the asparagus bed and the beautiful fig trees with their delicious figs, and the wild pear tree and your detached garden of tulips, &c. &c., which float on my fancy and which existed more than seventy years ago in all their luxuriance and attractive forms. What a contrast is this to the present Vicarial parterre, even when I saw it in its incipient state.'[4]

Stories are told of vehement exchanges between old Henry Michell and Dr. Samuel Johnson[5] and on one occasion 'when the war of words waxed uncommon warm, 'tis said that his alarmed companion', his son John Henry Michell (1759–1844), 'then a boy, took to pulling his father by the coat-tails, or whatever answered to these more modern appendages, to get him away'.[6]

On another occasion, 'The Thrales went to the rooms, and Dr. Johnson went there also. The weather was cold, and Michell and Johnson, meeting in an ante-room, they sat down near a fire to warm themselves and converse. For a time their conversation was amicably and peacefully exchanged; but, at last, some knotty and difficult question arose, and not being able to adjust the matter, Michell seized a poker, and Johnson the tongs, with which they enforced their arguments by thumping the grate violently and vociferating. The ladies, who most unscientifically were dancing, became alarmed; the country dance was interrupted; nor was it resumed until Wade, the Master of Ceremonies, and the politest man in the world, pacified the wranglers.'[7]

Michell became friendly with the Thrales, who stayed at Brighton regularly in the 1770's, and was at their house at Streatham in 1776. In a game of animal comparisons in 1779 they put down Johnson for the Elephant but 'Old Michell' for the Hog.[8] His daughter Anne Elizabeth Wagner (1757–1844) incidentally recalled her father's domestic discipline when she checked one of her sons as a child who 'was handing a book or doing something in a gauche or rude way . . . with the words "If my Father had seen you do that, he'd have knocked you down" '.

He died on the 31st of October 1789 and was buried in a vault in the old parish church of St. Nicholas, Brighton. His widow Faith (née Reade) survived him twenty years, living in the Old Steine, and dying aged 82 on the 18th of February 1809 was buried in the same vault. Of their sixteen children seven survived childhood, five sons and two daughters. Of the two sisters, Anne Elizabeth Wagner and Elizabeth (1760–1810), who never married, their brother James said 'Betsy has the wit, but Nancy has the sense'.[9] Betsy, of whom a charming crayon drawing in Downman's style (the pair to one of her mother) and a miniature survive, was a beauty but never married. 'A rejected admirer was Mr. Stanford of Preston, grandfather to Mrs. Fane-Benett-Stanford, & she wore the willow for a Mr. Charles Hayes or Hays (Probably the Charles Hayes who was J. H. M[ichell]'s School & College Contemporary, & also Sir William Browne's Medallist, & was Bursar of King's) who had property at or near Windsor. Hurt by a naive reply of hers, when he was taking leave after a visit to her at her brother's house in Fresh-

15

water, that "she was glad he was going", he broke off the engagement; while she, poor soul, had only meant that the house was a bad one for visitors, the hostess having become addicted to fits'. Two of the sons, William and Henry Chicheley, went as Writers in the Company's service to India, where William (1754-1838) was Resident of Nagore and Negapatam in the Madras Presidency from 1782 to 1794. Returning home at the age of 40 he married and settled in Norton Cottage, Freshwater, in the Isle of Wight. He brought back with him from India a natural son, by a Chinese or Malay mother, named Harry Dorset to whom he left the property called Frankwell in Ashburnham, left him by his father. Henry Wagner (GNQ 121-2) records that 'On his return from India, Uncle William entertained Brighton, in an enclosure, answering now to the Pavilion Grounds! (then a possibility!). Then as now, one had to pay upon entering the Chapel Royal: but when the Pew-opener suggested this to him, 'What, pay to enter a Christian place of Worship! never!' said he, and at once entered a pew, from wh. no one ventured to dislodge him, or offer further objection.' Henry Chicheley Michell (1761-1806), returning from India in 1796 settled at West Teignmouth, Devon.

John Henry Michell (1759-1844), the second surviving son, was a scholar and clergyman like his father. From 1768 to 1777 he was a King's Scholar at Eton, thence proceeding as a scholar, in 1778, to King's College, Cambridge, where in 1779 and 1780 he was awarded Sir William Browne's medal and became a Fellow (1781-1804) and Vice-Provost. He was a tutor successively in the families of the Dukes of Somerset and Newcastle (his future ducal pupils were at Eton 1783-91 and 1796-99 respectively). In one of these two households the sister of the future Sir Thomas Lawrence (1769-1830, P.R.A. 1820) was a governess and formed an attachment to John Michell from the violence of which she became quite ill. His sister, Mrs. M. H. Wagner used to ask her to the house frequently 'out of a feeling akin to pity'.[10] From 1803 to 1844 he was Rector of Buckland, Hertfordshire, where like his father he took private pupils, among whom were Edward Adolphus Seymour afterwards 12th Duke of Somerset (D. 1855), Henry Pelham, afterwards 4th Duke of Newcastle (D. 1851), his brother Lord Thomas Clinton, Henry Piper Sperling of Norbury Park, the Honourable Robert Samuel Leslie Melville and Francis Pym of Hassells, Bedfordshire, who on his death sought and obtained the gift of the diaries which J. H. Michell had kept in Latin. Charles Webb le Bas, principal of the East India College, Haileybury, said of him, 'There is a man within not many miles of here, who is the first classic now in England, & he is doing missionary work in a Village' [Buckland]. He is said to have refused the Head Mastership of Eton before Dr. Goodall was appointed in 1801.[11]

Twenty years after his sister had married, her brother, on 12 June 1804, married Margaret (1772-1849), daughter of George Wagner. They had a son and daughter. The former, William Antony Michell, was born at Buckland 18 November 1806 and died while at school at Eton 23 December 1819. A monument with a medallion portrait by Sir Francis Chantrey and verses by his father was erected in Buckland Church. The daughter, Margaret Henrietta (1811-1859) was born at Cambridge and baptized at Trinity Church there by that notable churchman, the Rev. Charles Simeon (1759-1836), a Fellow of King's like her father, of whom Henry Wagner notes that 'there was much in his thought and teaching, which struck a concord with the later Oxford Movement. *He* is not responsible, in less degree even than was Wesley, for his successors & "Trustees", who have been undeniably "too highly subjective and sectarian" '.

Margaret (Wagner) Michell, says Henry Wagner, 'had had little education, but she was gifted with great natural strength of mind. She had a firm mouth, speaking eyes; & was of a very argumentative disposition. She too must have been very peculiar—at least she was so in the way in wh. she showed her "love of air". When her son died, & was buried (at Buckland) she insisted upon an opening being made into the fresh air from out of the vault, protected by a grating; and was exceedingly wrathful at finding, upon her going down there some while after that this aperture had been stopped up. "You know, my dear, said she to Fanny [? Coombe, 1832–1924], fanning herself more violently than usual with her everlasting fan, "how fond of air I have always been, and I am sure Henry wld. wish the fresh air to reach him".'[12]

The daughter, Margaret Henrietta Michell (1811–1859) married 5 July 1842 Major Francis John Swaine Hepburn, late of H.M. 60th Rifles, who survived till 1863, living at Pelham Place, Brompton and later at 44 Cambridge Terrace, Hyde Park. He was 'a *made up* man, with a wig and pointed boots, &c. He was of good connexion, & with a distant prospect, wh. he afterwards attained, of an estate of £500 a year, but when he married, had only the worth of his Commission, and he evidently m[d.] for money (or as Mrs. L[uttman] Johnson phrased it of her daughter, "for the future"). Margaret was very peculiar, & fidgetted all about her, *except* her husband. Some 2 years before her death, she had a sun stroke, & had then to live some time "under care".'[13]

After he gave up duty at Buckland J. H. Michell and his wife went to live at 19 Queen Square, Bath. The inventory taken on his death there indicates his possession of several Wagner family portraits including a 'hare bracelet with miniature set with pearls', another 'miniature set with amethysts & diamonds', and, hanging in the drawing room, no less than '15 miniature profiles & miniatures' & again '13 small prints & two wax miniatures, as well as the portrait of Edward VI'.[14]

Margaret (Wagner) Michell's younger sister Mary (1774–1852) seems to have been still more eccentric. She at one time shared the house in Elysium Row, Fulham, with her brother George, but lived latterly and died at Bath. Henry Wagner records[15] 'that she chose thus to separate herself from her Family—She picked up a pretty hairdresser's dau., whom she thought she shd. like to have about her—& to her she left all she had, may be £7,000. Mr. Woodward, who was once curate there, & then visited her in her illness at Bath, wrote to say what an undue influence this person exercised over her. When my Grandmother died, she left £100 to each of her grandchildren (wh. £100 by the bye, with the House upon the cliff, was the ruin of Melchior Coombe, as he honoured its arrival with champagne—) & a little legacy of £20 to all her more immediate connexions & amongst them to Mary Wagner, who chose (probably because she intended to leave her own money away—) to *return* it to my Aunt, who thereupon gave it to poor in her name, & sent her an exact acc[t.] of how it had been distributed. She had once been very handsome & then thought no one good enough for her— Amongst her other traits, she was strong in her opinions, political among the rest —& in her fancies about people, wh. led to her frequently "finding them impertinent", & changing her lodgings'.

Mrs. J. H. Michell's elder sister Louisa Wagner (1756–1821) lived at one time with the J. H. Michells, eventually settling at Brighton. She was buried near by at Preston. There was 'a pretty portrait of her in crayons, pressing a dove'.[16]

The Michell male line was continued by the descendants of the two youngest sons of the Vicar of Brighton, Eardley Wilmot Lade Michell (1764–1834) and James Charles Michell (1767–1841). The former, who was named after his father's friend Sir John Eardley Wilmot (1709–1792), Chief Justice of the Common Pleas, was unsuccessful as a partner in the Old Bank (Shergold, Michell, Rice, Rice & Mills) at 103 North Street, Brighton. Later he lived at Wargroves, Herstmonceux, where he caused dissension, when 'the Rector not being to his liking, he introduced a conventicle, or at least its raison d'être, in the person of a Mr. Chapman, a Dissenting Minister. This unhappy proceeding engendered much strife & odium theologicum, & an acrimonious controversy ensued, in wh. the amenities were disregarded & we find Mr. & Mrs. Michell roundly charged with "the sin of Ananias & Sapphira"!' V. inter alia 'A short & sufficient answer to Mr. Brewer's scurrilous pamphlet on "The Hurstmonceux case" by Joseph Turnbull, Brighton, 1827'.[17]

James Charles Michell was a solicitor of Queen Square, Bloomsbury, and later at 68 East Street, Brighton.

Earlier he had 'lived at Iffley [near Oxford], holding some relation as man of business to Magdalen Coll.; but throwing this up suddenly, he then moved to Queen Square, London till Lady Hart left him the house at Brighton.[18] He was first married to Elizabeth, daughter of William Johnson, solicitor of Petworth, by Elizabeth Luttman. Her brother, the Rev. John Johnson, D.D., of Magdalen College, Oxford, made her son the Rev. Henry William Robinson Michell his heir on condition of his taking the name and arms of Luttman-Johnson, which he did by Royal Licence on 16 November 1831 and exemplification of 18 February 1832. J. C. Michell's second wife was the daughter of John Ahmuty of Grenada.

We return now to Melchior Henry Wagner (1749–1811) and Anne Elizabeth (Michell) (1757–1844) his wife. In 1810 he restored the family house in Pall Mall and set up on the garden front a stone with a Latin inscription to record the fact.

LIBERIS SUIS
POSTERISQUE EORUM
HAS AEDES PATERNAS
REFICI CURAVIT
M. H. WAGNER
M.D.C.C.C.X.

In 1908 the house, then part of the War Office, together with its neighbours was demolished to make room for the Royal Automobile Club. Henry Wagner acquired the stone and it was housed in various family gardens until 1968 when Sir Anthony Wagner removed it to Wyndham Cottage, Aldeburgh, to the north wall of which it is now fixed. A further Latin inscription was then composed by Sir Roger Mynors and carved by Mr. John Green to explain its peregrinations.

18

LAPIDEM ISTAM
WESTMONASTERII OLIM
POSITAM INDE MOVIT ANNO
MCMVIII HENRICUS WAGNER TRAIECIT
HUC ANTONIUS RICARDUS
WAGNER MCMLXIX

Early in the year after he had set up the stone, on the 17th of February 1811, Melchior Henry Wagner died aged 61, 'so suddenly that being taken ill in the middle of the night, 'tho his son George ran instantly for Dr. Heberden, who lived but a few doors off in Pall Mall, on his return with the Dr. he found him already dead'.

George Henry Malcolm Wagner[19] (1796-1868), the elder of Melchior Henry's two sons, succeeded to the hat business, but his apprenticeship in 1803 to his uncle J. C. Michell, attorney, of Brighthelmston suggests that his parents already had other views for him. A withdrawal from the business was at all events effected. Directories of 1818 show Wagner & Co. transformed into Wagner, Gale & Co., Hatters to the King, Army Cap Makers to their R.H. the Dukes of York, Kent & Cambridge & Manufacturers of Helmets & Accoutrements. In 1820 the firm becomes 'Wagner, Gale & Caterer'. In 1820-21 No. 93 Pall Mall was renumbered as No. 89 and there the firm remained at least to 1836. By 1839, however, the Globe Insurance Company was in occupation. In 1824 Wagner had dropped out, leaving Gale, Caterer & Co. In 1839 Gale goes and John Caterer & Sons, Hatters to Her Majesty, appear at 15 St. James's Street, are still there in 1840, but vanish in 1841. Whether John Francis Cater [sic], hat, cap and accoutrement maker, who was at 56 Pall Mall from 1839, was a successor is not clear. Henry Wagner thought that Christie, 'army hatters at the corner of Bond Street' had 'bought the Wagner business to get rid of a rival'.

Melchior Henry Wagner's widow Anne Elizabeth (Michell) continued to live at 93 Pall Mall until her elder son's marriage in 1814, when she moved into another house in Pall Mall, No. 10 (later No. 19). When her grandson Arthur Douglas Wagner (1824-1902) stayed there as an infant the building work on the Athenaeum Club opposite used to disturb his morning slumbers. The sketch book of Arthur's mother, Elizabeth Harriott (Douglas) Wagner, contains a pencil drawing of this Pall Mall house by Carlo Secandrei, who was, I think, the Italian servant of her husband Henry Michell Wagner. Ann Elizabeth was an intelligent, even an intellectual, woman. She had had from her father 'a boy's education, and knew Latin and Greek, but had the sense not to talk about it, except to her children, whom she grounded herself, knowing probably more than' her husband, 'who had only passed thro' Westminster. She used to repeat, with a remarkably beautiful intonation, many Odes of Horace—in her old age she amused herself with repeating much poetry, and some parts of Horace so often, that' her daughter Mary Ann, 'knowing nothing of Latin in the original, could repeat much also'.[20] On 27 April 1816 she wrote to the Duke of Norfolk to protest against his heightening a wall between Norfolk House, St. James's Square, and the back of her house in Pall Mall. Occupants of adjoining houses in Pall Mall were equally affected and one of them Chevalier Ruspini brought an action at law. Mrs. Wagner received a *sub poena* to give evidence and did so in Westminster Hall on

8 December 1817. 'The Chevrs Counsel accepted of 2000 as compensation for damages therefore the Nuisance of the Wall remains.'

She left four volumes of diaries which, though in the main impersonal or laconic, yet reveal her personality and life to us as no earlier member of the family is revealed. On Monday the 18th of July 1814 at half past nine, with her daughters Ann (1788-1844) and Mary (1791-1868), she began a journey 'in an hired chariot, with post horses, & the footman on the dickey', which took them 1,420 miles to Perthshire and back to London, where they arrived on the 13th of November after 17 weeks; having spent £373 10s. 6d. This was not the first such family expedition for Mrs. Wagner records that when they took a boat on Loch Lomond, 'the man who row'd us was the same who had rowed my sons four years before, to Ben Lomond & the woody Island. He spoke of them in the highest terms, & said how handsomely they had behaved to the bride and bridegroom & their friends, at whose wedding they had mixed in the dance. He was a very intelligent sensible old man, & explained everything to us'.

The route was by Barnet, St. Albans, Dunstable, Woburn, Newport Pagnell, Northampton, Market Harborough, Leicester, Loughborough, Derby, Matlock, Cromford, Haddon Hall, Chatsworth, the Peak, Buxton, Macclesfield, Knutsford, Northwich, Chester, Liverpool, Ormskirk, Preston, Gawton, Lancaster, Burton, Kendal, Windermere, Lowood, Derwent Water, Keswick, Penrith, Pooley Bridge, Lowther, Carlisle, Longtown, Lockerby, Moffatt, Douglas Mill Inn, Lanark, Hamilton, 'Glascow', Dumbarton, Loch Lomond, Arroquhar, Cairndow, Inverary, Dalmally, Tindrum, Luib, Killin, Hermitage, Kenmore, Taymouth, Nairn, Ballinger, Kenmore, Dunkeld, Perth, Stirling, Doune, Callendar, Alloa, Clackmannan, Edinburgh, 'Rossylin', Dalkeith, Melrose, Jedburgh, Edgerston, Kelso, Cornhill, Berwick, Belford, Alnwick, Morpeth, Newcastle, Sunderland, Durham, Raby, Auckland, Catterick, Ripon, Studley, Harrogate, York, Tadcaster, Ferry Bridge, Doncaster, Bawtry, Gainsborough, Lincoln, Sleaford, Folkingham, Market Deeping, Peterborough, Alkenbury, Cambridge, Buckland, Hertford and St. Albans back to London.

Scenery, architecture, localities and their manufactures and other activities are competently described in more or less detail in some thirty thousand words, with the attention one expects at this date to the picturesque and to noblemen's parks and houses. Occasionally there is mention of the hazards and adventures of travel and interesting or helpful encounters with individuals, especially friends or friends of friends. There is little, however, that is personal. However, a Mrs. Vernon, whom they met at the inn at Matlock 'discovered that she was related to us. Her name was Fisher before marriage, & her mother was first Cousin to my husbands Mother, consequently we were second Cousins'. Mrs. Vernon's mother, Mrs. Fisher, was in fact the sister of Lord Pigot and Mrs. Wagner's daughter Mary received, or at least admitted a deeper impression. 'My Aunt', wrote Henry Wagner about 1860, 'remembers, as she was travelling northwards with her mother & sister, meeting at an Inn Mrs. Vernon, who on seeing their names in the books, enquired if they were the Wagners of Pall Mall, & claimed them for cousins, & made them feed at a separate table with her party, wh. consisted of her husband, an oldish man, & 2 sons, one of 17 (who is now Mr. Vernon-Wentworth) & has (= Lady Augusta Brudenell B.) & the other, who was upon crutches, & is now dead—& further, on hearing they were going into the Highlands, asked them to

20

Wentworth Castle, upon their return'.[21] They did not go there but they did accept a 'pressing invitation when they were at Cambridge to stay with their friends Bishop and Mrs. Sparke at the Palace of Ely. Mrs. Sparke 'shew'd us the Palace which contains more good sleeping rooms, & greater comfort than I ever saw in any Nobleman's house before. The Bishop himself shew'd us the Cathedral, the choir of which is most beautiful, and highly finished'.

On the 4th of September the next year, 1815, Mrs. Wagner and her two daughters, with a man and maid servant, set out on their travels again, this time to Paris, now once more accessible to Britons since the victory of Waterloo on the 18th of June. They sailed from Dover to Dieppe, the ship rolling very much and making them seasick, but after breakfast on arrival 'agreed for an handsome coach lined with satin, to take us to Rouen for Nap. 5'. They passed through the village of Tôtes, 'where is a large Inn in which Mr. W. & myself had dined 28 yrs ago'. In Paris they lodged at No. 1 Rue Royale, 'named by Napoleon Rue de la Concorde, within one door of the Square of the Thuilleries. The suite of rooms was fitted up with taste, & some of the furniture costly'. Mrs. Wagner's son Henry, 'had call'd two or three times & had given us over', but soon came with his friends Mr. Luxmore and Mr. Burlton. Paris and surroundings were diligently explored and the sights seen are described. On the 1st of January 1816 they returned by hired coach to Dieppe and had this time a good crossing to Dover conversing with the Duke of Richmond and Lady Georgiana Lennox on board.

The diary continues to the end of 1817 and records time spent between Pall Mall and Brighton where on her sister Betsey's death in 1810 she had inherited the house on the Old Steine (then No. 49, later No. 47) where her mother had lived as a widow. This house was left to her daughter Mary Ann (1791 1868) and afterwards passed successively to her nieces Annie Wagner (1814-1865) and Emily de Wesselow (1819 1901). In 1817, however, Mrs. Wagner had also a house in Hastings, 'a large white one upon the farther cliff, or rather the lower slopes of the Castle Hill' (BN 109). Here it was that the Rev. Thomas Coombe began to pay his addresses to her daughter Anna Maria Wagner—as he told Henry Wagner on the spot some fifty years later. Here too her younger son Henry Michell Wagner made his appearance on returning suddenly from Italy in circumstances which must in due course be mentioned. In 1817, also, her elder son, George Henry Malcolm Wagner (1786-1868), took Herstmonceux Place, Sussex, of which two years later he had a long lease, and she visited him there on successive occasions, making day visits thence to her brother Eardley Michell at Wargroves, Herstmonceux, and her son in law and daughter, Thomas and Ann Maria Coombe at Carter's Corner, Hellingly. From time to time she mentions with evident pleasure one or another aspect of her son's country property. On 19 July 1828 she 'Walk'd with son to the Oast houses, nearly finished—saw his crops of corn & hops, all of which look'd beautifully'. On 14 October 1829 'Son had a ploughing match, 6 ploughs in the pack—Attempted to go, but came back on acc't of wind & rain. His two men, the 2 Isted won the first and third prizes'.

Calls on members of her family and their news, purchases at Christie's and other sales and at warehouses and shops and sermons heard at St. James's Piccadilly and elsewhere form the staple of her record; but especially when she is at Herstmonceux or Brighton visits to the poor and sick are not infrequent. The entries and comments are brief, but to the point and shrewd. At the beginning of

1827 after a nine year interval the diary is resumed and continues to the end of 1835 when the diarist was 78. 1827 finds her still at No. 10 Pall Mall, but in February 1829 the lease is given up and thereafter when visiting London she stays with her brother in law the Rev. George Wagner at Elysium Row, Fulham, coming into town thence by the coach or omnibus or in her carriage, but no longer, I think, on foot, as she sometimes had in earlier years. She notes arrangements made at Fulham for her comfort, a walk in the market gardens and by the river and in July 1829 going on the river for an hour, 'which was most delightful'. 'Brother George' enjoyed her visits but had ups and downs in health. On 25 May 1829 she took him in the carriage to Somerset House to see the Royal Academy exhibition: 'had much trouble in getting him up the stairs, & he groaned so much as to excite attention: neither did he seem interested in the pictures. It is the last time that he can go'.

Four days later she was up in London in her carriage with her daughter Mary and had called on Mrs. Brent and Mrs. Sparke, the Bishop of Ely's wife. 'In our way home the Coachman rang at Col. Rooke's bell, & the horses went off. He caught the reins but the lamp-post being in the way, dropped them. A mob of labourers began to throw up their hands, & hoot, wch terrified the horses so much that they went off in a gallop, then in a plunge—but the lamp-post getting between them threw them down, & we got out of the carriage—Two gentlemen offered to take us home in their gigs, & Mr. Halls partner sent a man & horse to take the carriage into his yard—& then sent for horses to take us home.—We return our humble thanks to God for this preservation. Those that saw us, say, they never saw such an escape we & the carr: might have been dashed.'

Mrs. Wagner was not at this time occupying her house on the Old Steine at Brighton and failing to let it satisfactorily seems to have decided either to enlarge or rebuild it. On 14 May 1828 she went there with her son Henry and 'Mr. Wylde, who brought the plan of the improvements which were excellent'. On 24 August, however, she heard that it was let for six months for 'very little'. On 29 January 1829 she agreed on a payment to 'Mr. Wilds' (presumably Amon Wilds) and on 27 February went first to 'Mew's' and 'then to the Steine, where the house was quite down'. On 2 March with Mary she called at Mr. Mew's, '& one of his pupils took the plans to Mr. . . . whose house we went over, & much admired . . . from thence, to Steine house where Mary laid the first stone'. On 27 April 1830 'went with dear Mary to Stein house much pleased with it' and the next day 'went with Mary to new house to meet Mew, & arrang'd about the papers, & best-room'. In May she was unpacking a trunk and china there.

However, after taking 26 Marine Parade for a month in June 1827, she seems to have made her home when in Brighton with her son at the Vicarage. Already on 11 February 1828 she 'had much conversation on the subject of enlarging the Vicarage'. The final decision was to build a new vicarage and the note that on 29 April 1833 'son Henry went to Town at 10 to meet Church Commissioners' may relate to this. On 29 October 1834 she went with her daughter Mary 'to new Vicarage, went over it' and noted a 'Great sacrifice of Western view in Chambers'. On 1 April 1835 she again 'Went with Mary to New Vicarage'. On 1 May she 'left the old Vicarage where I was born, with much regret—my sleep affected by it', and on the 5th 'Went to old Vicarage: most melancholy'. On the 9th she 'Went to Vicarage Garden: met son, & went over house with him: was astonish'd

22

at quantity of things brought up from Old Vicarage. Son insisted on my going home in a fly'. But, where, then, was 'home'?

Two days later 'Son dined at home & Arthur', i.e. Henry (the Vicar) and his son Arthur Douglas Wagner. 'After tea took a fly, went first to Chain Pier, then along the Cliffe, up Montpelier Road to Vicarage, got food for bird. After walking round Garden, returned, & set Henry down at the Cliff. In returning overtook Br. James, who went home with us in Fly'. Finally, after staying with her elder son George at Herstmonceux from 24 July, on 22 September she 'Arose early—Son, daur & 9 children all most kind.—Took affte leave of them— Horses arrived at 9: daurs C[oombe] 7 Mary went with self in carr: Annie & Tiz. in Dickie behind—much incommoded by Oxen & sheep at Lewes being Cattle fair—beautiful day, & had a most pleasant journey—arrived at Vicarage at 2— House & grounds very beautiful,—Son. H. gave us all a most kind reception'—The new Vicarage for the rest of her life was 'home' and she notes on 15 December 1835, shortly before her diary ends, 'Breakfasted for first time in Library'. Her daughter Mary Ann built a house hard by the new Vicarage, intended for her mother (p. 26), but she never went to live there.

Her views on the conduct of church services, preachers and sermons are regularly and firmly expressed. Her pride in her son Henry, the Vicar of Brighton, is evident. On 16 August 1827 'Son Henry took us all to see the New Church, which is very beautiful & much larger than expected. Wrote to daur. George.' On 7 November 1828 'Bishop of Chichester call'd and admired the alterations Henry had made'. On 13 January 1833 she 'Went in even^g. with Br. J. & Marg't, to St. Peter's: heard an excellent sermon from son: So God loved the world &c.' Two days later 'Son H. went to their Majestys' party. Her Majesty went to him & expressed concern at his illness'. Two years earlier on 28 Jan. 1831 she had noted 'Grand Ball & entertainment at the Pavilion—Son G.[George] & Br. James were there—did not return 'till after 2.' At St. Peter's on the evening of 24 November 1833 'Mr. Young (son of the Actor) read prayers remarkably well, but not devotionly—son preach'd. On 22 June 1834 she 'Went to Parish Church. Son preach'd an excellent sermon—Went in even to St. Peter's. Son did the whole duty, & preach'd one of the finest sermons I ever heard on the Subject of Prodigal Son. When finish'd, a gentleman in pew behind ask'd me if he were Mr. Wagner: I answer'd Yes. He said he had heard how much good he had done in the Parish, but this without exception was the finest sermon he had ever heard. I answered, it gave me peculiar pleasure to hear him say so, being his Mother. Madam, he answered, you must be proud of such a son, & I lament I did not take my two daurs here this even: Mr. Cooke got them seats this morn: I believe in Mr. W's pew'.

Politics are seldom mentioned, but when they are Mrs. Wagner makes her views clear. At Herstmonceux on 28 September 1828 Mr. Matthews 'gave us two very good sermons, but that in the morn: was rather calculated to raise the discontent of the poor, than to exercise the charity of the opulent'. On 9 October 1831 she and her brother James 'were both most thankful for the Reform Bill being thrown out of the House of Lords by majority of 41'. But on 19 May 1832 'Fear that ill consequences will attend the Reform Bill being passed—Thankful for having lived in the time of good K.G. the 3rd'.

23

For the last years of her life she occupied the ground floor in the new Vicarage known as the study and dying on the 27th of August 1844 aged 86 was buried beside her parents in the Michell family vault in St. Nicholas Brighton. In her will of 1 January 1838 she had asked for this in case she died at Brighton, but to be buried with her husband and daughter at Lee if she died elsewhere. She left her copyhold house in Black Lion Street, Brighton, to her son George, Trowhurst or Holes in Wartling (purchased by her husband of the Christmas family) to her son Henry, as also Tutty's Gill, a small farm of 41 acres, the copyholds on East Cliff and Little Castle Square to her daughter Anna Maria Coombe and those on the Steyne and in Steyne Court to her daughter Mary Anne Wagner, with remainder to the eldest daughter of her son George. She left £20 to her husband's cousin 'Miss Selina Godde—long separated from me but not forgotten'. When she was 85 she was painted by the miniature painter Stephen Poyntz Denning (1785–1864), curator of the Dulwich Gallery from 1821. She 'sometimes then', says Henry Wagner, 'had a weak look, wh. is just what Denning caught in his otherwise charming picture. Mr. Copley Fielding recommended Mr. D. to my Aunt'.[22]

Her elder son George Henry Malcolm Wagner (1786–1868) made with remarkable success the transition—not always easy—from West End tradesman to country gentleman. In 1817, as already mentioned, he took Herstmonceux Place and from 1819 to 1843 it was his home. By 1818 (see p. 19), he had taken partners in the Pall Mall business and by 1824 he was out of it. In 1819 he became a Deputy Lieutenant and in 1838 served as High Sheriff. This was through George (Wyndham), third Earl of Egremont (1751–1837), who was Lord Lieutenant of Sussex from 1819 to 1835, who used each year to offer George Wagner some shooting at Petworth, 'and would make him say where he wished to shoot, which had he declined to do, the invitation would not have been renewed'. Another of Lord Egremont's peculiarities was that he regularly enquired of his keepers and servants the amount of their vails, or as we should say nowadays, what they had been tipped. If he visited Mr. Johnson (p. 18) 'at Petworth, the servants had standing orders not to appear to notice his lordship's movements, & the latter would often pay a stealthy visit to the larder, when, if this was well stocked, no consequences would follow, but, if it seemed deficient, a haunch of venison, or some generous supply, was sure shortly to arrive from the big house'.[23]

George Wagner, being six years older than his brother Henry, 'a great difference at that time of life, used to ride down to·Eton to see him', when at school there between 1805 and 1812. 'He was very nearly missing "Kings"; but my uncle [George] having been informed that the Fellow next going off, wanted to do so immediately, in order to marry, but was prevented by the thought that he shd. lose some sum arising from his Fellowship, called on him, & finding it to be so, payed the arrears at once into his hands. On his leaving, he desired to 'dine' his friends in Windsor, & gave a long list of them,—many more than he supposed Keat wld. allow—into Uncle's hands, that he mt· do his best with the latter. Keat at once granted permission, say, for the first four, & with a little hesitation for a 2nd batch, but when Uncle proceeded to "ask leave" for more, he answered sans ceremonie, as his manner was, that if Uncle asked for these further ones, he wld. withdraw his permission for all the previous boys. Brighton, in his earliest remembrances, consisted of 7,000 inhabitants. The Prince first occupied a small house, with 2 bow windows, & a tiny garden, but afterwards bought the Duke of Marlboro's. George's [George Wagner 1818-1857, p. 95, *infra*] late Church was the ball-room of the Castle Hotel, & Uncle was often in it, in it's then character. At the theatre, & in Brighton Society, was a Miss Brenton, a very pretty girl, whom Uncle, a boy of little more than 16, used to spoon. Lord Craven, after endeavouring in vain to seduce her, actually proposed, & the Queen received her in her new rank of Countess, as she had been irreproachable'.[24]   This was Louisa (1785-1860) daughter of John Brunton (not Brenton), sometime a grocer in Drury Lane but subsequently an actor and manager of the theatre at Norwich, whom William, 2nd Earl of Craven (1770-1825) married by special licence on the 12th of December 1807.

George Wagner was for many years 'most active both as a magistrate and sportsman' and he and his family, 'being cultivated linguists and musicians', at intervals paid long visits to the continent, when 'they enjoyed to the full the excellent opportunities afforded in their Continental life, & saw much interesting & distinguished Society. Of the young ladies, the elder [Annie] was a charming harpist & the younger [Emily] played on the zither, while George had learnt the violoncello. Their father had *not* studied music, but his accuracy of ear was such as to enable him to sit down to the piano, on coming home from the opera, & to play off airs which he had only once heard'.[25]

On the 14th of April 1814 George Wagner married at Brighton Anne (1792-1878), daughter of John Penfold of Annington, Sussex, by Anne, daughter of the Rev. Miles Williams of Shermanbury and his wife Anne Michell. The Penfolds are traced back six generations before John, in Angmering and Sompting, to Richard Penfold, yeoman of Angmering, who died in 1608. In 1845, when on one of the family visits to the continent, which this time had lasted more than three years, George Wagner 'was crippled for life, by an accident to the family carriage, in which his leg was dreadfully shattered, at Tegern See, in the South Austrian highlands'.

Herstmonceux Place had been let in 1843 to Chevalier Bunsen, the Prussian Ambassador, and George Wagner moved to 77 Marina, St. Leonards on Sea, where he died on 11 October 1868, having celebrated his golden wedding in 1864. His nephew Henry Wagner recalled that he 'had an exhaustless fund of anecdotes and reminiscence, from which he was ever ready to bring forth things new and old, the latter, if not enjoying absolute freshness, regaining their youth, or at least a look of youth, from the vivacity of the narrator. His charm of manner and warmth of welcome made him a delightful host, and a visit to St. Leonards, as a nephew, who came upon the scene too late to have known Herstmonceux days, can testify, was at all times a treat to his younger relatives'. His widow died on the 10th of July 1878 and both are buried at Ore Cemetery near Hastings.

They had two sons, George (1818-1857) and John Henry (1821-1878) and two daughters, Anne (1814-1865) and Emily (1819-1901). Of George we shall have more to say (pp. 91-99). Anne did not marry, but devoted her life to George 'whose singular charm & grace of character she shared'. Emily married at St. Leonards on the 14th of December 1858 Francis Guillemard Simpkinson (1819-1906),[26] son of Sir Francis Augustus Simpkinson, Bencher and Treasurer of Lincoln's Inn, by Mary, daughter (and coheir with her sisters Mrs. Majendie of Hedingham Castle and Lady Franklin) of John Griffin of Bedford Place and

Jane Guillemard. Sir Francis was son of the Rev. John Simpkinson, Rector of Cliffe, Kent, by Renée, daughter and coheir of Abraham Wesselowski or de Wesselow, a Russian nobleman, who had been Peter the Great's ambassador at Vienna but did not return to St. Petersburg when summoned back in 1718 after the sentence and supposed violent death of the Czarevitch Alexis.[27] In 1869 F. G. Simpkinson took the additional name of De Wesselow. He and his wife lived at Cannes, where he built the villa La Cava in 1870, 'where he and his wife, with their keen interest in art and music, were well known alike to French residents and to English visitors ... His memory was remarkable. He could recall accurately the events of every month of his long life, and many friends will remember his graphic stories of early days in New South Wales and Tasmania (which he always spoke of as Van Diemen's Land), and of his experiences in a survey ship on the west coast of North America, where he entered the celebrated harbour of San Francisco through the Golden Gates when the site of the future city was marked only by a solitary farmhouse'.[28] He had served in the Royal Navy under his uncle Sir John Franklin and only absence on duty in Tasmania prevented his participation in the expedition to discover the North West Passage.

The only child of George Wagner to leave issue was his younger son John Henry (1821-1878), who was at Eton from 1835 to 1878, was for a short time in the army,[29] was a J.P. for Sussex, and married at St. Leonard's in 1851 Margaret, daughter of Henry Pearson and widow of the Rev. John Mossop, Rector of Hothfield, Kent, by whom she already had two children, John Henry Mossop (1846-1927)[30] and Mary Aynscombe (1844-1919), who in 1871 married Sir William Alexander Baillie-Hamilton, K.C.M.G. (1844-1920) and left two sons who died without issue. John Henry and his wife, who lived for a time at Great Sanders, Sedlescomb, Sussex, had two children, the last Wagners of the elder branch, Edith (1854-1947), who lived for many years at 36 Ovington Square, London, S.W., and Malcolm Wagner (1856-1933), who lived at 26 Walton Street near by.

After 1933 the only extant descendants of Melchior Henry Wagner (1749-1811) and Anne Elizabeth (Michell) were those of their daughter Ann Maria (1788-1844) and her husband the Rev. Thomas Coombe (1796-1876), sometime Rector of Girton, Cambridgeshire. They had four sons and four daughters, of whom Fanny (1832-1924), the youngest, was the principal legatee of her first cousin Arthur Douglas Wagner (pp. 100-136), whom she had looked after for many years.

Mrs. Coombe's younger sister Mary Ann Wagner (1791-1868) bought three acres of land on the adjoining downs at the time when her brother built the new Vicarage. There, on the part nearest the Vicarage in Montpelier Road, she built in the Jacobean style a house which from its fine open views she called Belvedere. A coloured engraving from a drawing by G. Earp, Junr., published by W. H. Mason, Repository of Arts, King's Road, Brighton, shows ladies and gentlemen strolling on the lawn, with the spire of St. Paul's Church (built 1848) and the sea in the background. The house was meant for her mother, who, however, never lived there (p. 23); Mary Ann let it for a girls' school and on her death in 1868 left it to her nephew the Rev. Arthur Douglas Wagner (1824-1902), who lived there for the rest of his life. On his death it passed to his first cousin Fanny Coombe (1832-1924) and on hers to her great nephew the Rev. Arthur Newman

26

Coombe (1894–1964), sometime Roman Catholic priest at Henfield, Sussex. On the southern part of the same field Mary Ann Wagner built the houses which now form Belvedere Terrace and part of Montpelier Place and Montpelier Terrace. These were left to different members of the family, the larger share passing to Arthur Douglas Wagner. Henry Wagner (1840–1926) lived and died at 7 Belvedere Terrace, which then passed to O. H. Wagner (1867–1955), who sold it in 1954. About 1850 Mary Ann Wagner gave a plot fronting on Montpelier Place for the re-erection there at her expense of the demolished Pavilion Chapel. This became St. Stephen's Church of which her nephew George Wagner became incumbent (p. 95). It had started life as the ballroom, designed in Adam-like classical style by John Crunden and built alongside the Castle Hotel in 1767. When Nash transformed the Pavilion for George IV, the ballroom was bought and converted into a chapel and consecrated in 1822. When the Town Commissioners bought the Pavilion in 1850, the Bishop claimed the Chapel as consecrated ground.[31] Thus it came about that George Wagner officiated as a priest in a building in which his father had once danced.

Mary Ann Wagner lived latterly at Brighton Vicarage, the home of her brother, caring for her mother till her death in 1844 and then and thereafter for the motherless sons of her brother, the Vicar, by his two marriages. These were Arthur Douglas Wagner (1824–1902), the son of his father's first marriage, of whom there will be much to say, and the two sons of the second marriage Joshua Watson Wagner (1839–1898) and Henry Wagner (1840–1926). Joshua, who was born at the house in Park Street, Westminster, of his grandfather Joshua Watson and baptized at St. Margaret's Westminster by H. H. Milman, afterwards Dean of St. Paul's, was sent to Eton in 1850 to the house of the Rev. J. L. Joynes. Joynes had married Fraulein Unger, Joshua's German former nursery governess and lived after retirement at 71 Montpelier Road, Brighton. Eton for Joshua was not a success and he was placed under the private tuition of the Rev. William Inge (1829–1903) in the house, Crayke Rectory, near Easingwold in the North Riding of Yorkshire, of Archdeacon Edward Churton (1800–1874), whose daughter, Susanna, William Inge married in 1859. Their elder son was William Ralph Inge, Dean of St. Paul's. Mrs. Edward Churton, born Caroline Watson, was the first cousin of Joshua's mother. Joshua's life must have been unhappy for he told Canon Charles Inge, younger brother of the Dean of St. Paul's, that his mother (Susanna Mary (Watson) Inge) was the only person who was ever kind to him. He entered Oriel College, Oxford in March 1858 and became B.A. in 1862. In 1863 he entered Lincoln's Inn as a student, but his health broke down and he died in 1898.

Chapter III

THE REV. HENRY MICHELL WAGNER

HENRY MICHELL WAGNER was the second son and fourth and youngest child of Melchior Henry Wagner, who has been the subject of pages 12–18, and his wife Anne Elizabeth Michell, who has also been described on pages 18–24. He was the grandson of the Rev. Henry Michell, who had been Vicar of Brighton from 1744 to 1789 (see pages 14–15). He was born at No. 93 Pall Mall, London, on the 16th November 1792 and baptised at St. James's Church, Piccadilly, on the 15th December 1792. He was educated at Eton from 1805 to 1812 and was a King's Scholar for the last four of these years. He went on to King's College, Cambridge, where he became a good classical scholar and was elected a Fellow in 1815. He retained his fellowship until 1824.

The conclusion of peace in 1814 having opened the continent to English travellers for the first time in eleven years, much of the next three years was spent in travelling abroad in order to acquire a knowledge of modern, as well as of classical, languages. In 1814 he was in Paris for 10 weeks and returned via Dieppe, Brussels, Amsterdam and Antwerp. On crossing an arm of the sea in Holland he and seven other passengers were overturned into the sea a mile and a half from the shore but were rescued by another boat. His principal loss was a box containing 90 louis d'or. There followed a very disagreeable passage from Helvoetsluys to Harwich. The day after he landed he was re-united with his family at Cambridge and accompanied his two sisters to a ball there.

He was again at Paris in September 1815, staying at a boarding-house in the rue Vaugeson, when his mother and sisters arrived on a visit. He accompanied them to the Louvre, to the Tuileries and to St. Cloud. In the Tuileries they watched the newly-restored Royal Family pass along the long gallery, and, as they stood very close, Wagner's mother recorded in her diary that she thought that the King and the duchesse d'Angoulême, knowing them to be English, 'regarded us with complacency'.[1]

In February of the next year he made his first recorded visit to Brighton. It included a disagreeable experience. He was stopped in one of Brighton's twittens, or narrow lanes, by a man who demanded money. His mother described the site in her diary as 'near the boats in the passage from Mr. Batcocks to Pool Lane',[2] (now Pool Valley). On his refusal to hand anything over the assailant fired a pistol at him and would have shot him in the head, had not Wagner put up his hand to protect his face. The ball lodged in his hand, and the assailant apparently escaped. The ball was soon extracted and the wound cleverly dressed by his servant, Joseph. As the condition of his hand subsequently grew worse and he was about to leave for France he consulted Sir Astley Cooper as to the propriety of travelling. Cooper advised him to go as his life was not in danger. But a piece of bone would in due course come away from the hand. This did in fact happen several months later. The wound was not fully healed until October.

Wagner embarked from Brighton on the 30th March in the sailing packet 'Union' commanded by Captain Wren. The passage to Dieppe took 38 hours. This visit to the continent was in fact for him his grand tour and lasted 18 months. He went at first to Fontainebleau, where he boarded with the family of a physician for the price of 7 napoleons a month. From there he moved on to Geneva, which he found full and expensive, and where he met several Eton acquaintances. Passing into Italy, he proceeded to Milan, Florence, Rome and eventually Sicily. Messina and Senegallia seem to have been the farthest points he reached. Thence he returned to Rome in September 1817. He would probably have spent the following winter in Rome, had he not been called home by an unexpected development.

The Duke of Wellington was looking for a tutor for his two sons. He first asked the advice of his elder brother, the Marquess Wellesley. The latter had been a school-fellow of Dr. Joseph Goodall, the Provost and former Headmaster of Eton, and so consulted him. Goodall recommended Wagner, and the Duke seems to have accepted the recommendation without further enquiry. Letters were sent at once to acquaint Wagner with his good fortune, but these did not reach him in Sicily as he changed his route. They eventually overtook him on his return to Rome. He set out at once for home and travelled via Leghorn, Genoa, Turin, Lyons, Paris and Dieppe.

On landing at Brighton he went first to his brother George's house at Herst-monceux, where he is said to have arrived in Italian costume, whatever that may mean, and accompanied by a servant named Carlo Secandrei, whom he had presumably picked up in Italy. He then went on to see his mother at Hastings before travelling to Eton to report to the Provost.

By this time the Duke of Wellington was in France, but he arranged for Wagner to go over there to be interviewed. After a good passage from Dover to Calais Wagner found both the Duke and Duchess of Wellington at Mont St. Martin near Cambrai. He was evidently accepted as suitable, and everything was arranged satisfactorily. He remained with them two days and then spent a week in Paris. The return passage from Dieppe to Brighton took 26 hours. Four days later he left for London in order to be introduced to his pupils by the Duchess of Wellington. The elder, the Marquess of Douro, later second Duke of Wellington, was then aged ten, the younger, Lord Charles Wellesley, nine.

Just over two years later a third pupil was added to his care. The Duke's younger brother, Henry, afterwards Lord Cowley, had married Lady Charlotte Cadogan. In 1809 she had run away with Henry, Lord Paget, the son and heir of the Earl of Uxbridge. He afterwards became Marquess of Anglesey. She had left four children behind. Gerald, the youngest of Lady Charlotte's sons, was born that year, and his paternity was repudiated by Henry Wellesley. In such a disastrous situation it was left to the kind-hearted Duchess of Wellington to adopt Gerald. He came to live at Stratfieldsaye. As he was only a year younger than Charles Wellesley Wagner assumed responsibility for teaching him from January 1820 onwards. Gerald Wellesley lived to be Dean of Windsor and the valued counsellor of Queen Victoria.

Another of the Duke's brothers, the Rev. Gerald Wellesley, was also deserted by his wife, Lady Emily Cadogan, who was the sister of his brother Henry's wife. A letter from him to Wagner dated the 28th April 1818 exists asking Wagner to comfort his son in these circumstances, as the latter was much attached to his mother but at the same time to intercept and forward to the father any letters passing between them. These rather contradictory requests must have been difficult to comply with, and it is evidence of the confidence felt in Wagner by the Wellesley family that such a letter was written.

At first Wagner must have lodged with his pupils at Stratfieldsaye. But in 1818 they went to Eton, and Wagner accompanied them thither. They started by being in Ragueneau's house, but towards the end of 1819 the Duke took for them a private house in Eton. Here Wagner lodged with them. There was a maid named Susan and, as Wagner kept a horse and gig, also a groom. He and his pupils frequently made visits to Stratfieldsaye and occasionally but not often to Apsley House. On these last occasions he usually took his pupils to the theatre. The Duke sometimes went with them.

Wagner's dealings with the Wellington family over the boys were naturally with the Duchess, who was a most affectionate and conscientious mother. To her Wagner wrote frequently, for the most part about her sons' health but sometimes about their scholastic progress. He clearly regarded her with the greatest respect and even affection. In June 1819 the Duchess gave him a silver ink-stand. He recorded in his diary[3] that the letter which accompanied this gave him the greatest pleasure that he had ever felt in his life. The Duchess reciprocated his feelings of cordiality, and two years later she wrote to him: 'My terms of gratitude and affection are all exhausted. I can only now say that I am the happiest of Mothers and that my Boys are most fortunate as well as the luckiest of Boys in possessing so active, so affectionate, so steady a friend as you. I write to each may their progress thro' life be blessed. I pray for them as I love them incessantly and with all my heart. To this I must add God bless you, Sir, believe me most gratefully yours, C. D. Wellington.'[4] The Duchess was a very religious lady, and the moral tone of her letters to Wagner and her principles for the upbringing of her sons were much more attuned to the Victorian age, into which she never lived, than to the Georgian and Regency periods, of which she formed part.

In the education of his sons the Duke was more a background figure or a court of appeal in important cases. But Wagner occasionally wrote to him and saw him often both at Eton, Stratfieldsaye and London. When in Stratfieldsaye he played tennis with the Duke, joined in the shooting parties and on one occasion was mounted by the Duke in order to hunt. Their relations were obviously cordial, though necessarily more distant than with the Duchess.

The tutor was for the most part satisfied with his pupils, though Charles was inclined to be lazy. They went up in class at the appropriate intervals to his satisfaction. Probably the highest praise that he ever gave them was to say that they were the best horsemen of their age that he ever saw. But this was recorded in his diary and not in a letter to the Duchess. Of their general behaviour, particularly that of the elder son, Douro, he was at times more critical. The severest occasion was in November 1822, when Douro's supercilious manner caused Wagner to strike him. He at once reported the incident rather angrily to the Duchess with the comment that Douro's manner 'would not be tolerated, were he in a different situation in life. His manner to servants is haughty in the extreme'.[5] For once Wagner was critical of the Duchess's attitude to the boys. He wrote:

'There is a veil before your eyes. You overlook Douro's faults . . . Your Grace takes a great responsibility upon yourself.'[6] The Duchess received this letter with complete understanding and sent a copy of it to Douro, who apologised and admitted his faults.

Of the unhappy relations between the Duke and Duchess of Wellington there are occasional echoes in Wagner's diary. In August 1819 the Duchess lost a paper entrusted to her by the Duke and 'was in great tribulation thereat'.[7] Wagner rode over to Reading from Stratfieldsaye for her with a letter to Martha Baxter, the house-keeper at Apsley House, to see whether the missing letter was in London. The following day he rode over again to fetch the reply, but he did not record whether the missing letter was found or not. Three years later he was sent on another errand from Stratfieldsaye, this time the whole way to London by coach, when the Duchess had read a report in a newspaper to the effect that the Duke had been assassinated at Brussels. Wagner went first to the Duke's brother, Lord Maryborough's, house and as the family were not at home, went on to the Ordnance Office. The Duke was Master-General of the Ordnance in the Liverpool Government at the time. Lord T. Somerset, whom he saw there, was not able to give him any information, and he went back to Stratfieldsaye the same evening, presumably no wiser than when he set out. But, as so often in his diary, he does not record the conclusion of an incident of which he related the beginning in detail.

On account of their relation to the Duke of Wellington Wagner's pupils and their tutor were frequently involved in events connected with the Royal Family. George IV invited them to parties and to Windsor races. On the 12th February Wagner rode over to Cumberland Lodge, Windsor, with Lady Bathurst to see the Duke of Kent lie in state. Only three days later he was privately admitted to see George III lie in state at Windsor. The next day he attended the old King's funeral in St. George's Chapel and even went into the vault afterwards. On the 29th April of the same year he and a party of friends, again including Lady Bathurst, walked or rode over to the new King George IV's cottage in Windsor Park. They were admitted to every room. But his comments are rather odd: 'Little interesting is to be seen, the furniture is beautiful in character and expressly made for the cottage. The chairs in the drawing-room are of beech cut in the forest'.[8] In later years Wagner must frequently have had occasion to compare these furnishings with those of the Royal Pavilion at Brighton after he became a resident there. Two years later (23rd March 1822) he and two of his pupils visited Frogmore and were taken round the house, garden and Hermitage by Princess Augusta, who had inherited the house from Queen Charlotte.

But the most interesting royal event recorded in Wagner's diary was George IV's coronation. To this he accompanied the Duchess and her family. The day before (18th July 1821) he hired the requisite court dress from the Regency equivalent of Moss Bros. for £5 5s. 0d. Then on the 19th he rose at 3 a.m. and 'dressed in misery in a broidered coat, waistcoat too large and breeches too short for me'.[9] At 6.45 a.m. he accompanied the family, including the Duke, to Westminster Hall. He was duly impressed by the magnificence of the costumes, particularly that of Prince Esterhazy, the Austrian Ambassador. He thought the Duke himself, Prince Leopold and Lord Castlereagh 'particularly distingué'.[10] The King entered the scene at 10 o'clock, when the officers of state, including the

Duke, assumed their insignia and formed a procession into the Abbey. Wagner then followed the Duchess and the boys into the Lord Steward's box in the Abbey. After the ceremony they all returned for the banquet to Westminster Hall, where 1,600 candles had been lighted. The King re-entered the Hall at 6 p.m., followed by the Champion—the last occasion when that officer performed his functions at a coronation. Soon afterwards Wagner himself came away 'Gratified and tired beyond measure'.[11]

Between the 22nd April 1819 and the 7th December 1824 Wagner kept a diary. Most of the entries are fairly pedestrian in character: the number of lines which he construed from Homer, Virgil or other classical authors; the chapters of the Bible and other authors like Clarendon which he read; the verses and compositions of his pupils which he looked over; the lessons he took; the letters he wrote; and his routine movements. But occasionally he expressed his feelings, though in a very restrained way. On some of these occasions he did so in Italian, French or Latin, rather like Pepys but with quite different motives for there was nothing improper in what he wrote. A typical comment of this kind when he had spent an evening at the house of Dr. Keate, the Headmaster of Eton, at which Wagner's future wife, Elizabeth Douglas, was present, was 'O qual gioja!'[12] On one occasion he even entered in Italian a list of clothes that he had to buy for his pupils, which reads like a washing list!

Wagner regularly took lessons on the flute. He took instruction in the riding-school with his pupils and was thrown on the 29th October 1819. In May 1820 he started lessons in Hebrew with teachers named Lyon and Meyer. On the 1st August 1821 Mr. Lyon took him over the Synagogue in London. When in friends' houses Wagner played billiards and cards; also fives and tennis when there were courts to play on.

The first notable event in his life which is recorded in the diary is when he took his M.A. at Cambridge on the 5th July 1819. This coincided with a visit to Cambridge by the Duke and Duchess of Gloucester and Princess Sophia. They were present in the Senate House at the degree ceremony. Wagner noted that he and nearly all the other graduates 'turned their backs on royalty making our descent from the throne'.[13] The next day he attended an oratorio in the Senate House and then went to a breakfast in Trinity College, for which 1,500 tickets at one guinea each had been sold. Part of this breakfast was to have been in the open air, but rain made this impossible. 'Nevertheless the effect of so many well dressed people was quelque chose d'étonnant'.[14] After dinner the Duke of Gloucester visited the hall and library, and dancing 'was attempted'.[15] On the 7th July the royal party attended a service in King's College chapel, for which they were an hour and a half late. They dined at the Provost's Lodgings before leaving Cambridge that night. Wagner remained there till the following day.

When his diary opens Wagner seems to have been rather interested in a Lady Bathurst, whom he constantly met for excursions to places near Eton. After one such trip on the 21st March 1820 he noted: 'Took leave of Lady B. Qual giorno infelice!' But she had a husband in the offing, Sir Frederick Bathurst. So it came to nothing.

His future wife, Elizabeth Harriott Douglas, makes her first appearance in the journal on the 13th November 1820, when he danced with her at a ball and afterwards in his diary wrote 'O qual piena!' She was the daughter of the Rev.

William Douglas (1768-1819) who had been Vicar of Gillingham in Dorset and Canon and Chancellor of Salisbury cathedral. Her grandfather, Dr. John Douglas, had started life as political agent to William Pulteney, later Earl of Bath. He had been a Canon of Windsor from 1762-1776, Canon of St. Paul's cathedral from 1776-1787, Bishop of Carlisle from 1787-1791, also Dean of Windsor from 1788 onwards and Bishop of Salisbury from 1791-1807. Elizabeth Douglas's father had died in 1819. His widow had been allotted a grace and favour residence in Windsor called Park Hill. She also had a house in Jermyn Street in London.

On the 4th March 1821 Wagner drove up to London to consult his mother and sister 'upon a subject that entirely engrossed my attention, and rec'd much satisfaction and good advice from my visit'.[16] From the context this consultation almost certainly related to Elizabeth Douglas. But his next reference to her in his diary is hardly complimentary. After spending two consecutive evenings with her he commented on the 29th July 1821: 'Quem deus vult perdere, prius dementit'. [sic]

There is no record in the diary of when he proposed to her. He did not communicate his engagement to the Duke of Wellington until the 5th December 1821. Their engagement was a long one, as was normal at the period. They were not married until 1823, and the Duchess of Gloucester only sent her congratulations in January of that year.

But in the intervening period Wagner's status had seriously changed, as he was ordained deacon. On the 30th August 1821 he asked the Duke of Wellington for a fortnight's leave in order to prepare himself for ordination with his uncle, the Rev. John Henry Michell, Rector of Buckland and Kelsall in Hertfordshire, as his occupation with the Wellesley pupils had deprived him of the opportunity which other candidates had enjoyed of reading divinity. On the 13th October Dr. Keate signed his testimonial and on the 27th October he went to Ely for ordination by the Bishop who was a friend of his mother's. He signed the thirty-nine articles and dined with the Bishop and Mrs. Sparke and the other ten candidates for ordination. After the other candidates had left the Palace at 8 p.m. Wagner played whist with the Bishop and Mrs. Sparke. He spent the night at the Deanery. He was ordained by the Bishop the next day and then returned to London via Cambridge. On the 4th November he took his first services in Clewer church, near Windsor, christened a child and churched a woman. Six days later he married his first couple in the same church.

In Wagner's diary after his ordination there is no noticeable change in his way of life. In fact in November 1821 there are two entries to the effect that he played cards until 1.15 a.m. and 3 a.m. respectively 'much to my annoyance'.[17] He also continued to play tennis and billiards and attend the theatre and the races on occasions. The day had not yet dawned when it was considered inappropriate for a clergyman to do such things. Bishop Grantley had not yet been succeeded by Bishop Proudie.

Preparations for Wagner's wedding began in January 1823. A connection of his fiancée's drew up a marriage settlement, and Wagner transferred £10,000 to his trustees of this. Another relation inspected the house at Eton which Wagner and his pupils already occupied and passed it as suitable for a married home. The Duchess of Wellington also approved of their living there. But there is no record of Elizabeth Douglas herself having inspected the house. The old carpets were taken up on the 14th March, and the painters and carpenters moved in four days later. Amongst the furnishings sent down to the house was a dinner service of 48 table plates, 12 soup plates, 24 soup tureens with covers, 4 sauce tureens on stands, 16 dishes, four of them with covers, and a salad bowl. The poor maid, Susan, was given notice for no more substantial reason than that, as she had not had a mistress for the past three years, she might not take kindly to one. Also as the household would require an additional maid, she might no longer be suitable. Wagner did, however, give her a present and offered to find her another place, but she replied that she was not in immediate need of one.

The Duke gave Wagner 26 days' leave to be married. On the 20th March he rose at 5 a.m. after a sleepless night and went to his mother's house, No. 10 (later No. 19) Pall Mall, though she was not there. He was married at 8.45 a.m. at St. James's, Piccadilly. The Bishop of Salisbury was not able to perform the ceremony on account of illness. The bride's mother was also unable to be present for the same reason. After the ceremony the company proceeded to Mrs. Wagner's house, for a large breakfast 'which was well conducted'.[18] The couple then left for Brighton at 11 a.m. It snowed all the way there. They arrived at 6 p.m. and found Wagner's mother ready to receive them at her Brighton house, No. 49 (later No. 47) Old Steine. The last entry in the journal for the day was 'At 9 went into a warm bath'.[19]

The weather continued bad, but two days later they walked nearly all over Brighton, which they found very agreeable. The 23rd March was a Sunday, and they attended a service at the Chapel Royal in North Street which was conducted by the Deans of Hereford and Salisbury. The Dean of Hereford, Dr. Robert James Carr, was also Vicar of Brighton at that time. The Wagners called on him the next day, as well as going to the Devil's Dyke.

They left Brighton on the 27th March and drove over to Wagner's brother George's house, Herstmonceux Place, 25 miles away. Here they remained eight nights. The 28th March was Good Friday. They attended church in the morning and then went—Elizabeth Wagner mounted on a pony—to inspect the ruins of Herstmonceux Castle, which Wagner had already described to the Duchess of Wellington as 'perhaps equal to any thing of the kind in England, and the place so beautiful that all strangers in the neighbourhood go to see it'.[20] On Easter Sunday Wagner read prayers at Herstmonceux church. They made a whole day excursion to Ashburnham Place, where they saw Charles I's shirt in the church, Battle Abbey and Hastings. Wagner's wife found this trip very fatiguing. They also visited Pevensey and Ticehurst and set out for Eastbourne but never reached it because of snow. They went back to London on the 4th April. The journey took nine hours. They stayed at Mrs. Wagner's house in Pall Mall and did not return to Eton until the 12th April. They found the servants all in readiness and the house much improved.

Eight days after the Wagners' return home the Duchess of Wellington wrote that she considered their marriage 'as a great blessing to my dear Children'[21] on account of the amiable society that they would now have around them. But a month later the Duchess took slight offence because, when the Wagners were in London at his mother's house, Elizabeth did not call on her and was actually for a few moments in Apsley House while her husband was in the house on a special errand. She did not have herself announced to the Duchess, and immediately afterwards they returned to Eton on the Duke's instructions. Wagner, however, apologised for any apparent misunderstanding, and the Duchess evidently accepted the explanation. She later became very friendly with Elizabeth Wagner.

In general the Wagners' married life seemed to pass uneventfully until early November, when Elizabeth's mother became seriously ill. She died on the 8th December and was buried in the Douglas family vault in St. George's chapel, Windsor.

The next event of any significance occurred early in the following year. On the 25th January 1824 Wagner's pupils awoke to find that two of their desks had been broken open during the preceding night. Wagner's reaction to this incident throws a good deal of light on his character. He at once set himself with the greatest diligence to investigate the crime and to discover the thief. The money stolen was two sovereigns from Douro's desk and a purse made by the Duchess of Wellington containing a few shillings from Charles Wellesley's. No plate belonging to either the Wagners or to the Duke of Wellington was taken, though this was to be found in a kitchen cupboard. Wagner's first step was to go before a magistrate, a former Mayor of Windsor named Bannister, and obtain the services of a police officer. At first the suspicion fell on the servants, but the policeman soon found evidence that the culprit had come from outside. Wagner was not content with official investigations only. He was aware of the existence of 'a set of men denominated cads'[22] whom he compared to the lazzaroni of Naples and to whom he and the boys had given money from time to time. He sought out one of these men and offered him a reward for the discovery of the thief. The man agreed to help out of a sense of past obligation. Either through the services of this informer or through Wagner's own efforts suspicion fell on one of the carpenters who were working in the house at the time named Joseph Flexon. Wagner and the police officer were in the process of examining another carpenter named Jacob, who had been drinking with Flexon until late the preceding night, when Flexon's father arrived to acknowledge his son's guilt. Meanwhile Flexon disappeared but was discovered by Wagner in a potato shed in Dr. Keate's garden. He was taken before a magistrate, Sir Charles Palmer, and confessed his guilt. He revealed that he had thrown the purse into a hay-loft, which had once belonged to Wagner.

At this point in the incident Wagner's reaction to the crime completely changed, and compassion became his dominant consideration. He was well aware that the penalty for any kind of burglary and for the theft of objects worth more than five shillings was death. He therefore concealed the existence of the two sovereigns in Douro's desk and declared the value of the money stolen as three shillings. He also endeavoured to see that the charge against Flexon was felony and not burglary. In this way he thought that the culprit would not run any risk to his life. To the Duchess of Wellington he wrote that it was their object 'only to transport Flexon, who is a thorough mauvais sujet, and if he had been successful in this his first attempt, there is reason to believe, from his character and habits, that he would have repeated such outrages, whenever opportunities offered and that he was in want of money'.[23]

Flexon had in fact been employed by Wagner as a groom for three years. During this period he 'on several occasions was guilty of improprieties for which I (Wagner) should have dismissed him instantly but for the

35

entreaty and tears of his Father'.[24] We do not know why or when he actually left Wagner's service, but he evidently continued in the same kind of conduct as his father later admitted that his son had gambled with his money, had run away from his later master's service and pawned everything except his last shirt which he had worn for a fortnight before the father found him at Hastings.

Flexon came up before the Assizes at Aylesbury on the 4th March. Wagner had informed the Duchess of Wellington before-hand that there was a possibility of his being compelled to prosecute for burglary but that he would not do so except under compulsion, though he did not mention what form this compulsion might take. He added that he was assured by their counsel that Flexon would at their instance be recommended to mercy and that there was no chance of capital punishment being applied. When it came to the point Wagner reported to the Duchess that he had been compelled to prosecute for burglary. But he had given Flexon a good character in court, despite his private reservations about the man. Flexon was duly convicted, but the jury added a rider to their verdict, recommending mercy. In view of the state of the law until it was altered by Sir Robert Peel four years later the judge had no option but to pass sentence of death. But when Wagner left the court he still felt able to assure the Duchess that the sentence which Flexon would actually serve would probably be very light.

After the trial the thief's distraught father cut up rough and accused Wagner of having given false evidence against his son. He even threatened to bring an action against Wagner for perjury. But he later said that he would not do so as he was a poor man. Despite the deliberate concealment by the prosecution of the theft of the two sovereigns in the hope of avoiding a capital charge, the father's real grievance seems to have been that any charge was made at all. He claimed that Wagner had told him that he did not wish to see his son either transported or hanged. The latter was certainly correct, but of the former there is direct contradiction in Wagner's letter to the Duchess of Wellington. Moreover it was not in character with the man that mercy should not be tempered with justice. Wagner evidently took Flexon senior's threat seriously as he consulted friends and counsel whether he should not anticipate Flexon senior by proceeding against him for defamation. However, they advised him to take no notice and to do nothing. Meanwhile the poor thief took a hand in the matter and wrote from Aylesbury gaol to 'Mr. Waggoner'[25] to say that he had induced his father to acknowledge that his accusation was unjustified. An apology from the father was actually published in a Windsor newspaper on the 5th May.

Soon afterwards Flexon was transferred from Aylesbury gaol to Portsmouth. In his pathetic letters to Wagner he seems not to have realised that the death sentence had not yet been commuted as he begged Wagner to get him off transportation in favour of imprisonment in England. A petition asking for clemency for Flexon was prepared and signed on the 12th April by Wagner and Charles Wellesley as the prosecutors after they had taken the Duke of Wellington's instructions. A number of the principal inhabitants of Eton also added their signatures. But this first petition seems not to have been successful for on the 4th May the Member of Parliament for Windsor named Ramsbottom forwarded to Wagner another petition with the request that he should transmit this to the Duke of Wellington for presentation to the King.

Wagner did this, and the Duke acknowledged that he had passed it on. Such a step was no formality at the time as George IV was a very merciful man and loved to find reasons for commuting death sentences to lesser punishments. In fact when Sir Robert Peel as Home Secretary was staying with him in the Royal Pavilion at Brighton he sometimes caused Peel to be woken up in the middle of the night when the King himself could not sleep in order to go through with Peel the list of condemned felons to see which of them could be reprieved. Flexon was in fact reprieved from the death sentence, but whether he was transported or not is not clear from Wagner's diary. The last entry about the matter was on the 1st June, when he copied into it a letter from John Dashwood King to Flexon senior, saying that, though the petition of the visiting Justices had been unavailing, he (King) had solicited the Treasury that Flexon might be detained in England and had reason to believe that this petition 'would be attended to'.[26] But he thought that the case would be greatly strengthened if it was supported by Wagner and still more by the Duke of Wellington. Wagner made no comment as to whether or not he gave such support. He certainly did not bother the Duke any further in the matter. As so often in his diary he left the final outcome of the point in suspense.

This is understandable in the circumstances because by that time Wagner had become involved in matters that were of much greater importance to him personally. Dr. Robert James Carr, who had been Vicar of Brighton since 1804, also Dean of Hereford since 1820, had just been promoted to the see of Chichester. The living of Brighton therefore became vacant, though the new Bishop remained also Dean of Hereford. In such circumstances the next presentation to the living, which normally was in the hands of the Bishop of Chichester, passed for that occasion only to the Crown. On the 12th May 1824 the Duke of Wellington sent for Wagner and told him that he was authorised to offer Wagner the Brighton living. This was more than routine preferment offered by a Cabinet Minister to a protégé. The living was worth only £150 a year. To this could be added another £150 a year from West Blatchington which had been united to Brighton since 1770. To a man of means like himself this £300 was not of significance. But the Duke knew from his own experience that this particular living would be specially acceptable to his friend. Wagner's grandfather, the Rev. Henry Michell, had been Vicar of Brighton from 1744-1789. He had kept an academy for young gentlemen in the old Vicarage. The Duke himself had been a pupil there in 1784 and had worshipped in St. Nicholas's church. His choice of this living in the Government's gift showed that he was most anxious to be of service to his protégé. But as the Duke had recently announced his intention to send his sons to Oxford and wished Wagner to go with them for a period of 18 months he did not envisage that Wagner should reside at Brighton. In fact he dismissed any question of this by saying that Wagner could 'get rid of that by application to the Bishop of Chichester'.[27] Wagner was much gratified by the cordiality of the Duke's manner in making the offer.

The possibility of such a living immediately determined Wagner to complete his ordination and the same day he called on the Bishop of Ely, who agreed to ordain him as priest. This he carried out at 8 p.m. on the 16th May in St. James's, Piccadilly. The question of residence, however, was not so easily disposed of. The new Bishop of Chichester, when he had been Vicar of Brighton, had not during his last four years resided there throughout the whole year as he had also been Dean of Hereford. But he had always spent part of each year in Brighton. When Wagner called on him in London on the 22nd May he said that he could not make any exception about residence but that the inhabitants of Brighton had recently talked of building or buying a new house for the Vicar, and a short absence might be justified on that score. The Duke of Wellington at first advised Wagner not to use the plea of a chaplaincy as a reason for non-residence. At a subsequent meeting at Wagner's mother's house in Pall Mall the Bishop was more accommodating. He said that he did not see any objection to what was proposed. The senior Curate named Taylor could well take duty for Wagner during his absences. However, another snag occurred. At a later interview with the Duke the latter mentioned that 'some of the Methodists had been with Lord L. (Liverpool, the Prime Minister) and had said that I had been found with another living'.[28] This was probably a reference to the fact that Wagner was already carrying out some kind of ecclesiastical duties at Winkfield near Bracknell in Berkshire. It was also a foretaste of much trouble that he was to have in the future. The Non-Conformist community in Brighton was very active and fairly numerous, and throughout Wagner's ministry in the town there were often to be clashes between him and them. In reply to this allegation the Duke took up his case 'with a degree of warmth that I c'd not have expected'.[29] He suggested that Wagner should obtain a written statement from the Bishop and Mr. Bates. It was not stated who Mr. Bates was but he was probably the Chairman of the Brighton Magistrates. Wagner travelled to Chichester to see the Bishop, 'who kindly offered to write everything that he recollected of the circumstances'.[30]

There the matter rested for three months. But in mid-September on the Duke's advice he made a formal application to the Bishop for a licence of non-residence in order to attend his pupils at Oxford. This was presumably granted, though there is no evidence of it in Wagner's diary or letters, except that he had another satisfactory interview with the Bishop of Chichester on the 27th September. The Curate, Taylor, accompanied him to this meeting. He began to take duties in Brighton at the end of July.

During this period of uncertainty Wagner also had other anxieties. His wife had been expecting a baby since 1823. Her labour began on the 12th June 1824, and Wagner immediately drove her to her family's house, Park Hill, in Windsor. He was able at the same time to send for his mother, who arrived from London by 10 p.m. The next day at 5.15 a.m. their son was born. By the 6th July the mother had recovered sufficiently to come downstairs and three days later took a carriage drive. But there was a subsequent setback, as on the 21st the doctor diagnosed that she was suffering from dropsy and recommended exercise, particularly on horseback.

On the 26th July the Wagners moved from Eton to Winkfield near Bracknell in Berkshire. The reason for this is not given in either the diary or the correspondence, but the Duchess had announced the move to her sons as far back as the 27th April. The Vicar was the Rev. William Lewis Rham who was a cousin of Elizabeth Harriott Wagner. Henry Wagner frequently took clerical duty in the church at Winkfield from June onwards and probably acted as an unpaid curate in the parish. His connection with this parish may, however, have been sufficient to account for the reference by the Non-Conformists of Brighton to the fact that Wagner had been provided with another living.

38

On the 6th August his son was christened in Winkfield church. He was called Arthur after the Duke of Wellington and Douglas after his mother's family. With the consent of the Duke and Duchess their eldest son, Lord Douro, acted as one of the sponsors. The others were the Vicar of Winkfield, the Rev. W. L. Rham, and the mother's sister, Annie Douglas, in whose house the child had been born. The Duchess herself arrived the same evening, and the church bells were rung in her honour.

The Wellesley boys went up to Christ Church, Oxford, in October and matriculated on the 16th of that month. Wagner and, it seems, his wife, went with them, though his time there was interspersed with visits to Brighton. The boys' career in Oxford, however, came to an abrupt end. On the night of the 18th–19th February 1825 the Dean of Christ Church's door was painted red, and caricatures of heads of houses were painted on other doors in Tom quad. Henry Wagner was not in Oxford at the time and according to a letter to him written by his brother, George, neither of the Wellesley boys was involved in this incident. But a month later after a supper party in Douro's room Charles joined other undergraduates in breaking out of the college gates. The Dean was extremely angry and in punishment rusticated Charles for one year.

The Duke of Wellington was not disturbed by the offence but took the sentence very badly. He considered it 'enormous . . . in comparison to the offence committed'.[31] He wrote at length to the Dean, the Rev. Samuel Smith,[32] to complain of the indiscipline in the college and of great irregularities being consistently permitted which were bound to lead to such incidents as had occurred. The sentence on Charles was eventually remitted but too late to curb the Duke's wrath. After considering the possibility of transferring both his sons to New College or Magdalen, Oxford, he eventually made the Olympian gesture of removing them both altogether from Oxford in order to fix 'the blame of the late transactions upon the authorities of the College'.[33] Douro was sent instead to Trinity College, Cambridge. Wagner was prepared to go with him, but the Duke also decided that it would be best for Charles to remain in Wagner's charge and go with him to Brighton for private tuition. In October Charles returned to Oxford to take his name off the college books. He had an interview with the Dean, who was quite friendly. He also inspected the college gates. The lock had been replaced but the doors not otherwise mended.

Wagner seems to have made periodic visits to Cambridge to look after Douro, and the latter joined Charles in Brighton during the vacations of at least 1825 and possibly 1826. In October the Duke wrote to Wagner to complain about his elder son's habits of indolence and listlessness. During a month that they had spent together the boy had not read a single book or followed any useful pursuit. He had been provided with German and Spanish masters and 'an officer versed in fortification',[34] but never went near them. Wagner also had to admonish Douro for not attending lectures at Cambridge.

Altogether Wagner's ministrations with the Duke's sons lasted at least eight years. Even when these ended he continued in touch with both the Duke and Duchess. For instance at the end of 1827 the Duke asked Wagner to find a tutor for his 'unfortunate nephews'.[35]

As long as Wagner's commitments to the Duke of Wellington's family lasted he had to fit in his new responsibilities at Brighton as best he could. He was inducted to the living on the 30th July 1824 and officiated for the first time at the morning and evening services in the parish church two days later. There were at that time two curates attached to the church. Neither was the kind of impecunious clergyman that the idea of a nineteenth century curate suggests. Both in due course acquired their own proprietary chapels and presented themselves to minister there. Indeed Brighton at that time seems to have attracted rich clergymen who were in a position to do this. During the next 20 years the town came to have about half a dozen such chapels of ease in which the minister was also the proprietor.

The senior Brighton Curate in 1824 was the Rev. Henry Joseph Taylor, who lived at No. 20 Grenville Place. Wagner was assisted by him in his negotiations with the Bishop about non-residence and evidently established good relations with him at once. The position was quite different in the case of the second Curate, the Rev. Dr. Edward Everard. The latter seems to have been the first person in Brighton to come up against Wagner, as was subsequently to be so common during the 46 years of Wagner's ministry there. At that time and since R. J. Carr had become Dean of Hereford in 1820 Everard was living in the Brighton Vicarage. This stood on the site of what is now Nile Street. The first post-reformation Vicarage on that site had incorporated part of the medieval chantry or grange of St. Bartholomew. This had been rebuilt in 1790 by the Rev. Thomas Hudson after the death of Wagner's grandfather, the Rev. Henry Michell. The new building was a simple Georgian house of three storeys, faced with cobbles or flints and ornamented with brick dressings and quoins. It had a fairly large garden. Wagner may not have fancied the house from the start or may have considered the site was too cramped because at this time he enquired from the Town Commissioners whether they would be interested in acquiring the Vicarage to give them more space for an enlarged market. However, they did not take up the offer, and the market was not rebuilt until 1830. Meanwhile Wagner moved into residence in the Vicarage some time before April 1826. Two years later he added two rooms and employed the local botanist, Henry Phillips, to improve the garden. Soon after the work had been completed the Bishop of Chichester called and admired the work that had been carried out by his successor. Wagner was to occupy the house for nine years until he built himself a larger Vicarage on the hill at Montpelier Road. The old house was demolished two years later, in 1837.

In 1824 the old parish church of St. Nicholas was a very picturesque building, though Horsfield in his history of Sussex described it as 'a tasteless and unsightly edifice . . . in all respects below mediocrity'.[36]

There had been a church in Brighthelmston at the time of the Domesday survey, but it is not known whether this was on the site of the existing church or was part of the old town below the cliff that had been destroyed by the sea during the sixteenth and seventeenth centuries. The existing building dated from the fourteenth century and comprised a chancel with a south chapel, a nave with aisles, a small south porch and a west tower. In the years since Brighton had become a fashionable resort the building itself had not been extended but in order to accommodate a congregation of 1,300 internal galleries had been put up in all available places, including the space above the chancel arch. These galleries were lit by dormer windows and entered by separate staircases from the outside.

Inside, the furnishings were those of a Georgian preaching-house. There was a three-decker pulpit which figured very prominently. This could be seen from all parts of the church, including the east gallery above the fifteenth century screen which turned its back on the altar. The seating comprised box pews, arranged in four blocks with cruciform aisles between them. In the centre of this crossing was the great treasure of the church: the circular Norman stone font carved with two scenes from the life of St. Nicholas, with the baptism of Christ and the Last Supper. In 1745 it had been placed on a brick base with a circular wooden seat round it. Above the seat the churchwardens of the date (H. Stanbridge and W. Bucholl) had caused their names to be inscribed. This had provoked Brighton's first historian, J. A. Erredge, to say that the inscription was a 'monument of their vitiated taste, confirmed vanity and profound ignorance'.[37] Unfortunately the inscription has vanished in a later restoration, when the font was again moved. There was an organ in the west gallery and a hatchment above the east gallery. The reredos above the altar took the form of a board inscribed with the Ten Commandments. Altogether the appearance of the church at the time of Henry Wagner's arrival in Brighton must have been something like that of Whitby church in Yorkshire today.

West Blatchington, which is now in Hove, at this time consisted only of a large farm-house with its ancillary cottages and a windmill of unusual pattern as it stands on the roof of a barn. The total population was about 80. There had been a medieval church there, but this was in ruins at that date and was not restored until 1894.

In 1824 Brighton already had three other places of worship belonging to the Church of England, two public and one private. The first was the Chapel Royal in North Street. This had been built by the then Vicar, the Rev. Thomas Hudson, as a proprietary chapel, partly with the hope of attracting to it the Prince of Wales who had made very few appearances at services at St. Nicholas's church. The Prince himself laid the foundation stone of the chapel on the 25th November 1793, and it was opened on the 3rd April 1795. It was designed by Thomas Saunders and was a simple stuccoed classical building with a colonnade at the east end.[38] The Prince did attend services there from time to time. But in 1822 when the Castle Hotel was demolished the King, as he had by then become, purchased the building and converted its former ball-room into his private chapel. This had been designed by John Crunden in Adam style and was a most un-chapel-like building. It was always called the Royal Chapel to distinguish it from the Chapel Royal.

In 1803 an Act of Parliament had been passed to regularise the position of the Chapel Royal, and it became a chapel of ease to the parish church. After Thomas Hudson left Brighton the freehold of it was acquired jointly by the existing Perpetual Curate, the Rev. John Portis, and the new Vicar of Brighton, the Rev. R. J. Carr. In 1824 the Perpetual Curate was the Rev. Dr. E. R. Butcher. The latter seems to have been another of the clergymen in Brighton in 1824 to whom Wagner did not take kindly, possibly because he was also a lawyer. There are references in Wagner's diary in 1824 to the possibility of Butcher defying his authority. The terms of the references make it clear that Wagner would have welcomed Butcher's resignation. However, this was not forthcoming. Whatever was the issue between them was settled satisfactorily in October, and Butcher remained the Perpetual Curate of the Chapel Royal until 1830.

The third of the three Church of England chapels that existed in 1824 was St. James's chapel in St. James's Street. This had been built in 1810–1813 and was intended to be a chapel of ease to the parish church. But the curate proposed for it had not been approved by the then Vicar of Brighton. The proprietors therefore had no option but to run it as a dissenting chapel. In 1817 it was bought by Nathaniel Kemp of Ovingdean Hall and was consecrated for Anglican services. In 1826 it was placed on a regular basis by a private Act of Parliament which authorised Nathaniel Kemp to appoint the Minister for the next 40 years. The Rev. C. D. Maitland held the position from 1828-1865. It was rebuilt by Edmund Scott in 1875.

A number of dissenting chapels already existed in Brighton in 1824. The most important was the Union chapel in Union Street, which was the oldest non-conformist meeting house in Brighton. From 1698 onwards for a hundred years this had been a Presbyterian chapel, but it then passed to the Congregationalists. It was rebuilt by Amon Wilds in 1810 and is now the Elim chapel. Its Minister, the Rev. John Nelson Goulty, was an exact contemporary of Wagner's. He was born in 1788, had preached his first sermon in Brighton on the 9th November 1832 and held the position of Minister at the chapel from 1824–1861. He died on the 18th January 1870 aged 82. During his ministry he was to become one of the principal spokesmen for the Non-Conformist community and was sometimes amongst Wagner's opponents in the town, but never in a malicious manner.

There was a Wesleyan chapel in Dorset Gardens dating from 1818. Lady Huntingdon had built a chapel in North Street in 1761 for her connexion. This building had already been enlarged on three occasions prior to 1824 and was to be rebuilt again later in the century. A directory of 1824 mentions also a Huntingdonian chapel in Union Street as distinct from the Union chapel in the same road. There was a Particular Baptist Chapel in Church Street dating from 1810. The Unitarians had as recently as 1820 commissioned Amon Henry Wilds to construct for them a fine meeting-place in Doric style in New Road. The Society of Friends had in 1805 built themselves a meeting-house, which still exists, in Ship Street, when their burial ground in North Street had been sold to the Prince of Wales as part of the transactions that led to the opening of New Road. In addition there was a small Roman Catholic church in High Street and a Synagogue in Devonshire Place, which, prior to 1823, had been in West Street.

Such was the ecclesiastical establishment at the time of Wagner's arrival in Brighton. But the town was already fairly large, and the 10 years from 1820-1830 were to see the biggest increase of population during any decade of the century. More places of worship were therefore needed, and five chapels of ease in the Church of England were under construction or in contemplation at that moment, as well as one other in the adjoining parish of Hove.

The most advanced of these and the first one to give Wagner any trouble was St. Margaret's behind Regency Square. This was the property of a jack-of-all-trades named Barnard Gregory who would have been likely to upset a much less difficult character than Wagner. At different times he was a chemist, wine-merchant, banker, journalist, newspaper-proprietor and actor. In 1824 he was the Manager of the County Bank of Tamplin, Creasy and Gregory at the corner of Castle Square[39] and the Managing Director of the Sussex County General

Fire and Life Assurance Company in North Street. He was also Editor of the 'Brighton Gazette' and the proprietor of a scurrilous London newspaper named 'The Satirist'. This last involved him in several libel actions, as the result of which he went to prison. In fact it earned him so many enemies that, when he turned to acting, he was frequently hooted off the stage. The building of St. Margaret's chapel, to serve Regency Square and its surrounding streets, was purely a financial speculation. It was called after his wife, whose Christian name was Margaret. She had laid the foundation stone on the 15th May 1824. The architect is only known as 'Mr. Clarke of London', but it was a most attractive classical building.[40]

Gregory wanted to nominate Edward Everard, who was one of the Curates at the parish church, as the first Perpetual Curate of his chapel. For some reason that cannot now be known Wagner did not wish Everard to be appointed and refused to give up his right of veto, though repeatedly pressed to do so. A long and complicated negotiation ensued between Gregory, Wagner, Everard, Taylor (the other Curate of the parish church), and Dr. Butcher of the Chapel Royal. Eventually Wagner had to lay all the correspondence before the Bishop of Chichester. Wagner's diary records many meetings but usually does not make clear what was discussed or agreed. Everard at one time admitted the truth of Wagner's statements and at another time apologised to him.

Eventually in November Gregory proposed that 'Everard, Taylor and Dr. B. sh'd retire' and that he would have no objection to the appointment of Anderson[41] under certain conditions.[42] The next day Wagner went to Chichester to see the Bishop who 'Wrote a strong letter and a complete contradiction to Gregory's assertions'.[43] This letter irritated Gregory, who then offered to elect Taylor, provided that Wagner would give up his right of veto. The next day Wagner felt 'very unwell and harassed'.[44] Gregory rejected his proposed terms. But on the 1st December agreement was at last reached. Everard drew up a paper which was signed by everyone, including Wagner in a desire to conciliate all parties. The terms of this agreement remain doubtful because the diary states that Dr. Butcher, who had previously been an obstacle to agreement with Gregory, might be prepared to retire from the Chapel Royal. If he did so Wagner expressed his willingness to 'elect Dr. Everard'.[45]

The implication of this wording is that Wagner should appoint Everard to the Chapel Royal instead of to St. Margaret's. But things did not work out like that. Dr. Butcher remained at the Chapel Royal until 1830, and Everard did in fact become the first Perpetual Curate of St. Margaret's. So in the agreement of the 1st December 1824 Wagner must have given way in an attempt to be conciliatory and must have accepted Everard for St. Margaret's. If so, this is the kind of concession which he would certainly not have made in later life.

Wagner's diary ended about a week after he made this agreement over St. Margaret's. So this is the last we hear of the dispute. But the preparation of the chapel went ahead, and it was opened for worship on the 26th December 1824 — apparently unconsecrated, though the Bishop of Chichester disliked the existence of unconsecrated churches in his diocese. Gregory duly obtained a private Act of Parliament dated the 10th June 1825 which regularised the affairs of the chapel. Being moved entirely by financial considerations, he had hoped to enjoy the right of presentation to the chapel indefinitely. But Wagner paid him £500 out of his own pocket to agree to the limitation of the proprietor's presentation to a period of 40 years, after which it would pass to the Vicar of Brighton. This was a provision which was included in all the other Acts for the erections of private chapels in Brighton at this period. The negotiations with Gregory gave Wagner an enduring dislike of proprietary chapels erected only for profit, and he never again agreed to any other such being built in Brighton during his incumbency after the completion of those which had been started before his arrival.

Edward Everard continued to play a fairly prominent part in Brighton life during the next 15 years. He remained Perpetual Curate of St. Margaret's until 1828. During this time he moved from the Brighton Vicarage to a house in Cannon Place. From 1825 to 1839 he was also Rector of Southwick and held both livings concurrently. When Brunswick Town was built he bought a plot of land there and erected the chapel of ease of St. Andrew's, Waterloo Street, Hove. In so doing he may well have had in mind to remove himself from Wagner's jurisdiction in the parish of Brighton. To this chapel he presented himself in 1828 and ministered there for 10 years. During this period he resided at Wick House, Hove, the original mansion of the Wick estate on which Brunswick Town had been built. This house belonged to another rich clergyman, the Rev. Thomas Scutt. In 1830 Everard was appointed by William IV Chaplain to the Royal Household, and he officiated at services in the Royal Chapel at Brighton whenever the court was in residence during that reign. In 1838 he was obliged by the Pluralities Act to give up St. Andrew's as he was also Rector of Southwick. He then moved from Wick House to No. 24 Brunswick Square.

When Everard gave up St. Margaret's he was succeeded by the Rev. J. Rooper. But two years later Gregory sold the freehold of the chapel to Everard's former colleague as Curate of Brighton, the Rev. H. J. Taylor, who presented himself to the perpetual curacy.

The next chapel of ease to be built was St. George's at the east end of the town. Its owner, Thomas Read Kemp, was a very different kind of person from Barnard Gregory. A gentleman and one of the Lords of the Manor in Brighton, he had taken the unusual course of reading divinity at Cambridge. Later he had had his unorthodox phase by seceding from the Church of England in 1816 and together with several members of his first wife's family had founded a dissenting sect of his own. But in 1823 he returned to the Church of England. At this time he began to build Kemp Town, and St. George's chapel was intended to be its place of worship.

Kemp obtained a private Act of Parliament dated the 3rd June 1824 to regulate the affairs of the chapel. The building was designed by Charles Augustus Busby, one of the architects of Kemp Town, and consecrated by the Bishop of Chichester, Dr. R. J. Carr, formerly Vicar of Brighton, on the 30th December 1825. It was opened for worship two days later. The first Perpetual Curate was the Rev. George Siveright. But three years later he was succeeded by a minister who was more important to Brighton life, the Rev. James Stuart Murray Anderson, who had been for a short time one of Wagner's curates. He was amongst other things Chaplain Ordinary to Queen Adelaide from 1833 onwards, and the Queen frequently attended evensong at St. George's. He was later Chaplain to Queen Victoria and then officiated at the Royal Chapel in Brighton. He lived at No. 12 Arundel Terrace until 1851 and remained a friend of the Wagner family throughout this time. In 1830 or 1831 Kemp sold the freehold of St. George's to Lawrence Peel of No. 32 Sussex Square, the youngest brother of Sir Robert Peel. Lawrence Peel remained the proprietor of the chapel until his death in 1888.

The next private Act of Parliament to deal with ecclesiastical affairs in Brighton was dated the 22nd March 1826. It regularised the position relating to St. James's chapel, St. James's Street, as has already been mentioned, and also covered Trinity chapel, Ship Street (now Holy Trinity church). This had been built by Amon Wilds in 1817 as the meeting-place for Thomas Read Kemp's special sect. When Kemp returned to orthodoxy in 1823 he was succeeded in the ministry there by his solicitor, George Faithful, who was to be one of Brighton's first Members of Parliament in 1833. Two years later Kemp sold the freehold of the chapel to the Rev. Robert Anderson, brother of the Rev. J. S. M. Anderson, and Faithful built himself another chapel in Church Street. Trinity chapel was consecrated for Church of England services, and Robert Anderson presented himself to the living. He remained Perpetual Curate there until his death on the 22nd March 1843 aged 51. A few years after Anderson's death the chapel became the cause of one of Wagner's sharpest conflicts, which was with the then Perpetual Curate, the Rev. F. W. Robertson. The chapel itself was rebuilt in 1870 by Somers Clarke.

The same Act of Parliament that sanctioned the building of St. Margaret's chapel also authorised Barnard Gregory to erect another chapel in St. James's Street. This he never did. But Lord Egremont, who then had a house in Brighton on the site of what is now Egremont Place, gave a piece of land immediately adjoining his house for the chapel. This was given on the understanding that Lord Egremont himself should have a private pew in the chapel, that at least 240 free seats would be provided and that the living would be offered to Edward Everard. Everard, however, went to St. Margaret's in 1825, and Gregory sold the site of the new chapel in 1826 to Charles Elliott of Westfield Lodge, Brighton.

Elliott had been a partner in the firm of Davis & Elliott, later Elliott & Co., of New Bond Street, London, which was then the chief rival to Waring & Gillow as the best furniture suppliers in London. The firm sold many fine pieces to both George III and George IV. They were one of the first importers of French furniture and supplied £1,745's worth of furniture to the Prince of Wales for the first Royal Pavilion in Brighton. Elliott was a pious man and a member of the Clapham sect, of which the central figure was his brother-in-law, the Rev. John Venn, Rector of Clapham. He was also one of the founders of the Church Missionary Society.

Within a few months of Wagner's appointment to Brighton Elliott enquired from him about building a chapel there. Wagner's diary does not record the nature of his reply. But Elliott went ahead with the erection of such a building for his son, Henry Venn Elliott, who was destined for Holy Orders but at that time had not yet been ordained. Charles Elliott entered into a contract with a builder to erect a chapel for £2,000, but owing to 'the bankruptcy of the builder, the carelessness of the lawyer and the roguery of the vendor'[46] his son claimed afterwards that the building had cost £10,000. The architect was Amon Henry Wilds. The chapel was a replica of the temple of Nemesis at Athens with a fluted Doric portico somewhat similar to that of the Unitarian church in New Road. Later in the century when Gothic had become the obligatory church style the first St. Mary's did not find favour with the writers on ecclesiastical subjects. John Sawyer in 'The Churches of Brighton' called it in 1880 'one of the worse built public edifices ever erected, and went on to say that 'some floating idea possibly possessed the speculative architects—who some fifty years ago marked this town as their own and for a time wrought their fantastic will with it—that so fashionable a place was destined to become a sort of modern Athens'.

The chapel was consecrated on the 18th January 1827. Elliott immediately presented his son to the perpetual curacy and left him the freehold when he himself died in 1832. Henry Venn Elliott ministered there until his own death in 1865. He was succeeded by his son, the Rev. Julius Marshall Elliott, who was killed on the Schreckhorn in Switzerland in 1869. Wagner then appointed the Rev. W. W. Godden. The church was rebuilt in its present form by Sir William Emerson in 1877–9.

Two other members of the Elliott family made some mark in ecclesiastical affairs. Charles Elliott's younger son, the Rev. Edward Bishop Elliott, was Perpetual Curate of St. Mark's church, Brighton, from 1853 to 1875. His sister, Charlotte, was the author of the hymns 'Nearer my God, to thee' and 'Just as I am'. Charles, Henry Venn, Edward Bishop and Charlotte Elliott were all buried in the old Hove churchyard just south of St. Andrew's church.

Of the five chapels of ease that were under construction in Brighton in 1824, the most important to Wagner was naturally St. Peter's in the Valley Gardens as this was not a proprietary chapel but an official chapel of ease to the parish church, St. Nicholas's. As far back as 1818 the parish had decided to build another church. As that very year a general Act of Parliament had set up the Commissioners for Building New Churches the parish decided to proceed under the provisions of that Act, rather than to obtain their own private Act. The Vestry had sanctioned the expenditure of £15,000 and the Commissioners agreed to advance this sum free of interest, to be a charge upon the parish rates and to be repaid by annual instalments of £1,500.

In 1824 a competition for the design of the chapel was organised. The winner was the then unknown young architect, Charles Barry. The runner-up was the Wilds & Busby partnership. The result, as we know it, is one of the best early Gothic revival churches in England, despite the fact that the church was originally intended to have a spire that was never built. As late as 1841 Barry complained about the absence of the spire, and there is no doubt that the effect of the church, standing at the end of the long vista of the Valley Gardens with its Portland stone gleaming in the sunlight, would have been even more effective with a spire than the tower alone now is. No explanation has been given as to why the spire was never built. But this was almost certainly because the parish was unwilling to pay for it. In the same year, 1824, Barry was also given the commission to build the original portion of the Sussex County Hospital in Eastern Road. A few years later he was responsible for the design of St. Andrew's chapel, Waterloo Street, Hove, and of the Attree Villa in Brighton Park (now Queen's Park), which were the earliest examples of Italianate architecture in England.

The building of St. Peter's proved to be a stormy passage for all concerned, though the disputes which ensued do not seem to have been caused or increased by Wagner's actions or personality. They merely represented the fact that the parish wished to do the job as cheaply as possible and was determined not to exceed the original sum of £15,000 voted by them. This, however, proved insufficient. The architect's original estimate had been for £14,703 9s. 5d. But by 1828 the church had cost £20,365 5s. 0d. The Commissioners provided further sums of £3,000 and £700. The latter was unquestionably an outright grant. But there seems to have been some misunderstanding about the £3,000. The Vestry took it as a grant but the Commissioners evidently meant it as a loan and in 1836 issued a writ of mandamus against the parish to return it.

The church was intended to seat 1,800 people. Out of this total, 1,100 places were to be set aside as free seats. The Vestry wanted this number reduced and rented pews to be inserted in parts of the galleries. The Building Committee, headed by Wagner, refused to try and influence the Commissioners to agree to this arrangement on the grounds that the Commissioners had made their grants on the distinct understanding that the majority of the sittings would be free. The Commissioners did, however, agree to reduce the number of free sittings from 1,100 to 900. The Perpetual Curate's stipend was fixed at £550 a year and the Clerk's at £50, though it is doubtful whether the Curate ever received as much as that sum. Anything over and above that figure which the pew rents produced was to be used in reducing the outstanding debt on the church. In addition to these supplies from the Commissioners voluntary contributions were collected from the public. Thomas Read Kemp acted as Honorary Treasurer of this fund, and Lord Egremont, Sir David Scott and the Vicar as trustees. Wagner himself, his mother and his unmarried sister, Mary Ann Wagner, paid for the painted glass windows in the clerestory of the building.

The other internal fittings of the chapel caused difficulties. The Vestry had voted £1,500 for these in 1827, which was to include a clock in the tower illuminated by gas. When the church-wardens were prepared to accept an additional liability for the erection of chandeliers the Vestry reproved them for exceeding their authority. The Vestry also quarrelled with the architect because he would not hand over the working drawings of the church as this was contrary to custom and because they refused to pay the additional fees of £45 for designing an organ-case and £13 for alterations to the west gallery.

As a result of all these difficulties the building of St. Peter's took four years. The foundation stone had been laid on the 8th May 1824 by R. J. Carr as Vicar of Brighton. It was consecrated by him as Bishop of Chichester on the 25th January 1828. The day before Princess Augusta had attended a sacred concert in the building. As the first Perpetual Curate Wagner appointed the Rev. Thomas Cooke, who had been one of his curates for a few months before this. He was an exact contemporary, having been born in 1791. He was ordained in 1813 and had served as an army chaplain in the last campaign of the Peninsular War and at the battle of Waterloo. So he also had Wellingtonian connections. He was to prove one of Wagner's staunchest supporters during the 42 years of their joint incumbency. He outlived Wagner by 4 years and only resigned his charge at St. Peter's in 1873 in order to assist the reorganisation of the whole parish by Wagner's successor, whereby St. Peter's became henceforward the parish church.

Returning to Wagner's private life, Elizabeth Wagner, or Zimmie as she was called in the family, never really recovered from the birth of her son in 1824.

This left her with dropsy, which was described by her doctor as 'the only kind of dropsy over which medicine has no power, but at the same time it is the only one which does not affect the constitution and health'.[47] The doctor proved too sanguine. Her body swelled to such a size that her husband's mother actually thought at one time that she was going to have another baby. The fluid had to be removed by operations that needed the help of four, and on two occasions five, medical men. These tappings were repeated every two or three months and took away vast quantities of fluid, usually between 24 and 31 quarts. The Duchess of Wellington in a letter to Elizabeth's husband wrote that in this suffering her 'patience and perfect sweet temper deserve to be rewarded'.[48] Between the operations she was able to lead a fairly normal life and even travelled to London or to Herstmonceux to stay with other members of the Wagner family. In London she tried without success what was presumably a quack remedy of the time. Her mother-in-law's diary records that she went to 'La Beaume's, where she was electrified and recd. 64 strokes'.[49] But on her last visit to Herstmonceux her legs were so swollen that she found walking 'inconvenient',[50] which must have been something of an understatement. By September 1839 she was dangerously ill. She could not stand but was lifted daily from her bed to a couch and back. Wagner sent for his unmarried sister, Mary Ann, to help with the nursing. 'After an illness of more than ordinary trial'[51] she died 'without sigh or struggle'[52] at 10.15 p.m. on the 27th November 1829 at the old Vicarage in Brighton. She was only 32. She was buried in the Michell family vault in St. Nicholas's church.

Nine months before Elizabeth Wagner died the Vicar's mother had given up her house in Pall Mall, London. Her Brighton house, No. 49 Old Steine, was in course of being rebuilt by Amon Henry Wilds and was later let. Henry and Elizabeth Wagner therefore invited her to make her home with them. She had accepted this invitation at the time but owing to Elizabeth Wagner's illness had gone instead for a temporary period to her other son, George Wagner, at Herstmonceux Place, Sussex. As soon as Elizabeth Wagner died Henry's mother and sister became permanent members of the household at the Vicarage in Brighton.

The house did not prove big enough for an augmented household, despite the fact that it had been enlarged in 1828. So in 1833 Wagner obtained permission from the Ecclesiastical Commissioners to sell the Vicarage and build a new one at his own expense. He purchased a site of two acres to the west of Brighton on the hill which is now Montpelier Road but was then open land. He laid the foundation stone for a new house there on the 24th June 1834. It was designed by a Brighton builder named Mew and built by George Cheesman and Sons, who were responsible for the construction of most of the Brighton churches built by Wagner. The house cost less than £3,000. It is in Tudor style with three gables and three two-storeyed bay windows facing east. But it is faced with cement and so plain as to seem rather gaunt and uninteresting. In size it was more a mansion than a clergy-house. Some idea of its size can be gathered from the fact that there was room in the cellars for 40 tons of coal, and 25 tons were usually delivered at one time. The ground floor has an immense drawing-room at the north end, a large dining-room in the south east corner and two smaller rooms between which were probably a library and the Vicar's study. One chimney-piece is decorated with attractive classical roundels, but most have simple Gothic motifs. The staircase is impressive but rather austere in its plain Tudor manner.

After a stay of a few months at Anne Elizabeth Wagner's house, No. 49 Old Steine, the Vicar's household moved into the new Vicarage during the summer of 1835. It remained his home for the rest of his life. After his death the house proved too large for comfort. His four immediate successors continued to live there, presumably with increasing inconvenience as the years passed. Then in 1923 it was let as a school and subsequently sold. It now houses the Junior School of the Brighton and Hove High School, who maintain it well and treat it with respect. The principal rooms have been little altered.

At the same time as the new Brighton Vicarage was built Wagner was also responsible for erecting a house at Chichester. In April 1834 he was appointed by the Bishop of Chichester, Dr. Edward Maltby, as Treasurer of Chichester cathedral. The post carried with it a residence in the Close immediately adjoining the Bishop's palace. Wagner went over and looked at this house and evidently did not like what he saw for it was demolished immediately. In the same year he laid the foundation stone, which can still be seen, for a new house. It is smaller than the Brighton Vicarage but in the same style: Tudor Gothic. As it is faced with flints with stone dressings and has cusped gables and ornamental casement windows it is much more attractive than the Brighton house. Here presumably Wagner lived for a portion of each year while he did duty at the cathedral.

Three years after Wagner moved into the new Brighton Vicarage he married again. His bride was Mary Sikes Watson, the only surviving child of Joshua Watson, who was well-known in the High Church movement and was called by Charles Lloyd, Bishop of Oxford, 'the best layman in England'. He had started life as a wine merchant in Mincing Lane in London and had made a fortune. But in 1814 he retired from business in order to devote himself to charitable work. His brother, the Rev. John James Watson, was for 40 years Rector of Hackney. Joshua's wife, Mary Sikes, was a member of a leading High Church family. With their co-operation he started a high church party which was sometimes called 'the Hackney phalanx'. He founded the National Society for the Education of the Poor and also the Church Building Society. He was Honorary Treasurer of the Society for the Promotion of Christian Knowledge, of the Clergy Orphans School and of the Additional Curates Society. Together with Henry Handley Morris he purchased the journal 'The British Critic' in order to restore it to its original purpose as the organ of the high church party. Watson was in fact the link between high churchmen before and after the Oxford movement.

Mary Sikes Watson was as pious as her father. A number of letters from her to her future husband have survived which were written during the year of their marriage and the year before. There is nothing in them of love or courtship. They were all about the principles of religion, the building of churches, vestry meetings, the provision of curates and such matters. One is left with the impression that she was a rather managing lady of too great Victorian piety for comfort.

She bore the Vicar two sons: Joshua Watson Wagner, who was born at his grandfather's house, No. 6 Park Street, Westminster, on the 29th May 1839, and Henry Wagner, who was born at the Brighton Vicarage on the 16th July 1840. The mother was 38 when she was married. She fell a victim to the Victorians' lack of skill in obstetrics and died four days after the birth of her second son. She was buried in the Michell family vault in St. Nicholas's church.

At the time of Wagner's second marriage his sister, Mary Ann Wagner, who was a member of his household, bought a piece of land immediately adjoining the grounds of the Vicarage on the south. On this she built a house which was intended for her mother and herself. This was at first called "Belvedere" and was an essay in the Jacobean manner but built of red brick. It was much more elaborate and distinguished architecturally than the Vicarage. Neither she nor her mother in fact ever lived there. Both continued to inhabit the Vicarage till their deaths. The mother died on the 27th August 1844 and was buried in her own family's vault in St. Nicholas's church; the sister on the 31st July 1868 and is buried in the Lewes Road Cemetery. "Belvedere" was at first let as a girls' school. At her death Mary Ann Wagner left the house to the Vicar's eldest son, Arthur Douglas Wagner. He occupied the house until his own death in 1902. It subsequently became a hotel known as the Park Royal Hotel and was demolished to make way for a block of flats about 1965.

Wagner's connection with the Royal Family did not end with his arrival in Brighton. George IV came there seldom after 1824. But on William IV's accession Wagner was presented to him by the Duke of Wellington at the first levée which the new King held, on the 29th July 1830. This was on his appointment to the position of Chaplain in Ordinary to the King. Henceforward he frequently officiated at the Royal Chapel in Brighton whenever the Court was in residence at the Pavilion during that reign.

On the arrival of the Sovereign in Brighton the church bells were normally rung. But on one occasion William IV arrived on a Sunday, and the bells were silent. The King sent for Wagner and asked why the church bells had not been rung as usual. The Vicar replied that on the sabbath the church bells were only rung for the King of Kings. Queen Adelaide, who was very pious, is said to have approved of this reply.

Wagner was invited to parties at the Royal Pavilion during the King's reign and occasionally attended a drawing-room in London. On the 5th September 1830 Princess Augusta presented him to her sister and brother, the Landgravine of Hesse Homburg and the Duke of Cambridge. The Queen also agreed to accept the patronage of a "Fancy Fair" which was to be held in the parish on the 10th November. On another occasion (the 15th January 1833) the Queen expressed concern about Wagner's health as he had undergone an operation for the removal of a fistula a few months before.

Wagner never held the position of Chaplain to Queen Victoria, and there is no record of his association with her. But almost certainly he would have continued to be invited to the Royal Pavilion from time to time as long as her Court still came to Brighton.

The five chapels of ease that had been built in Brighton between 1824 and 1828 and the one in Hove were all intended for the use of the fashionable residents and visitors in the districts near the sea-front. They were also good financial speculations as the pew rents were let for handsome figures. There remained the problem of the poor, who, in a period of almost compulsory church-going, were expected to attend services as much as the rich. Wagner was concerned about this question and therefore had a survey made of its scope. It was estimated that there were a total number of about 18,000 poor people in Brighton and that there were only 3,000 free sittings in churches set aside for them. It seemed clear therefore that further churches were needed in the poorer districts of the town.

The largest of these areas was at the east end of Brighton around Eastern Road and behind Royal Crescent. Here Wagner built the first of the churches associated with his name: All Souls, Eastern Road. He himself laid the foundation stone on the 29th July 1833, and it was consecrated by the Bishop of Chichester, Dr. Edward Maltby, on the 4th April 1834. The Bishop stayed the nights before and after the ceremony at the Vicarage and there were large parties to dinner on both nights. Due economy was observed in the construction of the church, and it only cost £3,082 10s. 8d. Of this, £1,000 was given by the clergy of Brighton. The Vicar's own contribution was £150. His wife also gave £37 19s. 0d., his sister £11 and his brother, George, £10. The Society for the Building and Enlargement of Churches contributed £500, and Lawrence Peel of No. 32 Sussex Square £200. "Offerings liberal according to their means"[53] were made by the fishermen, the charity schools, privates of the First Dragoons and even "the poor of Pimlico". The thought of how such people must have pinched themselves to make a gift is daunting to a degree. The Registrar and Chancellor of the diocese waived the fees due to them. The sacramental plate, a bible and a prayer-book were sent anonymously to the Vicarage.

When the chapel was opened there was still a debt of several hundred pounds outstanding on it. As long as this lasted the Vicar required all the clergy in his parish to preach an appeal sermon once a year for the benefit of the church's funds. By August 1858 the debt had been reduced to £100. Presumably it had been completely eliminated by the time of the Vicar's death in 1870.

The architects of the chapel were Messrs. Mew, who also designed the new Brighton Vicarage, but the money did not run to architectural embellishments. Only the north elevation was exposed, and this received the simplest classical treatment, with a tower at the west end, decorated only with a clock-face. The interior reflected the meeting of the eighteenth and nineteenth centuries. It took the form of an old-fashioned preaching-house and had galleries on three sides and a three-decker pulpit. The Vicar's mother greatly admired the latter when she first saw it. But the details of decoration to the galleries and their columns were Gothic. The first Perpetual Curate appointed by Wagner was the Rev. Gilbert Henry Langdon, who had been one of his curates at St. Nicholas's. During Langdon's incumbency All Souls had the first surpliced choir in Brighton, which was trained by J. V. Bond, the organist of Trinity chapel, Ship Street. It was accompanied by a barrel-organ. Langdon went on to be Vicar of Oving near Chichester and was succeeded by the Rev. H. Ellison. Langdon died in 1853, and there is a memorial window to him in St. Paul's Church, Brighton. All Souls church was altered twice in the later nineteenth century. It was enlarged in 1858 at the cost of £1,040. The builder was named Winder of Grafton Cottage, Upper St. James's Street. It was later altered by Edmund Scott. The church was demolished as redundant in 1968.

The next church built by Wagner was Christ Church, Montpelier Road. It is rather surprising that this site was chosen as it was fairly close to St. Margaret's chapel, and the Montpelier and Clifton Hill estate to the north of Western Road had not yet been built. The construction of the church took less than a year, and it was consecrated by the Bishop of Chichester, Dr. William Otter, on the 26th

April 1838. The fact that the district was more elegant than that of All Souls was reflected in the larger cost of the building and its greater architectural distinction. The total cost was £4,600. The Vicar, his mother and sister, Mary Ann Wagner, all gave £200 each towards this; his brother George £20. Wagner also made himself responsible for the expense of the stained glass in the east window and for the construction of the vaults below the church. He took advantage of his connection with people in high places to obtain a gift of £50 from King William IV shortly before his death and of £50 from Queen Adelaide. Queen Victoria also gave £50 after her accession. The ever-generous Lawrence Peel contributed £200, Colonel Wyndham and Captain Hope £100 each. The Commissioners for Building New Churches and the Incorporated Society for the Building and Enlargement of Churches each gave £500.

The architect was George Cheesman junior and the builders Cheesman & Son. The building committee were so pleased with their work that they presented father and son with a piece of plate each. The style of the church was rather rudimentary thirteenth century Gothic, and the chief feature of the building is the tower with spire over it at the east end in Montpelier Road. Many Brighton churches are not rightly orientated from a ritual point of view, and it was intended to place the altar in Christ Church at the west end of the building. But this was not acceptable to the Commissioners for New Churches if they were to make a substantial contribution. The arrangement was therefore altered so that the main entrance is at the side of the altar. The church was described by Sawyer in his "Churches of Brighton" in 1880 as being "old-fashioned". In this it no doubt reflected the fact that the Vicar of Brighton, who was its begetter, was also old-fashioned. There were galleries, high pews, a three-decker pulpit and a reredos of the Lord's Prayer, the Creed and the Ten Commandments. The church seated 1,070 people. 620 of these were free seats. It was demolished in 1982.

As the first Perpetual Curate Wagner appointed one of his own curates, the Rev. James Vaughan, who had come to him from Chelsea in 1836. Vaughan remained at Christ Church for 43 years. He was almost the last Church of England clergyman in Brighton to preach in a black gown but did eventually agree to wear a surplice. However, he remained anti-ritualist and preached against ritualism on the Sunday following the opening of St. Bartholomew's church in 1874. In 1841 he built the charming little miniature Tudor Gothic Sunday School in Bedford Place adjoining the church, which was later spoiled by the addition of a much larger and more realistic extension behind it.

The third Wagner church was St. John the Evangelist's, Carlton Hill. This area probably was at the time and remained throughout the century and even beyond the poorest district in Brighton. Wagner in fact realised that a chapel there could never be self-supporting and that very little or nothing could be obtained from pew rents. He therefore aimed to provide an endowment for the church to take the place of pew-rents. The building cost £5,212 7s. 11d., of which all but £450 had been raised by the time that it was opened. The Wagner family was as generous as usual. The Vicar himself gave £200, his mother and sister £25 each, his brother, George, £10, the Vicar's wife £118 10s. 0d. and her father, Joshua Watson, no less than £265. Wagner again persuaded Queen Victoria to subscribe £50. The pious Marquess of Bristol, the Rev. J. S. M. Anderson, J. P. Morier and Miss Woods all contributed £100 each; Lawrence Peel again £50 and Sir Adolphus

Dalrymple, who had been Member of Parliament for Brighton from 1837 to 1841, £25. As in the case of Christ Church, the Commissioners for Building New Churches and the Incorporated Society for the Building and Enlargement of Churches provided help: the former as much as £1,000 and the latter £500. The Chichester Diocesan Society also gave £500. The amount of the endowment fund raised was £2,996 11s. 6d., of which the Royal Bounty Fund contributed £1,400.

The architect of St. John's, as of Christ Church, was George Cheesman junior, and the builders Cheesman and Son. John Sawyer says that the building of churches in classical style, which he so much disliked, was given the "coup-de-grace"[54] by the erection of St. John's, Carlton Hill. Like All Souls, the exterior, through poverty and the nearness of other buildings, was of the utmost simplicity. But the interior is a most elegant composition, again of the preaching-house variety, with galleries on three sides.

The church was consecrated on the 28th January 1840. The Bishop of Chichester, Dr. William Otter, was unable to officiate through illness, but his place was most appropriately taken by the Bishop of Worcester, Dr. R. J. Carr, who was staying in Brighton at the time and had himself been Vicar of Brighton from 1804 to 1824. Of the 1,200 seats, 650 were free. The first Perpetual Curate appointed by Wagner was the Rev. Wall Buckley. But he only stayed three years and was succeeded by the Rev. R. S. Drummond, who remained there from 1843 to 1861.

During Wagner's incumbency at Brighton five churches came into existence for whose construction he was not responsible. The first of these was St. Mark's, Kemp Town. Its erection was in issue during the eighteen forties. We do not know exactly what his relationship to the building was. The idea came from the Rev. Henry Venn Elliott, the Perpetual Curate of St. Mary's chapel. He had recently founded St. Mary's Hall school, which was opened on the 1st August 1836. He wished to have a church adjoining to serve as a chapel to the school. He therefore approached the Marquess of Bristol, who lived at Nos. 19 and 20 Sussex Square and owned the land between his house and the school. Lord Bristol's reaction was so enthusiastic that he set aside some land for the construction of the church and even began to build this at his own expense. But he did not obtain any official authorisation for erecting a church such as an Act of Parliament.

We know that Elliott approached Wagner, but we do not know what was the Vicar's reply. It looks as if, in their zeal, the Marquess and Elliott ran too far ahead and took his consent for granted, which was never a wise thing to do in Wagner's case. His future wife, Mary Sikes Watson, writing to him on the 17th April 1838, implied that Wagner's objection to the proposal was that he did not think the site suggested was the right place for a new church and that he also disliked the legal procedure which it was proposed to adopt for the construction of the building. The ecclesiastical climate was not then so favourable to the construction of proprietary chapels as it had been in the twenties. But Wagner was always on excellent terms with both the Marquess of Bristol and H. V. Elliott. Whatever may have been his feelings, the Commissioners for Building New Churches intervened—perhaps at his instigation—and, though Lord Bristol had spent £2,000 on the building, work on it was halted. It remained an empty carcass about 10 years. Accounts differ as to whether or not it had been glazed by this time.

In 1849 whatever had been the trouble was overcome. Perhaps by that time enough new streets had been built immediately adjoining the original Kemp Town on the west for Wagner to feel that a new church there was justified. The unfinished church was conveyed by Lord Bristol to the Trustees of St. Mary's Hall. The completion of the building cost £4,832 5s. 8d., of which Lord Bristol gave a further sum of £500. H. V. Elliott gave £1,500, and the remainder was raised by private subscriptions. The name of the architect is unknown, but it was probably George Cheesman, who designed Christ Church, Montpelier Road. The style of the two buildings is very similar. The church was consecrated on the 21st September 1849. Wagner was present at the ceremony. It is perhaps significant that presentations to the perpetual curacy were from the first made by the Bishop of Chichester and not by the Vicar of Brighton after the initial period of 40 years allotted to the original proprietor had expired. The first Perpetual Curate was the Rev. Frederick Reade, but he only remained there four years. Then in 1853 H. V. Elliott's brother, the Rev. Edward Bishop Elliott, took over St. Mark's and ministered there until his death in 1875. During his time St. Mark's superseded St. George's as the special church for Kemp Town.

Wagner's next venture in church-building—St. Paul's, West Street—was the most ambitious of any that he executed and the one which had the most lasting and widespread effects in his own lifetime and after. The site seems today slightly surprising as it is so near St. Nicholas's on the north, Trinity chapel and the Chapel Royal on the east and Christ Church on the west. But one has to remember that the old town (the rectangle between West, North and East Streets) was in 1845 much more densely populated than it is today and also that immediately adjoining West Street on the north west was Russell Street and a series of rather poor streets, where lived the major part of Brighton's fishing community. This community or "the fishery", as it was called, was described by Wagner in a contemporary sermon as "the descendants of the primitive people of Brighton, a class living much among themselves and standing in strong contrast from others".[55] It was for this community that Wagner designed St. Paul's. He even built them a reading-room attached to the church on the west. This had a huge fireplace with a colossal hood like the chimney-piece of a baronial hall. But Wagner had no success in drawing the fishermen away from the public-houses. So at a later date the room was converted into a vestry.

Only five years separate the conception of St. Paul's from the completion of St. John's, Carlton Hill, but the two buildings belong to different centuries. St. John's was the last of the Georgian classical preaching-houses which were part of Regency Brighton and which made the ecclesiastical climate of the first part of the nineteenth century so unacceptable to the rising generation of the clergy. The Brighton Gazette in 1874 described these churches as having been erected "on the most unseemly and degrading principles of art".[56] St. Paul's was to be a harbinger of a new age and the first of the great Gothic churches which, in time, were to be as important a part of Brighton's life and history as their classical predecessors had been earlier. The same article in the Brighton Gazette went on to say that St. Paul's was "a lasting rebuke of the barbarism of the past generation of church builders".[57]

Though Henry Wagner never belonged to any ecclesiastical party within the Church of England, since his second marriage in 1838 he had perhaps been influenced by his wife's father, Joshua Watson, who was a leader of the high church movement in England during the period before the Tractarians emerged into prominence. Also by 1846 Wagner's son by his first wife, Arthur Douglas Wagner, was 22. He was destined for Holy Orders, though he had not yet been ordained. He became in due course a leading Tractarian and ritualist. Over St. Paul's the father was entirely influenced by him. The church was intended to be for his ministry and was in all respects built according to his ideas.

On the site of the future church stood a Bethel Chapel that had been erected in 1830. It subsequently passed to the followers of Edward Irving. During their occupation Mrs. Anne Sober, the sister of Thomas Read Kemp, had preached in the building. In 1845 the chapel, two houses and a few shops were bought for £3,000. As builders Henry Wagner employed Cheesman & Son, who had proved so satisfactory in the construction of Christ Church and St. John's, Carlton Hill. But it was not good enough for Arthur Douglas Wagner that their junior partner, George Cheesman, should himself design the new building as well. He turned instead to one of the architects who was to be a high priest of the Tractarian movement, Richard Cromwell Carpenter. The church was one of Carpenter's earlier commissions in his relatively short life (1812–1855). The style chosen was late fourteenth century Gothic, then called "middle pointed". The exterior was faced with the local material of knapped flints. Great care was taken over such matters as the correct orientation of the church. As St. Paul's had to be approached from the eastern end in West Street, a long corridor was built along the south side to conduct the congregation into the building at the west end. The spire was added at a later date but this and the fittings of the church really belong to Arthur Douglas Wagner's story.

The church without its later embellishments cost £12,000. The Commissioners for Building New Churches and the Incorporated Society for the Building and Enlargement of Churches each made a grant. But neither Sawyer's "The Churches of Brighton", nor the local papers in describing the opening of the church record the amount of these gifts. The remaining sum was raised by public subscriptions. The Wagner family were as generous as usual. The Vicar contributed £1,475, plus the cost of the stained glass window at the east end. His wife gave £50 and her father, Joshua Watson, £805. The Vicar's mother subscribed another £50, his sister, Mary Ann Wagner, £310 and his son, Arthur, £10 10s. 0d. A further sum of £38 was provided by the Vicar's brother, George, and his wife, together with one of their sons and their two daughters.

The main work of construction took two years. The church was opened by licence on the 18th October 1848. The preacher at the first service was the Archdeacon of Chichester, the Rev. Henry Manning, who was Rector of East Lavington and Graffham in Sussex. At this time the church was only glazed with plain glass.

For the next year the church was administered from the nearby parish church by the Vicar himself and his curates. It was not consecrated at once in order to give time for the remainder of the money to be raised and also for A. D. Wagner to be ordained. The consecration ceremony was eventually performed by the Bishop of Chichester, Dr. A. T. Gilbert, on the 23rd October 1849 at 11.30 a.m. Afterwards at 4 p.m. the Bishop and clergy were entertained to "an elegant déjeuner"[58] at the Vicarage. A. D. Wagner, by now ordained, read the evening service, and the preacher was the Archdeacon of Lewes, the Rev. Julius Hare, who was Rector of Herstmonceux. Afterwards the choir was regaled by Arthur Wagner to tea and a magic-lantern show. He was appointed the first Perpetual Curate of St. Paul's in January 1850. The church seated 1,200. Arthur Wagner wanted all the sittings to be free, but this did not accord with the Georgian ideas of his father. So at first 460 seats were rented. These were, however, abolished in 1873.

The next church built by H. M. Wagner after St. Paul's was All Saints, Compton Avenue. Since the railway to London had opened in 1841 a number of streets of modest proportions had been built to the north west of Brighton Station extending up to Seven Dials. This church was intended to serve that district. It was in almost all respects a pale shadow of St. Paul's. It was designed by R. C. Carpenter in a similar style of Gothic and also built of flints, but was of smaller dimensions and much less cost. It was first projected in 1847 but not opened until 1852. The design provided for a tower at the north west end, but this was never built. Details of the expense have not survived except that the Vicar gave £300 towards this and that the Society for the Building and Enlargement of Churches made a grant.

The first Perpetual Curate was Henry Wagner's nephew, the Rev. Thomas Coombe. In October 1858 he made alterations to the sittings without any authority to do so, and tried to keep the Vicar out of church by instructing the Clerk not to admit anyone into the building. The Vicar suspected that these alterations were for the purpose of inserting pews for which rents could be charged. Such an action would have been a breach of the undertaking to provide a certain number of free seats that had been given to the Society for the Building and Enlargement of Churches when the church was built. But the Perpetual Curate refused to answer any question on the subject. The Vicar therefore requested the Bishop of Chichester, Dr. A. T. Gilbert, to require him to replace the beautiful woodwork of the chancel, which he had removed, and to give an undertaking that no such measure would be repeated and also that the Vicar would not be excluded from the church.

All Saints was always a modest building which attracted little attention during the hundred years of its existence and was quietly demolished in 1957.

To the same period as All Saints belongs St. Stephen's, Montpelier Place, though it was not one of H. M. Wagner's own churches. This was a new church made out of an old chapel. It had started life as the ball-room of the Castle Hotel in Castle Square. Then in 1822 it had been converted into the Royal Chapel of the Royal Pavilion. When the Pavilion was sold by the Commissioners of Woods and Forests to the Brighton Commissioners the chapel was claimed by ecclesiastical authorities and excepted from the sale. Instead the diocese of Chichester paid £3,000 for it. The Vicar's sister, Mary Ann Wagner, made a gift of a piece of land near to the new Vicarage on which the chapel was re-erected complete with its classical Adamesque interior. It was re-opened as St. Stephen's Church in 1853. But this really belongs to the story of the Vicar's nephew, George Wagner, who was the first Perpetual Curate of St. Stephen's.

In the eighteen fifties two offers of assistance in building a new church were received from outside the parish. The first was from an architect named George Morgan on behalf of the Conservative Land Society, which was then developing the Round Hill estate north of Park Crescent on the site of what had been Ireland's Gardens. He enquired whether the Vicar would approve of a new church being built nearby if a site was given for the purpose. Wagner replied rather stiffly with a list of questions as to their intentions, particularly as to their proposals for finishing the church. In a later letter he wrote that, as the population of the neighbourhood was rather scanty, he thought that a new church there would be "of comparatively little Spiritual advantage to my Parish".[59] But he added that he knew someone who might contribute £200 to an expenditure of about £2,500 if a church, other than a proprietary chapel, was built with a plan that was susceptible of enlargement if and when the population of the district increased. This unnamed person may well have been a member of his own family. But nothing more was heard of a church on that site for at least 10 years.

The second offer proceeded from the Rev. William Clarke, writing from Lympsham Rectory, Weston-super-Mare, in September 1858. He offered to build a Gothic chapel seating 300 people with 100 free seats and only so many rented pews as would be necessary to provide a stipend for the Perpetual Curate, with the aim of presenting himself to serve in that capacity. Wagner's sister replied on his behalf to the effect that the Vicar had an "insuperable objection to proprietary chapels".[60] William Clarke then varied the terms of his proposal to the effect that the funds for building such a chapel could be raised by public subscription and he would only reserve for himself sufficient pew-rents to bring in an income of £100 a year. He hoped that Wagner would not think him mercenary in making this reservation. After the interchange of several further letters the Vicar eventually wrote kindly but firmly to say that he did not consider his correspondent in any way mercenary but only that he did not seem to know his own mind as he had made four different proposals. He concluded with "my request that this correspondence may cease".[61]

If Wagner had an insuperable objection to proprietary chapels this was only on account of their being operated for financial gain. He clung firmly to the rights of presentation given to him as Vicar of Brighton after the first 40 years' existence of such chapels under the private Acts of Parliament that had already been passed. In May 1856 the Marquess of Blandford introduced into the House of Commons a Formation of Parishes bill which would have abolished Wagner's right of presentation under previous Acts to the Chapel Royal, St. Peter's, Trinity chapel, St. George's, St. Margaret's and St. Mary's. In the case of the two last he had even paid £500 to Barnard Gregory to secure this eventual right of presentation after 40 years. So he instructed his solicitor, Somers Clarke, to approach Lord Blandford to see whether the latter would accept any amendment to his bill whereby the presentation in these Brighton churches could be excluded from the bill. Lord Blandford refused the suggestion. Somers Clarke therefore enlisted the help of the two Brighton Members, Lord Alfred Hervey and Admiral Sir George Brooke Pechell. The latter had not always seen eye to eye with Wagner, particularly over church rates. But both Members agreed to assist him in this case and sponsored an amendment drafted by Somers Clarke. Wagner then approached the Bishop of Chichester, Dr. A. T. Gilbert, but was reassured by him that the bill had no chance of passing that session. Though it was referred to a select committee of the House of Lords, it did not in fact become law.

The last church in Brighton to be completed by H. M. Wagner was St. Anne's, Burlington Street. This was the most fashionable position of any Wagner church as it was very near to the sea-front and immediately behind Royal Crescent. It was erected in memory of the Rev. James Churchill, a former chaplain of the Extra-Mural Cemetery, in accordance with the will of his mother, Maria Cook, who had lived in Charlotte Street nearby, and on the condition that the church was built in that immediate district. She left an endowment of £6,600, which was supplemented by a lesser amount from her sister, Mrs. Welton. The Bishop of Chichester, Dr. A. T. Gilbert, and the Vicar of Brighton invited the Rev. Alfred Cooper to accept the responsibility for raising enough money to build the church and to be its first Perpetual Curate. Wagner with typical generosity headed the subscription list with a gift of £2,200 and Alfred Cooper himself gave £2,000. The Bishop of Chichester contributed £50, the Bishop of Winchester £10, the Incorporated Society for the Building and the Enlargement of Churches £300, the Chichester Diocesan Society £40 and Mrs. Welton £150. The total cost was £5,055. The architect was Benjamin Ferrey, who had been a pupil of A. W. Pugin. But he was on the whole a dull architect, and St. Anne's is no exception to the usual run of his work. The foundation stone was laid by the Vicar on the 16th June 1862 and it was consecrated by the Bishop of Chichester on the 13th June 1863.

Exactly contemporary with St. Anne's were three other churches for whose construction H. M. Wagner was not responsible, though they were built during his incumbency. The first of these was St. Michael and All Angels, St. Michael's Place. This was built to serve the Montpelier and Clifton Hill estate, which was developed from 1840 onwards but was never a poor district. The financial sponsors of the church were two sisters named Windle and friends of its first Perpetual Curate, the Rev. Charles Beanlands, who was previously a curate at St. Paul's. It was begun in 1860 and consecrated by the Bishop of Chichester, Dr. A. T. Gilbert, on St. Michael's day in 1862. The original portion, which is now the south aisle, was designed by George Frederick Bodley in a style that is usually described as north Italian Gothic, but Sawyer's "The Churches of Brighton" called it "Early English with some Byzantine features". An old-fashioned anti-quary like Mark Anthony Lower, who evidently preferred classical churches, in his "History of Sussex" called in "a continental hotel-de-ville". St. Michael's became one of the great ritualistic churches of Brighton. The north aisle was added in 1892 and is a posthumous work of William Burges. The other two churches of this period were St. Mary and St. Mary Magdalene and the Church of the Annunciation, which were built in 1862 and 1864 respectively. But as they were due to the initiative of Arthur Douglas Wagner, rather than that of his father, this story belongs to Chapter V.

Two other church projects of H. M. Wagner's never materialised in his lifetime. As has already been mentioned, there was no church at West Blatchington, which was then linked with the Brighton living. But the Vicar regularly arranged for one of his curates to hold services in one of the farm cottages. In 1855 he underwent a severe illness from which at first it was thought that he would not recover. When in fact he did so he formed the resolution to build at his own expense a new church at West Blatchington as a thank-offering for his recovery. He even went so far as obtaining a plan for this from G. F. Bodley—an architect no doubt suggested by his son, Arthur. All the land in the parish of West Blatchington then belonged to the Marquess of Abergavenny. The Vicar had necessarily to ask his permission. From his sick-bed he dictated a letter since his tremulous hand was still unequal to the use of a pen, asking the Marquess to donate two acres of land for the purpose of building a church with a grave-yard round it and a school for the poor and suggesting that he should surround the land with a rude dwarf wall. It seems likely from the content of the letters that the Vicar was taking the Marquess's consent for granted. Unexpectedly Lord Abergavenny refused to cooperate. He claimed to be not insensible to appeals for the increase of church accommodation when this was necessary or desirable. But this case did not seem to him to be either. He had consulted his tenants at the farm, M. H. and G. W. Hobson, who were unwilling to give up two acres of the land leased to them and did not like the idea of a grave-yard being created. The other inhabitants, who were their sub-tenants and employees and numbered about 80 in all, did not mind the walk of two miles to the nearest church at Hangleton, which Lord Abergavenny called "Hambledon" in his letter. He added that he was unable to sell any of his land without the consent of the Crown as it was entailed under an Act of Parliament of the reign of Philip and Mary—as any student of legal titles in Brighton knows.

Wagner accepted that Lord Abergavenny had no choice in view of his tenants' attitude, but he added: "I am quite sure that it is far from your Lordship's disposition to be insensible to appeals made for the increase of church accommodation".[62] In putting the phrase from Lord Abergavenny's letter in quotation marks in his reply one wonders if the Vicar was being slightly ironical. He informed the builder, George Cheesman, who would probably have built the church, had it materialised, that Bodley would have been entitled to £30, had the church been built. He felt that it was the proper and liberal thing to do to make some payment to Bodley despite the abandonment of the plans. He told Cheesman to inform the Vicar's sister, Mary Ann Wagner, of this and she would draw a cheque accordingly. Miss Wagner duly paid Bodley £10 10s. 0d.

The Vicar's second uncompleted project was to build another new church in a poor quarter of Brighton. At the time of his death he had set aside £3,000 for this plan, but no work on the building had been carried out. The money was in due course used by his sons for the purpose intended, and the sum supplemented by them to build St. Martin's church, Lewes Road, as a memorial to their father. But the history of this building belongs to the next chapter.

By 1864 there were in Brighton 19 churches belonging to the Church of England. Of these, 16 had been opened since Wagner came to Brighton in 1824, six had been built as the result of his personal initiative, two had been the work of his son and one had been sponsored by his sister. Until 1873, three years after his death, when the whole parish of Brighton was reorganised by his successor, the Rev. John Hannah, none of these churches except St. Nicholas's had been allotted parishes or districts. Therefore the whole town of Brighton was still one vast parish. In addition in most cases, save during the first 40 years of existence for proprietary chapels, the presentation of the perpetual curacies rested with the Vicar of Brighton. So it is not surprising that Brighton was designated by one of Wagner's contemporary bishops of Chichester as "a bishopric within a bishopric" and one moreover in which the presiding cleric had rather more power than the actual bishop had in the remainder of his diocese. Such a position gave full scope for the domination of a masterful character like Wagner. In consequence it led to a great deal of discord in the parish.

But this strife never in any way affected the bishop of the diocese. During the 46 years of Wagner's incumbency there were no less than six bishops of Chichester. With all of them Wagner's relations were excellent. The last but one of these, Dr. Ashurst Turner Gilbert, lasted the longest as he was in office from 1842 to 1870. In writing to this bishop on the 16th July 1856 to offer 150 guineas for the decoration of a window in Chichester cathedral Wagner said that this gift was intended "to mark the affectionate respect and gratitude of one who during a long course of years in the discharge of somewhat difficult parochial duties has received the benefit of the invaluable counsel and uniform encouragement of his Diocesan".[63]

Wagner's disputes were always within the parish of Brighton itself. There were three causes of such strife. The first and possibly the most common was nothing but a clash of personalities. Wagner never belonged to any party within the church. Writing to Sidney Gurney of No. 63 Montpelier Road, Brighton, in 1856 he commented that the Brighton clergy were "living representations of all shades and phases of opinion which obtain among the ministry of our Church".[64] He added: "I have my views but a sense of duty has prompted me not to narrow or restrict myself to the selection of those Clergymen alone who sympathise with my views".[65] In the last 25 years of his life, possibly as the result of the influence of his father-in-law, Joshua Watson, but still more on account of his son, Arthur, he turned a kindly eye towards the high church movement. But he never became a ritualist himself. He remained always a Georgian clergyman at heart.

So when, as frequently happened, he quarrelled with another clergyman this was not, save in one instance, on account of ecclesiastical attitudes but as the result of general behaviour. For instance when, in 1853, he fell out with the Rev. F. W. Robertson over the appointment of a curate to Trinity chapel the disagreement was not about the curate's religious suitability but only concerned his behaviour towards Wagner in the past. Wagner's obituaries emphasise that he strongly held the view that "he who is not with me is against me", and the forgiving of trespasses was not a Christian virtue which he greatly practised.

The second cause of strife was political. Eight years' association with the Duke of Wellington had left Wagner, if he was not before, a high Tory. This he remained all his life, and Conservatism is an outlook which normally increases with age. This adherence went down very badly in mid-nineteenth century Brighton, save with "The Brighton Gazette". In the seventeen eighties, when the Prince of Wales had first made Brighton fashionable, the Prince had been a supporter of the Whig party. The town had followed him in this allegiance. When as Prince Regent in 1811 he changed sides and continued the Tory Government in power the town had not followed this change of heart, though it always remained strongly Royalist. Throughout the whole period of Wagner's incumbency Brighton remained not only Whig but even Radical in sympathies. The Vestry vehemently supported the Reform bill of 1831–2 through all its stages and even pasted a copy of the People's Charter in the Vestry minute-book in 1841. It was not until about 15 years after Wagner's death that Brighton passed into the realm of the normal seaside Conservatism. As Wagner's voice was one of the few high Tory notes to be heard in Brighton during this period of Whig or Radical supremacy he was naturally involved in many controversies. These tended to spill over into activities beyond the normal political sphere and to generate great ill-feeling.

One such case was recorded by Wagner's mother in her diary for 1835. On the 15th December the Vicar, his sister, Mary Ann, and his son Arthur, attended a meeting in the Old Ship Assembly Rooms held to raise money for poor Irish clergy. Anne Elizabeth Wagner had subscribed £10 towards the appeal. She noted: "The radical party had issued a publication to appoint Good the hairdresser to the Chair instead of L'd Teignmouth or the Vicar; an Uproar arose; the Ladies made all haste to quit the room as also all the respectable persons in the room when the Upstart Good took the Chair. Arthur came home and said that I was lucky not to have gone as my life might have been in danger."[66] One must remember that, like her son, she also was a high Tory. Next day she added "Good behaved violently ill. The Vicar left the meeting early in expectation they wd. have stay'd late but it broke up."[67]

The third and most bitter cause of strife between Wagner and some elements of the local community was financial. As the law then stood the parish as a whole, i.e. the rate-payers, were responsible for the upkeep of the parish church and, in Brighton's case, also St. Peter's chapel as an official chapel of ease to it, and the provision of Divine Service there. This was hard on members of other religious communities who also had their own places of worship to look after. But the plea of injustice was one which found little sympathy with Wagner as, in his view, it was offset by the fact that the liability was the law of the land. The Roman Catholics and the Jews seemed not to have been disturbed by this obligation, but the Dissenters, who were far more numerous in Brighton at the time, were bitterly hostile to the arrangement. In 1836 they went so far as to form a local branch of the Metropolitan Society for the Abolition of Church Rates. On the 20th December Joseph Hume, the Radical Member of Parliament, addressed a meeting at which Thomas Read Kemp, M.P., took the chair. A petition embodying the resolution that was passed at the meeting was presented to the House of Commons by one of the Members of Parliament for Brighton, Isaac Newton Wigney, with the support of the other Member, Captain Pechell, and of Kemp as one of the Members for Lewes and of H. B. Curteis of Windmill Hill Place, who was one of the Members for the county. A Dissenting Minister named Turnbull became the Honorary Secretary of the new branch of the society.

This meeting had followed the first open clash between the Vestry and the Vicar in the preceding year. On the 17th December 1835 the church-wardens, acting no doubt on the Vicar's instructions, called a public meeting of the Vestry in the Town Hall in order to levy a church rate. At this meeting, with the Vicar in the chair, a rate of one penny in the pound was proposed by one of the church-wardens, James Cordy. The opposition countered with an amendment to the effect that a church rate would be "very unjust and oppressive towards the Dissenters"[68] and suggested that a committee should be formed to find private funds to pay the organist and pew-openers. The amendment was carried on a show of hands. James Cordy thereupon demanded a poll. This was held forthwith. But while it was proceeding the Vicar, who was in the chair, said that he must leave the meeting and appointed John Ade, the Vice-Chairman, to take his place in the chair and continue to record the votes. At that stage 186 votes had been given for the amendment and only eight against it. The opposition protested that if the Vicar left the chair the poll was thereby automatically closed. 120 people who were present added their signatures to the minutes of the meeting to that effect. John Ade expressed his willingness to continue recording votes, but none were tendered. So he announced that the poll would be continued on the two days following.

The result of the complete poll was that 1,521 people voted for the amendment and 1,244 against it. So the church rate was thrown out. The Brighton Gazette claimed that the poll was improperly conducted and that at least 200 people had voted who either had not paid their existing poor-rates and/or were not resident in the parish. So a scrutiny was demanded. This took place but did not find any irregularities. This incident was to be the first of many similar unruly scenes at parish meetings in the Town Hall during the next 17 years. As the result of the resolution funds were in fact raised privately to pay the organist, the pew-openers and the sexton at St. Peter's.

Another clash occurred in 1836. On the 24th November the church-wardens called a Vestry meeting in order to propose a church rate of 1½d. in the pound. The opposition immediately brought forward an amendment to defer consideration of the matter for 6 months. This was carried on a show of hands, whereupon the church-wardens demanded a poll. This was held on the two days following and produced a vote of 1,709 for the rate and 1,389 against it.

No further church rate was demanded until 1839, when exactly the same procedure was followed. At a Vestry meeting on the 2nd May a rate of 1½d. in the pound was proposed. But an amendment to defer the matter for 12 months was passed by 148 votes to 38 on a show of hands. A poll was again demanded, at which the rate of 1½d. was confirmed by 1,157 votes to 747.

In 1840 the churchwardens were more demanding as money was needed to buy land for an extension to the church-yard on the west side of Church Hill, now Dyke Road. On the 9th January they asked for a rate of 3d. in the pound. The opposition countered with an amendment to the effect that the matter should be referred back to a committee that had been investigating different sites. One of these sites was part of the land attached to the Workhouse on the east side of Church Hill. The opposition contended that this site could be used without involving the parish in the cost of buying additional land. This particular Vestry meeting was poorly attended, and the amendment was carried by 56 votes to 28. A poll was held the same day and on the two days following, when the original motion for a 3d. rate was carried by 737 votes to 62. This was followed by a further public meeting on the 23rd January, at which a petition was drawn up for presentation to Parliament saying that "church rates are unjust in principle and a violation of the rights of conscience and a continual source of discord amongst the Inhabitants of this parish and ought to be abolished".[69] The meeting appointed a committee to examine the legality of the decision made at the Vestry meeting on the 9th January and at the ensuing poll.

1841 was a particularly contentious year. At a Vestry meeting on the 9th March the church-wardens proposed a church rate of 2d. in the pound in order to pay for lighting St. Peter's church with gas and for laying out the church-yard round it. The opposition's move on this occasion was to bring forward an amendment requesting the production of the legal opinion that had been obtained from Sir William Follett about the legality or otherwise of such works being a charge on the rates. The amendment was carried on a show of hands. So inevitably a poll followed during the next two days. The result was a vote of 804 for the rate and 236 against.

At a subsequent meeting of the Vestry on the 22nd April the anti-church party were successful in carrying a motion to be presented to Parliament to the effect that all compulsory exactions for religious purposes were "prejudicial to the interests of religion, an infringement of the right of conscience and the freedom of religious opinion and, if abolished, would conduce to the peace and strength of the nation".[70] Captain Pechell attended the meeting and undertook to present the petition to the House of Commons.

The church-wardens were evidently feeling in a confident mood that year because as soon afterwards as the 26th October they summoned another Vestry meeting to pass another church rate of one penny in the pound. This meeting was packed by the opposition, and the rate was thrown out on a straight vote by 214 votes to 19. A committee was also appointed to examine the church-wardens' accounts. A poll was demanded in the usual way and on this occasion confirmed the rejection. The proposed rate was negatived by 1,617 votes to 1,275. Following the minutes of the meeting there is an entry in the minute-book "That a vote of censure be passed against the Vicar for his improper conduct in the chair and that the Vestry clerk be ordered to enter such a vote in the parish book immediately after the minutes of the meeting."[71]

This time the opposition's blood was really up. When the special committee reported on the 9th November they recorded that Sergeant Talfourd, who lived in Brighton, had advised that the use of church rates for laying-out a burial ground and for embellishments of a church was illegal. Therefore the amounts included for these purposes in the rate passed at the meeting on the 9th March were "a malappropriation little short of a fraud upon the rate-payers and that all monies laid out for ornamental purposes is illegal". The sums of £200 intended for the lay-out of St. Peter's church-yard and £51 3s. 0d. for embellishments of the church were struck out of the church-wardens' accounts. The committee went on to express the hope that the decision of the 26th October would convince the church-wardens that "the Parishioners can and will defend their just rights against the exercise of unjust power and arbitrary influence".[72]

At the conclusion of the Vestry meeting Dr. Edward Everard, who was in the Chair, announced the birth of the Queen's second child who was destined to be Prince of Wales. The announcement was greeted with laughter. When he expressed surprise at this one voice exclaimed "A president for four years for me." This sentiment was most unusual in Brighton at the time, because, although the town was then strongly Radical in sympathies, it was also strongly Royalist. In fact only three days later the Vestry duly passed a loyal address congratulating the Queen on the birth of the prince.

The difficulties at Vestry meetings were in fact caused by a small but resolute and clamant minority who stuck at nothing in order to get their own way. The leaders at this period who were present on nearly all occasions were a trio: Matthew Stocks, John Hilton and an individual who rejoiced in the almost unbelievable name of Lieutenant-Colonel Thomas Trusty Trickey. He seemed to live up to both parts of his name according to whichever side you were on. Equally vocal was the Rev. James Edwards, who was Minister of the Hanover Presbyterian chapel in Church Street and had suffered distraint on his goods at one time as the result of refusing to pay a church rate. Usually associated with these four men was Isaac Grey Bass, a prominent Quaker who owned a lot of property in the old town and in 1835 had bought the old Vicarage and demolished it two years later. Then there was a solicitor named John Colbatch, who was Clerk to the Brighton Magistrates and also the owner of the Albion Hotel in Old Steine. He was an awkward customer who was constantly at loggerheads with the Brighton Commissioners, though he was himself a member of that body.

The tactics of this group were to speak at inordinate length and wear down the patience of the other people present. As a result the meetings lasted for anything up to seven hours. They used most unparliamentary language in speaking of or to the Vicar in the chair. The atmosphere often became so stormy that one authority[73] went so far as to say that the Vicar sometimes risked being thrown down the stairs of the Town Hall. He was, however, never moved to reply in kind but always treated his adversaries in a public meeting with the courtesy of a clergyman and a gentleman. In her diary for the 14th May 1835 the Vicar's mother quoted the Brighton Gazette, which was always favourable to Wagner, as saying that he "appeared to much advantage from the great command of temper when opposed with much violence by a set of radical commissioners".[74] But it cannot be denied that he was often high-handed in his actions as a chairman of public meetings. He was handicapped by the fact that what could be called the church party was not as vocal or as well-organised as his opponents. He had principally to rely on the church-wardens, who changed from year to year. The most regular and stalwart of these were James Cordy and a jeweller named D. M. Folkard. The silent majority usually supported the Vicar at the polls which followed Vestry meetings. But even here the total vote recorded was usually less than 3,000. This is a small proportion of the then population of about 46,000, even allowing for the fact that only householders could vote. The position was in fact very similar to the meetings of some trade unions today, when militant extremists monopolise the proceedings to the extent of producing results which in no way reflect the opinions of the majority.

One irony of the Vestry meetings was that, when the Vicar was in the chair and the resulting vote went in favour of his party, the meeting concluded with a vote of thanks to the chairman "for his able and impartial conduct in the chair". When he was not present the chair was usually taken by the High Constable for the year. If the vote went in favour of the opposition the minutes similarly recorded a vote of thanks to the chairman in the same words. In both cases one imagines that the word "impartial" related only to the fact that the party of the chairman of the day had won that particular round of the contest.

The rejection of the church rate at the Vestry meeting on the 26th October 1841 led to the most notorious incident of Wagner's incumbency in Brighton. When the church-wardens' accounts were examined an item of £10 7s. 6d. for winding the clock in the tower of St. Peter's church was struck out. Therefore when the clock came to a halt at six minutes past 5 a.m. on the 13th November the church-wardens naturally made no arrangements for it to be rewound. The Brighton Herald's comments were: 'We do not believe that the clock of St.

Peter's would be guilty of felo de se—that it would turn its own hands against itself—we believe that there has been some foul play and the Vicar and church-wardens must look into it."[75] Colonel Trickey had the nerve, after securing the excision from the accounts of the expense in question, to write to the Bishop of Chichester, complaining that the Vicar had stopped the clock. Someone who lived nearby also offered to pay for its winding on a voluntary basis. The church-wardens indignantly replied that no-one had stopped the clock but, as they had been personally charged with the rejected expense of £10 7s. 6d., they would take no steps to have it rewound until there was some assurance that the cost would be paid out of public funds. The voluntary principle, they considered, was not suitable for use in matters of public convenience, and it was totally in-admissible for those who objected to paying church rates on the grounds that they could not benefit from them to complain about the cessation of the one church amenity which suited their convenience. The Brighton Herald remained unconvinced by the church-wardens' explanation. "They would not stop a church mouse, much less a church clock, without instructions from their Lord and Master."[76] There is little doubt that the paper was not referring to God.

This controversy about the clock in St. Peter's tower generated so much ill-feeling that small boys began to follow the Vicar about and even to throw stones at him. This came to a head on Saturday the 15th January 1842 between three and four in the afternoon when the Vicar was riding along Upper North Street. A group of children was playing in the street. As the Vicar rode by a boy aged seven called after him "Who stopped the clock?" and then darted into his own house, No. 60 Upper North Street. Wagner had evidently had enough of this petty persecution. It was not for nothing that he had been associated with the Duke of Wellington for eight years. He could have been equally successful in a military as in a clerical career. So he hurriedly dismounted, gave the reins of his horse to another boy to hold and pursued the culprit into the house. There at the end of the passage he found the boy's mother doing her washing. He asked her whose child the boy was and was told that the boy belonged to her. Mean-while the child had hidden himself in the back room of the house and had bolted the door. Wagner commanded him to come out. As the boy did not do so Wagner put his shoulder to the door and burst it open. It had no lock on it, only a bolt. The Vicar then gave the boy four or five strokes with his riding-crop. The mother was so much daunted by the invasion of this stern clerical figure that she went so far as to tell her son that it served him right for having been saucy. The Vicar then departed, after giving a penny to the boy who had held his horse.

Soon afterwards the boy's father, Stephen Grover, who was a bricklayer, returned home. He reproached his wife for having allowed anyone but themselves to chastise their son. He proceeded to take the boy off to the Vicarage and asked to see the Vicar. Whether his intention was to apologise for the boy's misdeed or to demand an explanation of the Vicar's intrusion into his house is not recorded. But in either case Wagner, in his high-handed manner, refused to see them. The year being 1842, there the matter might well have rested—but not in Brighton, where political and religious feeling ran so high. We have no means of knowing whether Stephen Grover was himself a Dissenter or a supporter of the Whig party. But even if he was not, word of the fracas must have swiftly gone round the town. This brought him into touch with a solicitor named Sidney Walsingham

Bennett of No. 63 Middle Street who was bursting with ill-will towards the Vicar. He openly boasted that he had stopped the Vicar once—presumably over the church rate in October 1841—and would do so again.

Bennett took Stephen Grover down to the Town Hall on the following Monday and demanded the issue of a summons for assault against the Vicar. The magistrates sitting that morning were George Basevi of No. 37 Brunswick Square, who was an uncle of Benjamin Disraeli, and Major Allen. Both of them were colleagues of Wagner's on the Board of Governors of the Sussex County Hospital. They were consequently most reluctant to take any official action and thought the matter ought to be settled out of court. Basevi observed that if the matter was drawn to the Vicar's attention and he had done wrong or had injured the child he was sure that the Vicar would take appropriate action. A settlement out of court was the last thing that Bennett wanted. Indeed he had instructed his client that, if he was approached by the other side at home, he should have nothing to do with them. What Bennett was out for was the maximum publicity and to whip up ill-feeling against the Vicar. He persisted in his demand for a summons. So the Magistrates had no option but to issue one. Wagner was represented in court by a solicitor named George Dempster of No. 51 Ship Street. The latter asked that the hearing of the summons should be as soon as possible. So the date fixed was therefore the following Thursday. Stephen Grover, being a poor man, could not pay the fee of 4s. 0d. which was required before the summons could be issued. But Sidney Bennett had great satisfaction in paying the fee on his behalf.

The hearing took place on the 20th January. The Bench on that day comprised Isaac Newton Wigney, M.P., George Basevi, Major Allen and Captain Millard. Sir Richard Hunter, the High Sheriff of Sussex, was also present but took no part in the proceedings. Presumably he was a friend of Wagner's who felt that he ought not to sit on the Bench on that occasion. It was also very doubtful whether Isaac Wigney should have done so—for the opposite reason, as he was a notorious opponent of Wagner's. The Vicar's mother had described him in her diary when he was first elected to Parliament in 1832 as "that rabble Wigney and Faithful"[77] (George Faithful, the solicitor). He was a strong supporter of the Society for the Abolition of Church Rates. He had clashed with Wagner on another occasion in a meeting of the Directors and Guardians of the Poor only a few weeks beforehand and as a result of this difference of opinion had written Wagner a rude letter which, at Wigney's request, had been published in the Brighton Herald. However, he did not think fit to stand down on this occasion. In fact he conducted the proceedings in a reasonably fair manner and twice reproved Grover's solicitor for the improper expressions which he used concerning the Vicar. Bennett went so far as to say: "You never saw a man whose countenance was a better index to his mind than the Vicar of Brighton. You cannot look at him without imagining that every evil passion that haunts the human mind dwells therein."[78] Wigney compelled Bennett to apologise for this expression and to withdraw it. Isaac Wigney had incidentally a very short time left to him to enjoy such prominence as sitting on the Bench. Within a few months of this hearing his bank, Wigney & Co., failed. He was declared bankrupt and had to resign from the House of Commons.

Naturally two versions of the incident in Upper North Street were related in court. In Bennett's version the Vicar, in a great passion, had brutally assaulted a small child, hitting him on the face and head with the result that the boy had a black eye and an injured thumb when he had put up his hand to protect his face. Had he not been wearing a cap at the time, his injuries would have been serious. Actually the boy was asked in court only five days after the incident occurred to display his eye and thumb, but the injuries seem not to have made much impression on the Bench nor to have been easily visible. Wagner was represented at the hearing by a solicitor named Charles Cooper of No. 57 Ship Street, though George Dempster was also present in court. Cooper's version of the incident was that the thrashing represented only moderate and wholesome correction administered with the mother's approval.

The facts were not in dispute. Therefore the Magistrates had no option but to convict for assault. But instead of the maximum fine of £5 demanded by Bennett they imposed a fine of £2, plus costs. That was the end of the incident. Henry Wagner's son, Arthur, would probably have sought out the boy afterwards and have made him some amends. But that was not in the Vicar's nature. The assault, however, did Wagner a lot of harm in Brighton. It was remembered for nearly 30 years afterwards and was even mentioned in his obituaries at his death in 1870.

Unfortunately for Wagner this incident coincided with another dispute that also injured his reputation. He quarrelled with one of his curates named Berkeley Addison, who left Brighton in February 1842. We do not know the cause of the disagreement. The Brighton Herald said that Addison would not "undo out of the pulpit what he had been striving to do in the pulpit" and "would not become a canvasser and coercer—a partisan and a parasite".[79] But this had no significance because the paper was implacably hostile to the Vicar. It is safe to say that the cause would have had nothing to do with ecclesiastical opinions but almost certainly related to personal behaviour. However, Addison was a popular young man, and according to Sawyer's "The Churches of Brighton" the quarrel added greatly to Wagner's unpopularity in Brighton.

As the church-wardens had been without funds since October 1841 and the pews of St. Peter's needed repair they called another Vestry meeting on the 19th May 1842 in order to try and levy a church rate. The meeting was not well attended. Of the Vicar's principal opponents, the only ones who were present were James Edwards and Isaac Bass. Even so there was a slight filibuster, but the meeting seems to have been much influenced by a mechanic named Dudman who said that he had had enough of such disturbances and had changed sides. Though he seldom went to church, he had found out who were the best friends of the working classes and that it cost him more to object to a church rate than to vote for one. A. H. Wilds' resolution for a penny rate was therefore passed on a straight vote by 69 votes to 53 and without recourse to a poll.

The next row took place on the 12th December 1843. The Vicar had ceased to attend Vestry meetings in protest against past bad behaviour. So John Hilton, who was one of his opponents, was voted into the chair. Before the church-wardens could even propose a rate the opposition brought forward a motion for the adjournment of the meeting. The church-wardens were therefore obliged to propose a church rate of 2d. in the pound as an amendment to the motion, instead of as a substantive resolution. The money was needed for repairs to both churches and for the salaries of the parish officers (the clerk £31 10s. 0d., the sexton £10, the pew-openers at St. Nicholas's £15, the organist £40, the beadles at St. Peter's £15, the porter £2 12s. 0d., the gardener £10 and the clock winder £10). Apparently the clock was by this time in working order again and chimed the quarters but did not strike the hours. Isaac Bass and a Dissenting Minister named Treago protested strongly because certain members of the Society of Friends had suffered distraint for failure to pay the last church rate and were not mollified by the church-wardens' reply to the effect that they intended to proceed against all defaulters and had only used these Quakers as a test case because Quakers claimed special exemption. Bass and another Dissenter named Wilkins offered voluntary contributions of an unspecified amount and enquired whether the church-wardens would accept such a method of raising the funds which were required. The church-wardens named Alger and Folkard replied that if Bass and Wilkins were offering to present all the money required, which amounted to about £1,400, then the church-wardens would accept it, but they could not accept a few guineas in hand and then have to beg the rest elsewhere. The amendment in support of a rate was defeated by a large majority on a show of hands. At the poll which ensued on the same day and the two days following the rejection was confirmed by 1,416 votes to 1,286.

For the following year therefore none of the parish officers received any salary, though they had been officially confirmed in office by a Vestry meeting. However, unlike twentieth century characters, they were such devoted servants that they seemed to have continued to carry out their duties without payment. To regularise the position the church-wardens called another Vestry meeting on the 27th June 1844, this time with rather better results. The same clique as usual attended, and John Hilton again took the chair. The rate was rejected by a large majority at the meeting. But at the poll which followed on the next two days the rate was accepted by 1,132 votes to 803.

This rate lasted for two years. By this time St. Nicholas's church was in serious need of repairs, and the only way of providing for these was to carry a larger church rate than usual. On the 4th June 1846 the church-wardens therefore summoned a Vestry meeting and presented to it an estimate for £4,305 to cover the general running of the two churches, plus the repairs needed by St. Nicholas's. James Cordy took the chair, and the rate was proposed by George Dempster. He stated that St. Nicholas's, which contained 1,300 seats, was the only free church in the parish, in fact the poor man's church. Brighton had grown so much in recent years that several hundred people were turned away from the church every Sunday. It was essential that the building should be both restored and enlarged. The opposition, consisting of the usual names, contended that it was unreasonable to enlarge St. Nicholas's when St. Paul's church, so close at hand, was still in the building. They even tried to make capital out of the fact that the meeting had been called at 11 a.m., when no working man could attend. Almost all the speakers were opposed to the motion, and an amendment to adjourn the meeting for six months was carried by a large majority. Dempster demanded a poll, at which the voting was 754 for the rate and 1,132 against it. After the chairman had declared the meeting closed the dissenting party, with only George Dempster to champion the official view, held a meeting of their own at which Isaac Bass counselled them to continue with their opposition year after year until the church party eventually tired of persisting further. He proposed that a committee should be formed to promote further opposition, but as no one came forward who was prepared to act as its honorary secretary the idea never got off the ground.

The church-wardens, being without funds, were obliged to try again fairly soon. A meeting of the Vestry was therefore held on the 7th June 1847, John Hilton was voted into the chair and before anyone else could speak took it upon himself to say that the time was inappropriate for levying a church rate when the last poor rate had been particularly heavy and in any case had not been fully collected and when many people had been thrown out of work by the recent heavy frosts. The Brighton Gazette subsequently maintained that Hilton himself had not paid his rates and therefore that the proceedings of the meeting were invalidated. James Cordy and D. M. Folkard proposed a rate of 1½d. in the pound to cover an estimate of £110 0s. 0d. expenses. Colonel Trickey, with his usual nerve, maintained that the Vicar should have asked the Archdeacon of Lewes to inspect the building and produce a schedule of its condition before money was asked for. A Dissenting minister named Caiger spoke at such length that even Isaac Bass interrupted and silenced him. The proceedings lasted from 11 a.m. till 4.30 p.m. The usual amendment to adjourn the matter for 6 months was carried by a large majority and at the ensuing poll also won the day by 1,040 votes to 706.

At this stage in the proceedings the Vicar's hand was greatly strengthened by several decisions of the High Court on the question of compulsory church rates. At Braintree in Essex an exactly similar situation to that in Brighton had existed and the matter had been referred to the courts. Lord Denman, the Lord Chief Justice, held that the parish was responsible for the repair of the parish church and the decent celebration of Divine Service. It was not for the Vestry to determine whether to repair their church but only how and when it was most expedient to do this. In a similar case at the Norfolk assizes Mr. Justice Patteson had given the same ruling and in his judgment had said that "it was not proper and becoming in any one man doggedly to set up his own private views and opinions against the law".[80] Such had certainly been the case with the militant group of people in Brighton. Mr. Justice Coleridge had also given a similar decision on the subject.

Therefore when the church-wardens summoned the next Vestry meeting in Brighton for the 6th May 1847 they noted in the advertisement that "the ancient Law of the land that the repair of the church and the providing of things necessary for Divine Service therein is the imperative duty of the Parishioners has been recently affirmed by the highest judicial authority after a very expensive and protracted litigation".[81] They went on to hope that the parish might be saved from "similar litigation and its consequent expense".[82] This had the true Wagner ring about it. The church-wardens proposed a rate of 1½d. in the pound and read to the meeting a letter from the organist of St. Nicholas's who had been regularly appointed by the parish in the normal manner, saying that he had been an invalid for three years and it was therefore such a great hardship to him not to have received his salary of £40 a year during that period that he had almost been reduced to receiving parish relief himself. The vociferous opposition brushed this aside and carried by a large majority an amendment to defer for six months consideration of the accounts and estimates. The church-wardens wearily demanded a poll, at which they were again defeated by 1,227 votes to 1,030.

This meeting brought the Vicar back into action with all his guns firing. He obtained a citation from the Archdeacon of Lewes, Julius Hare, to hold a special Vestry meeting for the purpose of levying a church rate of one penny in the pound. Outside the door of the room in the Town Hall where the meeting was held a barrier was set up, and only those parishioners were admitted who had paid their previous poor rate. This annoyed the opposition greatly as previously they had only had to show that they had paid the rate before they voted in a poll. The Vicar himself took the chair, as was his statutory right. The church-wardens set before the meeting an estimate of £800 10s. 0d., of which £466 9s. 8d. related to St. Nicholas's and £259 1s. 1d. to St. Peter's. Anticipating that the opposition would, as usual, propose an amendment to the effect that the meeting should be adjourned for six months or more the Vicar came armed with several opinions from learned counsel which he had obtained at his own expense. These were to the effect that amendments for adjournment on a proposal for a church rate were illegal. The first amendment in the names of Messrs. Treago and Feist actually proposed that the repairs and upkeep of both churches should be undertaken by voluntary subscriptions "in accordance with the statute law of the land",[83] —a very dubious plea incidentally. The Vicar refused to accept the amendment. A second amendment was then proposed by William Coningham of No. 26 Sussex Square. He had been one of the unsuccessful candidates at the last parliamentary election in Brighton and was to be later elected as one of the Brighton Members in 1857 and 1859 and to represent the Borough until 1864. His amendment was the usual one to the effect that consideration of the matter should be deferred for six months. In his speech Coningham called compulsory church rates "Anglican popery".[84] The Vicar refused to accept this amendment also as being illegal. He then put to the meeting the substantive motion in favour of a penny rate. This was rejected by 90 votes to 47. However, he announced that "the votes against the motion were illegal and thrown away"[85] and therefore declared the motion to be carried. This was thereafter always called by the opposition "the minority rate".

In such circumstances no question of a poll arose, and the church-wardens proceeded to collect the rate. But another meeting of the Vestry was requisitioned by 73 signatures. This was held on the 21st December 1847 and was attended by between 200 and 300 people. At this a resolution, proposed by William Coningham and seconded by Jonathan Streeter, was carried which stated that "the compulsory imposition of Church Rates is contrary to the great principles of civil and religious liberty and interference of the Civil Government in matters of religion which the State has no right to exercise, a source of bitterness and dissension in the community and that the immediate abolition of this obnoxious impost has become absolutely necessary for the peace and well-being of Her Majesty's subjects".[86] Captain Pechell, M.P. attended the meeting and agreed to present the resolution to the House of Commons in the form of a petition.

The rate voted in 1847 lasted for two years. But the rates seem to have been collected in a very inefficient manner. Some of the householders who did not pay suffered distraint on their goods. Others did not. It is difficult to tell on which principle, if any, the discrimination was made as to whether to prosecute or not. Summonses were issued against nine people in September 1849. One of these defendants told the Magistrates that it was his intention to dispute the rate in the ecclesiastical courts, though he had not as yet taken any action to do so. The Bench held that, in view of this plea, they could not grant any summons.

A week later, on the 27th September, the church-wardens called another Vestry meeting to make a demand for a penny rate. The chair was taken by John Good of the church party. The estimate put before the meeting amounted to £992 7s. 6d., of which £603 14s. 8d. was for St. Nicholas's and £313 12s. 10d. for St. Peter's. Part of the north wall of the new cemetery had collapsed and if allowance for a new fence around it, amounting to between £500 and £600, had been included, the rate would have had to be 1½d. But the opposition contended that only about two thirds of the previous rate had been collected and that something in the nature of £200 was still outstanding. They moved an amendment to the effect that it was not expedient to levy a new rate when the old one had not been fully collected. This was carried by a large majority. The church-wardens for once did not demand a poll.

They even waited another period of two years before trying again. A Vestry meeting was eventually summoned for the 4th December 1851. A long statement signed by the Vicar appeared in "The Brighton Gazette" on the day of the meeting. In this he pointed out that, like the church-wardens themselves, he was not personally in favour of the present position whereby the upkeep of the parish church was a compulsory charge on all householders, but that it was the law of the land and, as such, must necessarily be supported. He said that he quite understood the conscientious objection expressed by members of one religious community to the idea of contributing to the support of another religious community but he could not accept this when it was used for political ends, as he implied was the case in Brighton. He added that the adjoining parish of Hove had recently passed a church rate for the building of a new church. This would be St. John's church adjoining Palmeira Square. The Vicar took the chair at the meeting on the 4th December, and a rate of one penny in the pound was duly proposed to provide for an estimate of £820 14s. 6d. (being £492 7s. 6d. for St. Nicholas's and £273 7s. 0d. for St. Peter's). The same old body of objectors put forward an amendment which was most confusedly worded, though they said that they had taken legal advice in bringing it forward. This claimed that a new rate would be unjust to those who had paid the previous rate "now in course of litigation in as much as a large proportion of the parishioners who had paid the rate are at present by its legal position exempt from its liability".[87] The church-wardens' accounts were rejected, and the amendment was carried on a show of hands by 143 votes to 32. James Cordy duly demanded a poll. The result entered in the minutes was "under protest from Mr. Cordy for the rate 1,120 and against the rate and the clear undoubted and established law of the land 1,244".[88] The Vicar then declared the proceedings of the day at an end. But after he had done so William Coningham "mounted the table and proposed three cheers for something" (presumably inaudible to the reporter in the uproar) "and three groans for the Vicar".[89] There was no seconder, and therefore the "crowd moved off gradually and growlingly".[90]

The church-wardens only waited 5 months before trying again. They presented exactly the same estimates to a meeting of the Vestry on the 17th May 1852 and again demanded a penny rate. This time it was claimed that only about one third of the previous rate had been collected, and the church-wardens admitted that they had been hampered in the collection by the pending litigation. The opposition consequently proposed an amendment with exactly the same wording as in the previous year. This was carried by 147 votes to 33. But at the ensuing poll which was held on the four days from the 18th to the 21st May the opposition was substantially defeated by 1,901 votes to 1,347. This was not only the largest majority which the church party had ever received but was also much the biggest number of votes ever recorded in a parish poll on the subject. The opposition characteristically objected to the existence of the plural vote, whereby those householders with an assessment of over £50 had extra votes for every £25 of their assessment up to a maximum of 6 votes and also to the fact that women householders were able to vote in parish polls, as of course they could not do in parliamentary elections.

One of the most stalwart members of the opposition was an elderly Dissenter named Jonathan Streeter. On a previous occasion when a church rate had been levied he had refused to pay this, and a valuable clock belonging to him had been seized in distraint, in order to satisfy the rate. At the Vestry meeting on the 17th May 1852 he gave vent to the following observations about the Vicar who was in the chair: "Mr. Chairman, you have no occasion to look so serious at me, but I will say this, although you have many faults, I am proud of you because you, like myself, are not a sprig of the aristocracy. You come of a respectable tradesman, which shows that talent is not confined to the aristocracy. Your father was a great military hatter in London and when he placed you in the Church he made a great mistake, for, if you had gone into the army, you would, with your indomitable energy and your great ability, have made a second Wellington."[91]

It is doubtful whether the Vicar would have greatly relished this unsolicited testimonial. But at least it showed that the speaker had a good heart and no malice. One cannot say as much for the rest of the opposition. They had on their side the principle that it is not just for the members of one religious community (or none, though this was not then considered), to be forced to contribute to the support of another community. But though they mouthed the words "democracy" and "majority" with great readiness like the left-wing extremists of today, one has the impression that they were a thoroughly unpleasant and even malicious lot who were only interested in getting their own way and not in the least in finding out or following what was really the wish of the majority of their fellow citizens.

The opposition frequently urged the Vicar to adopt the voluntary system for maintaining the two churches under his control and gave instances of where it worked very well. His reply was that "when that system is brought into action they who are advocates for it are not often found to be its most prominent supporters".[92] Nevertheless more and more towns like Cheltenham, where there was a large community of Dissenters, were adopting the voluntary method of maintaining the parish church. With the exception of the year 1846 the rate demanded in Brighton had always been very small: either 1d. or 2d. in the pound. This was only for the general running of both churches. Meanwhile St. Nicholas's church, which was a medieval building, had not been properly restored or repaired during the whole period of nearly 30 years that Wagner had been its incumbent. The building was becoming more and more dilapidated, as parishioners sometimes mentioned at the Vestry meetings. In fact in 1849 one speaker had said that one of the windows in the chancel was boarded up. The rather ridiculous process of advance and retreat which had been pursued by the Vestry for the last 17 years might have continued indefinitely till the church fell absolutely into ruins, and there was little probability that the Vicar would ever have been able to secure a substantial church rate such as 6d. in the pound, which would have been needed to effect a proper restoration and enlargement of the church. So he might well have been forced in the end to turn over to the voluntary system anyhow. Then on the 14th September 1852 the Duke of Wellington most timely died.

The Vicar immediately put forward the idea of a full restoration of St. Nicholas's church on a voluntary basis as a memorial to the Duke, who had worshipped there as a boy. It is said that this was not Wagner's own idea but that it had been suggested to him by a friend some time beforehand. If that is so, then he kept the idea in store until the timely moment and brought it forward without any delay. Two days after the Duke died Wagner wrote to the principal inhabitants of Brighton inviting them to meet him at the Town Hall on Monday the 20th September at 12 noon "to consider the best means of testifying our respect for the memory of His Grace the Duke of Wellington".[93]

When the meeting took place the Vicar was voted into the chair. He reminded the company of the then largely forgotten circumstance that the Duke, as a boy, had been a pupil at the academy for young gentlemen kept by Wagner's grandfather, the Rev. Henry Michell, at the Old Vicarage, and had therefore once been amongst the congregation of St. Nicholas's. In view of this fact and of the Duke's known predilection for practical propositions he felt that the Duke himself would much prefer his memorial in Brighton to take the form of the restoration and enlargement of the parish church, rather than the erection of a column or obelisk, such as might be put up by other towns. Those who attended the meeting were for the most part supporters of Wagner's party locally and/or of the Tory party politically. So after one amendment had been proposed and subsequently withdrawn to the effect that the memorial should also be associated with the name of Sir Robert Peel, the meeting unanimously agreed to a resolution that "the restoration and enlargement of the parish church, wherein His Grace the Duke of Wellington at an early period of his life was wont to worship, would be an appropriate and enduring monument of our gratitude and veneration for his memory".

With characteristic generosity the Vicar headed the subscription list with a gift of £1,000. Nearly £100 came from other members of his family. The Bishop of Chichester and the Marquess of Bristol each gave £100 immediately after the meeting. Miss Burdett Coutts, who was a friend of the Vicar's, gave a hundred guineas. The Archbishop of Canterbury also made a contribution. The total sum finally raised reached £4,948 1s. 6d. But when the subscription list was eventually published it was noticeable that none of Wagner's noted opponents, who had frequently expressed their willingness to make a contribution on a voluntary basis had done so, despite the added inducement of a memorial to the Duke. One anonymous gift of £40 from "a Dissenter" was however included.

In 1846 the church-wardens had obtained an estimate for the necessary repair of the church. Under the influence of his son the Vicar had turned for this to R. C. Carpenter, who was then building St. Paul's church for them. Carpenter's estimate was for £4,305. The stability of the times was such that the church-wardens were confident that the work would still cost little more in 1852. Carpenter had been paid a fee of 2% for the plans and would charge another 3% for the executed work. They thought that the total cost would therefore be about £5,000.

A faculty for the repairs was issued by the Bishop's court at Lewes on the 15th April 1853. This actually empowered the parish authorities to take down the church or the greater part thereof and build a new one on the same site or immediately adjacent to it. Fortunately they took less drastic action. The church was closed from the 14th May onwards. Six tenders were received. The lowest, from Messrs. Bushby of Littlehampton, amounted to £2,986 0s. 0d. This was accepted. But in the usual way, when the church was opened up, the fabric was found to be in a much worse condition than had been thought. There was a crack in the west wall of the tower, and the foundations needed attention. The total cost proved to be £5,769 18s. 7d. Work began on the 3rd June and lasted until the 10th March 1854. The average number of workmen employed on the job at one time was 50. The church was re-opened on the 8th April 1854 in the presence of the Bishop of Chichester, Dr. A. T. Gilbert.

R. C. Carpenter was an excellent architect in original work, as St. Paul's, Brighton, and St. Peter the Great, West Street, Chichester, show. But in the "restoration" of medieval buildings he showed the same insensitivity as most pre-Morris nineteenth century architects. They all thought their own work could improve upon the middle ages. Though they despised classical churches, they nevertheless applied to the restorations which they undertook something of the tidiness and symmetry of classical buildings. Carpenter's handling of St. Nicholas's, Brighton, was no exception. He treated the building with such a heavy hand that little medieval work survived, in fact only the tower, the arcades of the nave, the chancel arch, the screen and the font. But in view of the terms of the faculty it is fortunate that any medieval work at all was spared. Forty years later the Brighton architect, Somers Clarke, lifted the roof and inserted a clerestory. The results of both restorations together is that the church has far more a nineteenth century than a medieval atmosphere.

With the aim of enlarging the accommodation available Carpenter increased the width of the aisles by 15 feet in all. Moreover he added to the length of the north aisle by extending it nearly up to the level of the west wall of the tower. But the south chapel of the chancel, which was a later addition to the church, he reduced in width. To the north of the chancel he added an organ-chamber and a vestry. Inside, he converted the division between the chancel and the south chapel from two arches into one. He also designed a new east window. The old interior had abounded in those things which the Tractarians most hated, namely galleries, box-pews and a three-decker pulpit. These were all swept away and replaced by open pews and a plain pulpit of one tier only. All the wall monuments, some of which were of great historical interest, were moved to the darkest portion of the church at the west end of the aisles. The old organ was too large to be moved from the west gallery to the new position north of the chancel. So a new one was installed. The screen was spared, but repainted. The font was moved from the centre of the church to a position in the south aisle just west of the main doorway.

These alterations, though they did slightly increase the amount of seating on the ground, actually reduced the total accommodation available from 1,300 to 900, owing to the abolition of the galleries. It is surprising that so Georgian a character as the Vicar was prepared to accept such a ruthless treatment of the building committed to his care. But in doing so he evidently relied on the taste and influence of his son, Arthur, who was a relentless champion of the new ecclesiastical ideas.

Carpenter himself made one fine contribution to the church. This was the Wellington memorial. It was designed by him and carved by "Mr. Philip of Vauxhall".[94] It takes the form of a stone Eleanor cross of several tiers surmounted by pinnacles. It was placed at the east end of the new south chapel or aisle. In the next century when all things Victorian were undervalued and even despised, the memorial was banished to the west and darkest corner of the north aisle, where, owing to the sloping roof, there was no room for the topmost section and this was barbarously cut off and lain by its side. It is greatly to be hoped that this memorial will soon receive the treatment which such a beautiful object deserves and will be moved again to a more worthy and prominent position.

Carpenter himself died soon after the restoration was completed. So in the step leading from the south aisle to the south chapel a small brass was inserted which read "In memory of R. C. Carpenter who but a short time survived the completion of his design, the restoration of the church MDCCCLV." A later generation, which had even less historical sensitivity than he had, removed this brass, and it can no longer be seen.

In the same year as the restoration of St. Nicholas's was undertaken (1853) occurred another quarrel which did Wagner a great deal of harm. The Rev. Frederick William Robertson had been Perpetual Curate at Trinity chapel, Ship Street, since 1847. He had become the most popular preacher in Brighton. But in May 1853 he entered into one of those mysterious declines that abound in Victorian social history. They would probably be called nervous breakdowns today, except that they often led to death, as in Robertson's case, which nervous breakdowns do not. His parish, thinking that he was overworked, offered to be responsible for the expenses of a curate. Robertson nominated the Rev. Ernest Tower, who at the time was a curate at Hurstpierpoint in Sussex. The appointment had, however, to be approved by Wagner as Vicar of Brighton. This approval he declined to give. There was no disagreement as to doctrinal or other ecclesiastical matters. Robertson wrote to him: "You yourself admit him (Tower) to be in conduct and doctrine an exemplary minister."[95] But about three years previously Tower and Wagner had clashed in the affairs of the Christian Knowledge Society. The former, dissatisfied with the management of the Brighton branch, withdrew from the Lewes Deanery and founded a new branch which in due course was recognised by the headquarters of the society. Wagner claimed that Tower's behaviour to him over the matter had been unbecoming.

The Vicar evidently did not attach much importance to the veto which he imposed and expected Robertson to nominate someone else. Presumably in an attempt to be helpful he attended matins at the Trinity chapel on Trinity Sunday and spoke to Robertson on the subject after the service. Robertson's nervous condition was such that he was looking for slights everywhere. Consequently he alleged that Wagner, together with a witness, had forced himself upon Robertson, who wanted to go home to rest. As a result Robertson had been unable to officiate at the afternoon service. He subsequently wrote that Wagner's attitude was that of "permanent unforgivingness" and that he could "offer no other nominee because I cannot admit your right of objection on personal grounds".[96] The matter remained unsolved when Robertson died on the 15th August. The cause of death was then given as brain-fever.

It would seem that the Vicar's stand was a somewhat hard and unreasonable one. But on the other hand Robertson's own biographer, Frederick Arnold, later wrote that he felt Robertson's refusal to nominate any other clergyman was "childish and self-willed".[97] He thought that there were faults of temper on both sides and that they were faults of the same nature. He even quoted Robertson's successor as saying after Wagner's death: "The good wishes and kindly words this aged man more than once expressed to me concerning the future of my ministry remain in all their freshness and have, through his death, acquired a new and richer value and importance."[98] Wagner's enemies on the other hand did not scruple to allege that his arbitrary and dictatorial attitude had hastened Robertson's death. The quarrel probably did Wagner's reputation more harm than any other single incident during the 46 years of his Brighton incumbency.

The last seventeen years of Henry Wagner's life were much more peaceful than the first twenty-nine years of his Brighton incumbency had been. No more was heard of church rates after 1852. Another matter which had troubled the local scene was settled in 1854. This was incorporation of the town. Feeling in favour of and against the proposal had run very high. Unlike his predecessor, Dr. Carr, Wagner had never been a member of the Brighton Commissioners, but he sided with those who were opposed to incorporation on the strange grounds that this would be undignified. However, he never took a very active part in the controversy. But the grant of a charter of incorporation in April 1854 put an end to his having to take the chair at stormy Vestry meetings.

After this date there is no record of any personal quarrels between the Vicar and other clergymen or prominent Brighton laymen. No doubt Wagner mellowed, as men do over the age of 65. But towards the end of his life he was involved against his will in two other disputes, both of an ecclesiastical nature. In this sphere he was always the most tolerant of men, and in both cases he was most reluctant to intervene.

The less momentous of these issues concerned the church of St. Michael and All Angels in St. Michael's Place. This church had been built during Wagner's incumbency but was not one of those for which he had been himself responsible. The leading spirit in its construction had been one of his own curates, the Rev. Charles Beanlands, who became its first Perpetual Curate. He had worked with Arthur Wagner at St. Paul's and had imbibed from him the high church spirit. To assist him at St. Michael's he had a curate named the Rev. Thomas Walter Perry, who was later to be a member of the Royal Commission which considered the whole question of Rubrics, Orders and Directions for regulating public worship in the Church of England. When the church opened in 1862 such high church practices as the eastward position for the celebration of Holy Communion and a mixed chalice of wine and water were adopted, but no vestments were at first used. There was Gregorian music, but no incense. A year later the surplices of the clergy were replaced by chasubles. Then in 1865 a whole set of Eucharistic vestments embroidered to the designs of C. E. Kempe were introduced and the ritual increased. At the time of the Royal Commission in 1867 one of the witnesses who gave evidence at it, Theodore Thomas Ford of the Church Association, was to claim that he had not seen any church "quite so advanced as St. Michael's".[99] He claimed to have seen the elevation and adoration of the Host and other anomalies such as flowers in the shape of crosses, but his evidence was reduced to confusion by cross-examination.

The increased ritual which was introduced in 1865 prompted the Vicar to challenge Charles Beanlands to produce a requisition in favour of this ritual signed by twelve householders who were also members of the congregation. But this was a false move on Wagner's part, and he was hopelessly defeated. T. W. Perry countered with a petition in favour of the ritual signed by a hundred householders. So the Vicar took no further action in this case.

The second and much more serious dispute related to St. James's chapel in St. James's Street. In 1865 the Rev. C. D. Maitland, who had been its Perpetual Curate since 1828, died. It was at first proposed to appoint the Rev. Stopford A. Brooke as his successor, but he was unacceptable to the Vicar of Brighton. Wagner's enemies suggested that this was only because Stopford Brooke had written a life of the Rev. F. W. Robertson, with whom Wagner had quarrelled. But this seems unlikely to have been the sole reason. It was therefore necessary to find another candidate.

The freehold of the building belonged to trustees, one of whom was abroad. It proved difficult to track down the ownership, and the formalities of a transfer were prolonged. But they were completed just before the expiration of the period of 40 years, during which the presentation remained in private hands. After that time it passed to the Vicar of Brighton. The building was actually bought by one of Wagner's own curates, the Rev. John Purchas. He had worked with Arthur Wagner at St. Paul's and had no doubt absorbed there all the ritualist ideas which Purchas was later to carry much further at St. James's. But at the time he assured the Vicar that he did not belong to the advanced school of ritualism. The relations between Purchas and the Vicar had always been so good that Wagner was afterwards to say that "not a passing cloud ever dimmed our intercourse".[100] So the Vicar gave his consent to Purchas's appointment on the very last day of the 40 year period. Purchas was afterwards to claim angrily that the Vicar could do no other than agree to the appointment of one of his own curates. But Wagner had actually intended to appoint to Rev. H. H. Wyatt, had the presentation passed to him. So if he had been at all unreasonable or dilatory he could have prevented Purchas's appointment. As there were no parochial duties attached to St. James's and only two services a week to take the Bishop of Chichester, Dr. A. T. Gilbert, suggested that Purchas should continue as a curate at St. Nicholas's. Wagner was quite agreeable to this arrangement.

The former services at St. James's were of an evangelical nature. So Purchas read himself in, wearing a black gown, and at first continued the services as they had been in C. D. Maitland's time. But after a while he closed the chapel in order to adapt it for ritualist services. It was re-opened on the 2nd September 1866 with a special service which he afterwards claimed was not intended to be the normal pattern of weekly worship. There was a choir in scarlet cassocks, several officiating priests dressed in vestments, altar-lights and incense. He himself was dressed in a claret-coloured cope and carried a biretta.

There was an immediate outcry. Seven Brighton clergymen, including the Rev. Thomas Coombe of All Saints church, who was H. M. Wagner's nephew, and the Rev. E. B. Elliott of St. Mark's, sent the Vicar a protest against the introduction into another Brighton church of "an ultra-ritualistic and sacerdotalising system of worship",[101] which was intended to "un-Protestantize our Protestant Church".[102] Varied vestments, altar lights and other such novelties, they felt, were only intended to do honour to what the Roman Church called "the real presence". An address to the same effect was also presented to the Vicar by the laity. One anonymous correspondent in the Brighton Herald stated openly that the Vicar had "introduced the seeds of division (into the Church in Brighton) in the person of his own son".[103]

Throughout the whole Purchas affair or that part of it which transpired before his death in 1870 the Vicar of Brighton was at his very best. In his replies to these addresses he showed a tolerance, a restraint, a wisdom and a kindness which would have done credit to any contemporary clergyman. Indeed if such had been displayed by a majority of the clergy who then (or at any other time) existed the history of the Church would have been a good deal happier. He agreed that the recent ceremonial at St. James's chapel was "carried to the highest order"[104] and that therefore the time had come to end Purchas's curacy at St. Nicholas's, which he had effected with the agreement of the Bishop of Chichester, Dr. A. T. Gilbert. He had "no time for gorgeous vestments and incense"[105] and had offered "faithful and kindly remonstrances"[106] to those who used them. He went on to say that he had sought to provide in Brighton "that not one section only of the Church but each and every phase of religious opinion within her pale shall be represented. . . . The consequence is that every person, be he in high or humble life, is not compelled to accept likings and dislikings of others but is at liberty to act according to his conscience and free will".[107] To the laity he added significantly: "The darkest page of history is the record of the evils which have sprung from intolerance and from the religious animosities of Christendom."[108]

Purchas was naturally annoyed at being dismissed from St. Nicholas's and said so. He had hoped to show that a very high church clergyman, as he now admitted himself to be, and one of moderate views could work together. However, he gave an assurance that the services at St. James's would henceforward cause the Vicar no anxiety and that he would conform to the statutory requirements of the first rubric of the Book of Common Prayer. On the 15th November in a letter to the Brighton Gazette he went further and said that he had decided to give up all vestments and incense there in the interest of unity and goodwill.

Unity and goodwill, however, did not result. In February 1868 the Brighton Church Union presented a petition signed by 3,110 people to the Archbishop of Canterbury, Dr. Charles Thomas Longley, against what they again called "the whole ritualistic and sacerdotalising system".[109] Purchas therefore thought better of his undertaking and, to commemorate the anniversary of his re-opening of St. James's chapel, he arranged a special service on Wednesday 9th September 1868 at 8.30 p.m., for which 1,500 tickets were issued in advance. At this service, incense, vestments and all the former ceremonial reappeared. The preacher was

Father Ignatius, who was dressed in the robe of the Benedictine order and prostrated himself before the altar before entering the pulpit. It can be imagined what effect such a gesture would have in Victorian England. It even produced adverse comment from "The Thunderer". Wagner too felt called upon for further action. He called on Purchas at St. James's and expressed great dissatisfaction with the altar lights there and all the other recent ceremonial arrangements. He announced his intention of preaching in the chapel the following Sunday and that he would bring his own choir with him. To this Purchas replied that this would not suit his arrangements at all and that, as the chapel was his own private property, he was not prepared to agree to the proposal. Wagner could do no other than retire, temporarily discomfited. But he immediately made the Bishop of Chichester aware of the whole matter. The Bishop wrote to Purchas but received the same reply, which Purchas reiterated throughout the whole affair, namely that the chapel was his own private property and that he could therefore do whatever he liked within it.

The next step was a petition to the Bishop, signed by 648 people, asking him to "restrain proceedings which are decidedly opposed to the teaching and spirit of our reformed and Protestant Church of England".[110] A copy of this petition was sent to the Vicar. Wagner replied that, while the petitioners were talking, he had already acted and that a copy of the Church Discipline Act was before him. He agreed that the ritualistic practices "deserve a much severer censure than that of ritualistic. They are often profanely irreverent violations of the rubrics and doctrines of our Church".[111] One wonders what his son, Arthur, must have thought of this pronouncement, but he was quite silent in the matter until after the Vicar's death.

Meanwhile another incident of an opposite nature occurred in Brighton. An evangelical clergyman named the Rev. J. Knapp, incumbent of St. John's church, Portsea in Hampshire, preached at the new Baptist chapel in Norfolk Street, which later became the evangelical church of Emmanuel in the Church of England. As a result he was inhibited by the Bishop of Chichester from preaching in the diocese of Chichester. The evangelical party complained that this severity contrasted very unfairly with the leniency shown by the authorities to John Purchas. Wagner replied that Knapp had actually committed a statutory offence and pertinently asked what Knapp's supporters would have said of an Anglican clergyman who had preached in a Roman Catholic church. Chichester was not Knapp's own diocese, and all other dioceses were open to him. As far as Purchas was concerned, the Bishop had already condemned ritualism and had disassociated himself from Purchas's actions. He (Wagner) felt that the Bishop would be unwise to take any further action in view of the pending appeal to the Judicial Committee of the Privy Council by the Rev. A. H. Mackonochie of St. Alban's church, Holborn.

However, the Bishop did take further action and also inhibited Purchas from preaching or from celebrating Holy Communion in his diocese. The Archdeacons, the Rural Deans and many clergy of the diocese signed a memorial to the Bishop supporting his action. But Purchas paid no attention to this official pronouncement and maintained that he was justified in so doing. Feeling rose so high that there was rioting in St. James's Street outside the chapel. On the 25th October 1868 Edward Martin of No. 41 Borough Road, Brighton, made a disturbance in the chapel during a service. He displayed a placard and started gesticulating violently. He was soon put outside, but in the uproar several people fainted. To prevent a repetition of such behaviour Purchas prosecuted Martin for the lesser of two offences open to him to plead: indecent behaviour in a church. Martin pleaded guilty and was fined by the magistrates 20s. 0d. and 12s. 0d. costs.

Purchas then appealed to the people of Brighton to protect his congregation against hired ruffians. On the following Sunday 20 policemen guarded the chapel during the morning service, but a stone was thrown through a window. When the service was over Purchas left by a side door in Chapel Street but was recognised in St. James's Street and mobbed by about 500 people. He managed, with police help, to make his way into Old Steine, where he secured a cab that conveyed him safely back to his home at No. 7 Montpelier Villas, though the driver received a cut in the face from a stone thrown at the carriage by one of the rioters.

As Purchas ignored the Bishop's inhibition and continued to conduct services at St. James's chapel in exactly the same manner as before his opponents urged the Bishop to take stronger action. This the Bishop declined to do himself. He said that he was content to leave his inhibition untested, but if the opponents wished to proceed further the courts were open to them and he would not oppose any such action there. Consequently the next step was an action in the ecclesiastical court. Colonel Charles James Elphinstone, with the tacit concurrence of the Bishop, brought thirty three charges against Purchas in the Court of Arches. The main charges were the wearing of copes, albs and other vestments; the celebration of Holy Communion from the eastward position with the priest's back turned to the congregation; the use of a ceremonially mixed chalice, altar lights and a veiled crucifix; and other rights and ceremonies not appointed by the ecclesiastical law. The last included the distribution to the congregation of candles which had been blessed and sprinkled with holy water; the use of a stuffed skin of a dove; the existence of a modelled figure of the infant Christ; and the rubbing of consecrated ashes on the foreheads of the officiating clergy on Ash Wednesday. Even as long as eleven years later this last charge could be transformed in Sawyer's "The Churches of Brighton" into that of rubbing black powder on the heads of the congregation as if it had been a witch trial of the early seventeenth century!

The Dean of Arches, Sir R. J. Phillimore, gave judgment on the 3rd February 1870. He pronounced that the use of Eucharistic vestments, wafer bread, a ceremonially mixed chalice and the eastward position in the celebration of Holy Communion could be justified, but that all the other practices cited were illegal. Purchas was condemned to pay the costs of the action. The judgment dissatisfied both parties. Purchas ignored it, as he had ignored the inhibition of the Bishop of Chichester. The evangelical party on the other hand considered that the most important issues were the very ones that had been given against them. They therefore appealed to the highest ecclesiastical court, the Judicial Committee of the Privy Council. But before the case could be heard Colonel Elphinstone died, and his place had to be taken by Henry Hibbert. Purchas entered into a legal appearance against the substitution of this new name. But this was the only time in which he recognised the jurisdiction of the courts at all.

Judgment was not pronounced until March 1871. By this time there had been a change also in two other actors in the scene. During 1870 both Dr. Gilbert,

Bishop of Chichester, and the Rev. Henry Michell Wagner died. So the sequel belongs to the story of the latter's son, Arthur Wagner. He had not previously taken any part in the proceedings but, when the judgment of the Court of Arches and subsequently of the Judicial Committee of the Privy Council condemned Purchas on most of the charges preferred against him, Arthur Wagner was unable to accept the validity of a secular court's pronouncement on matters of doctrine and worship in the Church of England and went into print to that effect.

The whole Purchas case must have greatly disturbed the last four years of Henry Wagner's life. But apart from this incident, the later part of his incumbency was relatively peaceful. This left him free to carry out his charitable activities which probably formed the best side of his work in Brighton. As early as June 1834 his mother had recorded in her diary her satisfaction at being told in church by a complete stranger, who did not know that she was the Vicar's mother, how much good the Vicar had done in the parish. This stranger added that the sermon on the subject of the prodigal son, which Wagner had just delivered, was the finest sermon that he had ever heard.

When Wagner came to Brighton in 1824 the Sussex County Hospital was in the process of formation. Thomas Read Kemp had given the site for it in Eastern Road, together with a donation of £1,000. Lord Egremont, the Lord Lieutenant of Sussex, had contributed £4,000 later supplemented by the further sum of £1,000 to make a fever ward. Wagner took an active part in raising the remaining amount of £9,000 that was needed to build the hospital. He gave 50 guineas himself and his brother George of Herstmonceux Place 25 guineas. In the light of this donation he became a Governor for Life and was also a member of the General Court of Management that met half-yearly. At the first meeting of this body on the 29th June 1828 he seconded the nomination of Lord Egremont as President of the hospital. For the rest of his life the Vicar quite often attended meetings of the Board of Governors.

He was not elected to the Committee of Management that supervised the daily running of the hospital but attended their meeting of the 24th June 1828 when they asked his advice about the appointment of a chaplain for the hospital. He recommended his friend, the Rev. J. S. M. Anderson, who was also the Perpetual Curate of the nearest church in Brighton to the hospital, namely St. George's. Anderson was duly appointed Chaplain to the Hospital by the Board of Governors on the 25th July at a salary of £50 a year. Wagner was again consulted about the Chaplain's salary in 1847 and recommended that this should be increased to at least £100 a year. But it is not clear whether this advice was taken by the Board at the time or not. Wagner continued his support of the hospital throughout his life and often required his clergy to make an annual appeal for its funds from their pulpits. Members of his family were also subscribers personally.

Another charity with which Wagner was connected was the Brighton Dispensary. This had been started in 1809 in premises in Nile Street adjoining the old Vicarage. It subsequently moved to North Street and then to Middle Street, where the Sussex General Infirmary was added to it in 1812. The latter was closed when the new County Hospital, with 72 beds, was opened in 1828. But the Dispensary continued in existence and in 1850 moved to more capacious premises in Queen's Road. The Vicar played a leading part in the enlargement of the scope of this institution. The Dispensary continued in existence until this century and the fine building which it occupied was only demolished after the 1939–45 war.

Perhaps the charity nearest to the Vicar's heart was the National Schools. None existed in Brighton on his arrival. So he set about founding one at once. In 1829 Stroud and Mew designed for him an extremely fine building in Regency Gothic style in Church Street at the north end of New Road. This was opened in the following year. Anne Elizabeth Wagner's diary records how the Vicar always examined the children himself once a year and, when they were given a treat, presided over the tea. The National Schools building continued in existence until our time. The building was scandalously and most unnecessarily demolished by Brighton Corporation in 1971 during a postal strike. A bust of H. M. Wagner by J. E. Carew stood in the building but disappeared at the time of the demolition.

The Church Street building was only the first of its kind in Brighton. Several others followed, and by the Vicar's death in 1870 there were no less than nine National Schools in Brighton, all started by him or under his influence before compulsory education was introduced. For these schools he required all the clergy in his parish to preach an annual appeal sermon. The only other charity for which he made the same annual requirement was one of rather similar aims, namely the local branch of the Society for the Promotion of Christian Knowledge.

Brighton, not being a medieval town, was not well provided with almshouses. The only such establishment of any age comprised six small houses in rudimentary Gothic style at the junction of Lewes Road and Elm Grove. These had been built in 1795 by Mrs. Marriott in memory of her friends, Dorothea and Philadelphia Percy. They were for six poor widows of the Church of England. In 1859 Henry Wagner and his sister Mary Ann, who lived with him, financed the addition to this row of six more houses. Three were added at each end of the block in the same style. These twelve almshouses have recently been restored and modernised by conversion into six larger dwellings.

Henry Wagner was also a Trustee and Vice-President of the Eye Infirmary in Queen's Road and President of the Asylums for the Deaf and Dumb and the Blind, both in Eastern Road. The last of these was built rather late in his life, in 1865, and was a very interesting Venetian Gothic building designed by the Brighton architect, Somers Clarke, who was the son of the Vestry clerk of the same name. The building was unfortunately demolished in 1957 to make way for the new building of the Royal Sussex County Hospital.

Another building in which the Vicar and Somers Clarke were associated was the new Swan Downer School. Swan Downer was a Brightonian in origin who had made a fortune as a merchant in London. He died in 1816 and left £7,100 for the foundation of a school for 20 poor girls in Brighton. Its first premises had been at No. 12 Gardner Street. Wagner had always taken an interest in this school. In 1867 he was instrumental in securing its removal to a larger building at No. 11 Dyke Road. Somers Clarke was the architect of the new Gothic building.

Another and more unusual charity with which Wagner was connected was the Royal Society for the Prevention of Cruelty to Animals. In January 1842 he arranged for the Society to send one of its officers to Brighton once a quarter in return for the receipt of an annual subscription from him of £20. In 1869 a county branch of the Society was formed, and Wagner became a Vice-President of this.

In 1850 occurred the so-called papal aggression, when the Pope redivided England into Roman Catholic dioceses, as had not been done since the reformation. This produced a hysterical reaction in many parts of the country. With Wagner's cosmopolitan background and tolerant attitude to differences within the Church of England, one would have expected him to view this development without dismay. But he seems to have shown some concern. On the 14th November 1850 a Vestry meeting was held, at which the Vicar took the chair. The Rev. H. V. Elliott, Perpetual Curate of St. Mary's church, representing the evangelical movement within the Church of England, and the Rev. J. N. Goulty on behalf of the Dissenters, brought forward a petition to Parliament on the subject. The meeting recorded that the Pope's decree "obviously contemplates the extension of Popery with all its vital errors in our Protestant Kingdom, and it is further an Act based on the arrogant assumption that neither the sovereign of this mighty empire nor any other individual among the many millions of Protestant subjects has any right to be accounted a Member of the true Church of Christ or any inheritor of His Heavenly Kingdom! A more audacious attempt to bind under the chains of an unlawful thraldom the dearest spiritual birthrights of the people of this land has not been made since these chains were broken asunder at the reformation".[112] Any thought that an adherent of the Church of Rome should feel entitled to consider himself a member of "the true Church of Christ" never entered their heads.

The Vestry went on to express amazement that there should be no existing law which permitted "this insolent aggression" to be resisted. But if none such existed they petitioned the Queen in Parliament to enact a law which, while "leaving to the adherents of the Church and Court of Rome the liberty now enjoyed by them of exercising with the most perfect freedom their own religious worship, shall teach them to respect the rights of others and preserve Your Majesty's United Kingdom and Your Gracious Colonies from any real or nominal subjection to the Pope and his Cardinals".[113] The proceedings closed with a vote of thanks to the Vicar in the chair for having concurred in the convening of the meeting and for his "courteous, able and impartial conduct in the Chair".[114] In the light of political and religious feeling in Brighton at the time such a vote of thanks would have been impossible if the Vicar had not manifested some measure of agreement with the subject matter of the petition.

Despite Wagner's early life and Georgian outlook in most matters, it seems that he was to some extent a sabbatarian, like most Victorian clergymen. In 1856 he agreed to become a Vice-President of the local branch of the Early Closing Association. The objects of this society were entirely sabbatarian. They thought that the long hours during which shops were open on weekdays encouraged young men to encroach on the sabbath and "make that day a day of pleasure and recreation".[115]

Two years later a copy of a petition to Parliament was pasted in Wagner's letter-book which protested against the opening of the National Galleries and Museums and the Crystal Palace on Sunday afternoons. There is no record that he actually signed this petition, but it can more reasonably be inferred that he did so rather than the contrary, from the fact that it appears in his letter-book at all.

In 1856 a Scripture Readers Association was formed in Brighton. Wagner agreed to send them a subscription of £10 10s. 0d. after being reassured as to the qualifications of the members of the committee who would select the readers and that, when selected, the readers would be presented by the minister who would be using their services to him as Vicar of Brighton for appointment.

In 1855 Wagner had a severe illness. The nature of it is unknown, except that it involved fever. At one time it was thought that he would not recover. But he was nursed through it by his devoted housekeeper, Emma Andrews. By October he was through the worst, though still too weak to hold a pen. As a thank-offering for his recovery he first attempted to build a new church at West Blatchington, now in Hove, but then attached to the Brighton living. But this enterprise was thwarted by the Marquess of Abergavenny's unexpected refusal to provide the necessary land for the purpose. Instead Wagner gave 150 guineas to the Dean and Chapter of Chichester to erect a stained glass window in Chichester cathedral. This was designed by John Reginald Clayton of Clayton & Bell and depicted Christ restoring sight to the blind and healing a man at the pool of Bethesda and also St. Paul healing a cripple. The window was placed in the north aisle of the cathedral but was blown out during the 1939–45 war.

To assist his recovery the Vicar was advised by his doctor to seek a warmer climate. So at the approach of the following winter he set out on what proved to be quite a hazardous journey to Malta and Egypt. During the journey he kept a journal which he illustrated with charming pencil sketches of people whom he noticed as part of the scene. In it he described himself as "aged and in ill health",[116] though he was only 64 at the time.

He was accompanied by his youngest son, Henry, aged 16, and two men-servants named Andreas and John. They had twelve pieces of luggage between them. They left home on the 10th November and crossed the channel from Newhaven to Dieppe. They stayed one night at the Hotel du Louvre in Paris and then proceeded across France by train in the daytime, stopping the nights at Fontainebleau, Dijon, Lyons, Avignon and Marseilles. At Fontainebleau, which Wagner had visited in 1816, they were allowed to see over the chateau, though the arrival of the Emperor was imminent. Between Lyons and Valence they noticed that two of their packages were missing: a portmanteau containing most of the Vicar's clothes, linen and books and a leather bag. They reported the loss at both Avignon and Marseilles stations and claimed that the value of the contents was £40 or 986 francs. The Sous-Inspecteur du Chemin de Fer at Marseilles promptly handed over 1,000 francs (instead of the 986 claimed!) which was to be refunded if the bags were subsequently found and forwarded to Malta. This in fact happened. It was reported by electric telegraph the next day that the missing pieces had been discovered in Paris. They were forwarded to Malta on the next steamer and when received by the Wagners on the 30th November, the compensation of 1,000 francs was refunded.

The party left Marseilles on the 20th November on the French steamer "Indus" with 60 first class passengers on board. The passage lasted three days, during which they sighted Corsica, Sardinia and Sicily off Marsala. They arrived at Valetta on the 23rd November and stayed a week with the Vicar's nephew, the Rev. George Wagner, and his sister, Anne. George Wagner had been sent to Malta for the benefit of his health. They landed on a Sunday and went at once to the Anglican church, now St. John's Anglican Cathedral, which had been built by Queen Adelaide at her own expense and at a cost of about £16,000 after her visit to the island in 1838-9. Three days later the Vicar called on the Governor, Sir W. Reade, who told him that the Maltese "desire municipal institutions without municipal taxes such as an import of water, lighting, etc".[117] Wagner might have added from his own experience that the people of Brighton thought on much the same lines.

There were no berths to be had on the French steamer that had brought their missing bags from Marseilles. So instead they travelled on to Alexandria on a P. & O. steamer "Colombo". They had to share a cabin with three other men whose conversation Wagner described as "low and disgraceful".[118] The Vicar had much talk on board with Sir James Outram, who had been appointed to command "the Persian expedition",[119] "Box and Cox" was also performed—not the Sullivan operetta, which had not yet been written, but the play by Maddison Morton.

They reached Alexandria on the 6th December and went on to Cairo by train. They stayed at Shepheard's Hotel, which Wagner found "abundantly redolent of onion and tobacco".[120] There they spent 27 nights. During part of the time the Vicar was "much disordered".[121] In fact he had to send for the doctor and spent five days in bed. Their most interesting excursion was to the Pyramids and the Sphinx. They left at 7.45 a.m. on the 30th December and were back in the hotel by 5 p.m. Transport was by litter drawn by donkeys and across the Nile by the ferry. But occasionally they had to be carried by Arabs over water and black mud, when the litter was unharnessed and the donkeys driven across. All the arrangements were made by Mr. Shepheard of the hotel, who actually accompanied them on the trip. On arrival at the great Pyramid Wagner felt the challenge of the occasion, despite the fact that it was only four days since he had been confined to bed. So he determined to make the ascent and reached the summit pulled and pushed by three Arabs in the usual manner. Arrived at the top "Mr. Shepheard erased his own name and carved mine in the sand upon the apex with the date of the month and of the year".[122] Of the descent he wrote that it "raised a palpitation dissimilar to that of the indifference of the homme blasé".[123]

Wagner had intended to go on from Egypt to Jerusalem and, while in Cairo, wrote to the British consul at Jaffa to enquire about the possibility of securing a litter for the journey. But he does not record any reply or why the plan was abandoned. Perhaps this was due to his illness. Instead the party left Cairo by train en route for home on the 2nd January 1857 and went on board the steamer "Arcadia" at Alexandria the next day. The passage to Malta took 5 days. The food on board was lamentable. Insufficient bread had been provided. There was no yeast to make more. The meat was so hard that Wagner was not able to masticate it. For the whole journey he had to live on water gruel, hard biscuit softened in water and tea made with some kind of preserved substitute for milk. As the result, when he arrived at Valetta he was so weak that he had to be carried in a chair. He stayed nearly a fortnight with George and Anne Wagner, on the ground floor in order to avoid the stairs. He found his nephew very weak and in fact George died soon afterwards.

On the 21st January the party boarded the steamer "Cairo" for Marseilles. The passage took 71 hours. Wagner was very sick during the first part of the voyage. From Marseilles they moved across France much more quickly than on the way out. They travelled at night, breaking their journey during the day at Lyons and Paris. They reached Boulogne at 7 a.m. on the 27th January and left again three hours later in a high sea and a snow-storm. The crossing took two and a half hours. They returned home via Ashford and St. Leonards, where Wagner's brother, George, had a house, and where they spent their first night in a bed since they had left Malta. They had been away for two and a half months. In spite of the extreme efficiency of the compensation paid for the lost luggage, which no travel of today would provide, the conditions outside France generally sounded most primitive and the discomfort considerable.

Thereafter the Vicar's life in Brighton followed a regular pattern. He rose at 3 a.m. each day, having retired to rest the night before between 8 p.m. and 9 p.m. He often appeared at the Post Office at the time when this opened with a pile of letters that he had already written that morning. He showed considerable business faculties in his management of the parish, was methodical to a degree and punctual to the minute in appointments and meetings. To the very end of his life, when he was often somewhat debilitated, he was indefatigable in visiting the sick in all weathers, despite the fact that at that time he had about 5 or 6 curates.

He conducted the services in St. Nicholas's and St. Peter's churches with great dignity. One picturesque story emphasising this in the early part of Wagner's incumbency in Brighton is related by Frederick Arnold in his life of the Rev. F. W. Robertson. On one occasion during evensong at St. Peter's church the Vicar noticed two young officers conducting themselves in what he thought was an unbecoming manner. He strode down the aisle in his surplice and stationed himself between them for the rest of the service. When it was over the officers demanded an apology from him on the grounds that he had made them conspicuous and embarrassed. He is said to have replied "Gentlemen, I know the Duke of Wellington. I may say that I know him very well. It is you who owe me an apology, not that I owe you one. Unless you sit down immediately and write me an ample apology for your improper behaviour I shall immediately write to the Duke and complain that you have acted in a way unbecoming officers and gentlemen."[124] However, the actual incident may have been slightly less dramatic. Wagner's mother referred to it in her diary for the 12th January 1834. All she said was that after the service Henry "had two of the Dragoons summoned to ye Vestry and reprimanded them for talking during Divine Service. They behaved impertinently".[125] Arnold's version of the incident is ben trovato, even if embellished, and quite in character with Wagner.

All accounts agree that he was an excellent preacher. His sermons were "short, terse, almost epigrammatical but clear, pointed and vigorous".[126] He was also a good speaker at lay meetings. At a public meeting held in Brighton to move an address of condolence on the assassination of Abraham Lincoln he made a speech which was said to be more moving than any on the same subject delivered at the time in the House of Commons.

Even his enemies agreed that his great forte was appeals, whether from the pulpit or the platform. Here he was unsurpassed. This was probably because example is always more forceful than exhortation and, as he usually gave more than anyone else in whatever appeal was in question, he was in a good position to urge others to be generous also, and they consequently proved to be so. He and his son Arthur almost certainly raised more money for all kinds of charities in

1a. Melchior Wagner, 1685-1764.
Miniature by Philipp Jakob de Loutherbourg.

1b. George Wagner, 1722-1796

2a.   George Wagner, 1722-1796.

2b.   Mary Wilhelmina Wagner, 1731-1808. Daughter
of Henry Godde, wife of George Wagner.

3a. Melchior Henry Wagner, 1749-1811.

3b. Anne Elizabeth Wagner, 1757-1844. Daughter of the Rev. Henry Michell, wife of Melchior Henry Wagner.

4a.   Anne Elizabeth Wagner, 1757-1844.
By Stephen Poyntz Denning.

4b.   Mary Ann Wagner, 1791-1868.
Miniature by Jean Pierre Frédéric Barrois.

5a. The Rev. Henry Michell Wagner (1792-1870) as a young man. Miniature by his mother in law Mrs Douglas.

5b. The Rev. Henry Michell Wagner in old age.

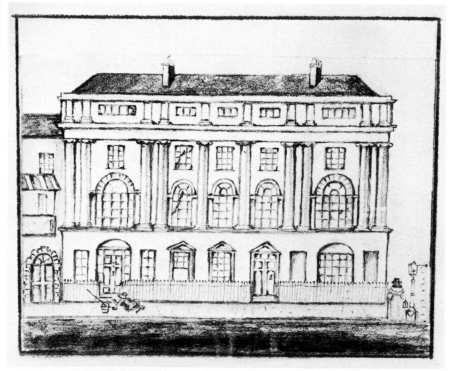

6a. (*above*) The old parish church of St Nicholas, Brighton, before the restoration of 1853. Exterior.

6b. (*left*) No. 10 (later 19) Pall Mall. Drawing by Carlo Secandrei.

7a. (*right*) Interior of the old church of St Nicholas, Brighton, before the restoration of 1853.

7b. (*below*) The old vicarage in Nile Street, Brighton, built in 1790. From a drawing in the Brighton Library reproduced by kind permission of the Chief Librarian, East Sussex County Council.

1. (*opposite above*) St Peter's church, Brighton, as designed.

2. (*opposite below*) St John's church, Carlton Hill, Brighton.

3. (*above*) St Peter's church, Brighton, as built.

4. (*right*) St Paul's church, Brighton, as designed, from a print reproduced by kind permission of the Rev. J. Milburn, vicar of St Paul's church.

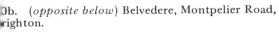

10a. (*opposite above*) The Vicarage in Montpelier Road, Brighton, built in 1835.

10b. (*opposite below*) Belvedere, Montpelier Road, Brighton.

11a. (*above*) The Rev. Arthur Douglas Wagner, 1824-1902, as a young man.

11b. (*left*) The Rev. Arthur Douglas Wagner in old age.

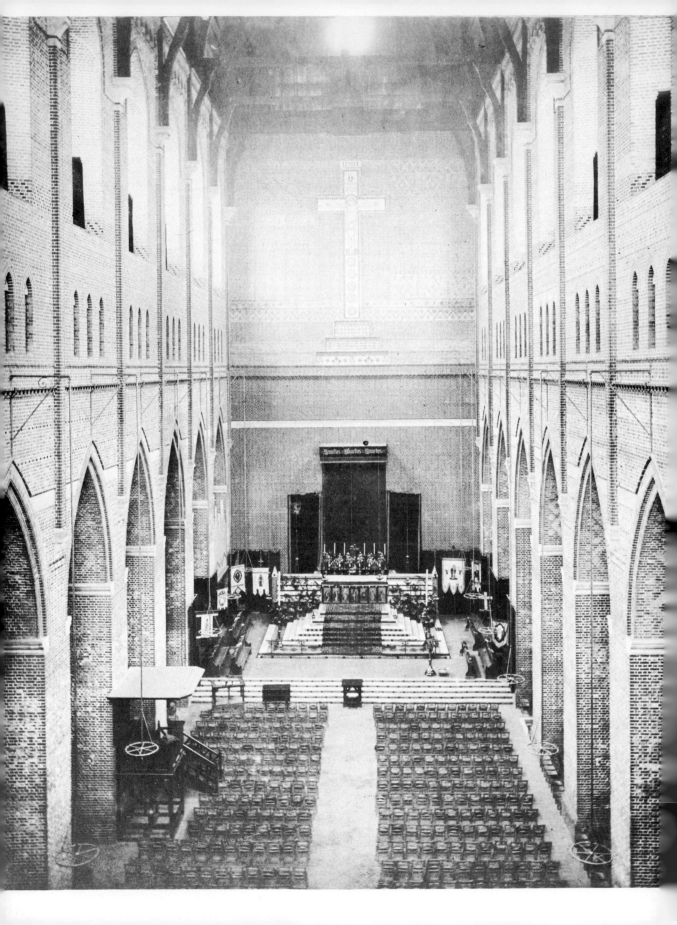

2a. (*above left*) St Bartholomew's church, Brighton. Reproduced by kind permission of the National Monuments Record.

2b. (*opposite left*) St Bartholomew's church, Brighton, interior. Reproduced by kind permission of r. Williams Parker, Honorary Archivist of St Bartholomew's church.

3a. (*above right*) Henry Wagner, 1840-1926.

3b. (*right*) St Martin's church, Brighton. Reproduced by kind permission of the Rev. Beaumont Brandie, Vicar of St Martin's church.

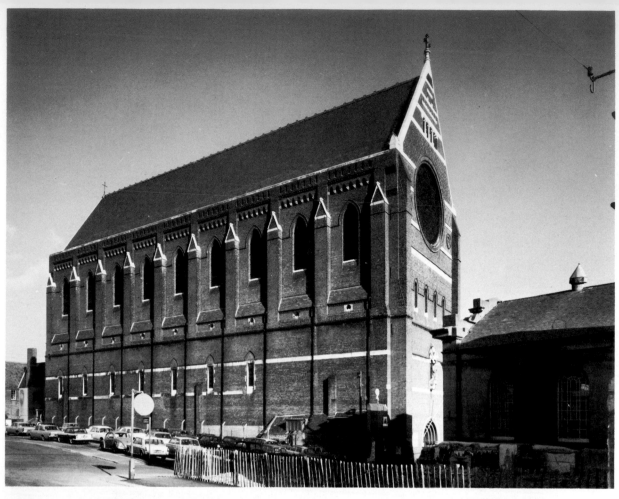

15a. (*left*) Anthony Wagner, 1770-1847. By T. Arrowsmith.

15b. (*below*) Thomas Jepson Wagner, 1810-1864. From a photograph of a miniature.

(*opposite above*) St Bartholomew's church, ...hton. Reproduced by kind permission of the ...onal Monuments Record.

(*opposite below*) No. 13 Half Moon Street, ...dilly, interior.

16a. (*left*) Orlando Henry Wagner, 1843-1909.

16b. (*below*) Orlando Henry Wagner, 1867-1956.

Brighton than any other person in the whole of the nineteenth century. His own contributions for the building of new churches and the restoration of St. Nicholas's together came to £3,327, without including the cost of several stained glass windows that he provided, and the gifts of other members of his family during his life to no less than £2,236.

There is little doubt that Wagner's own private and personal charities will have been on a proportional scale, but necessarily no record of them has survived. One incident, however, does give a glimpse of his kindness of heart together with his unsentimental and un-Victorian approach to such matters. In May 1859 a Mrs. A. Harvey, writing from the Rev. H. V. Elliott's house, No. 31 Brunswick Square, Hove, asked him to help the four children of her late coachman who were in the Workhouse at the time. He went to see them there and reported that one of the girls aged 9 was about to be transferred to the Girls Orphan Asylum. Her removal would be a sore trial to the other girl who would remain. He thought that it would be a great charity—he repeated the word twice—to place this remaining one in the Diocesan Training School for Servants. He added "I do not pretend to sensibility; indeed I have a dislike to the term, but I confess That I was rather touched by the spectacle of the four poor little ones".[127] He offered to provide 5s. 0d. a week to help rescue the child from "the peril and in some measure that reality of which Charles Dickens draws a portraiture somewhat overcoloured".[128] He may perhaps have thought that "Oliver Twist" was an exaggeration. But there had been grave scandals at Brighton Workhouse in 1838, during his incumbency, and he clearly felt that enough resemblance remained to make it desirable to remove this little girl at once. This was in fact done. Nothing was said about the two poor brothers. They were presumably apprenticed to a trade in due course, as happened to all the boys in the Workhouse.

The Vicar was a member of the Board of Directors and Guardians of the Poor during the whole of his period in Brighton. So no doubt he often had the opportunity to do similar good turns to other boys and girls who were in need of help.

In early life Wagner was an athletic man who had engaged in most sports. Although he left Eton in 1812, six years later at a match against Harrow at Lord's only three of the real team turned up and eight substitutes played. Wagner was one of these. In his first years at Brighton he would sometimes play cricket for a whole day at a time. He remained always a bold rider and in October 1834 had a fall from his horse. Only six weeks before this (the 22nd August) he had been involved in a carriage accident. When just outside Brighton at the beginning of a journey to Dublin the axle of the carriage broke. He was sitting in the box beside the coachman and was thrown off but not injured.

One of the peculiarities recorded of Wagner is that, when there was a parliamentary or other election, he was always the first to vote. The ballot was not introduced into elections until after his death. So this involved casting a vote publicly on the hustings. As his Tory views were well-known and the prevailing feelings of the district were wholly Whig and largely Radical he had often to pass through a howling mob of opponents in order to record his vote. He did so with the same obvious disdain as the Duke of Wellington had shown to the rioters at the time of Queen Caroline's trial and during the Reform bill crisis of 1831-2.

Wagner's vote in Brighton would have mainly been thrown away because the candidates whom he supported seldom stood a chance. The only exception was in 1837, when Colonel Sir Adolphus Dalrymple was elected by a majority of 18 votes. Dalrymple was a friend of Wagner's, as was Sir David Scott, another prominent Brighton Tory. But on almost all other occasions the Whig candidates triumphed. These were at first Isaac Newton Wigney and George Faithful, who were both Radicals. The longest spell in the House of Commons as a Brighton Member was held by Captain, later Admiral, Sir George Brooke Pechell, who represented the borough from 1835 until his death in 1860. He was not a Radical but supported the campaigns against church rates. When Wigney went bankrupt in 1842 his place was taken by Lord Alfred Hervey. Though he was a Whig, Hervey may have been more acceptable to Wagner as the son of his old friend, the Marquess of Bristol. But in 1857 Lord Alfred was defeated by William Coningham, another Radical who had been one of Wagner's main opponents over church rates at Vestry meetings. Coningham resigned from the House of Commons in 1864, and his place was taken by a barrister named Henry Moor of No. 5 Clarendon Place and later of No. 4 Sussex Square. Although he was a Liberal, Moor was supported by Wagner in his candidature.

In later life the Vicar suffered much from gout. Like Horace Walpole, this was no doubt the result of having too many prosperous ancestors. It affected both his hands and his feet and re-occurred so frequently that it eventually shortened one of his legs and gave him a slight limp. Another illness occurred in 1864. But he continued valiantly with his activities until very shortly before his death and was often to be seen walking on the West Pier, which had opened in 1866.

As late as the 10th August 1870 he was able to take the chair at a public meeting at the Town Hall which was held in aid of the Disestablished Church in Jamaica. The last meeting which he attended was on the 19th September, when he proposed a vote of thanks to the new Bishop of Chichester, Dr. Richard Durnford, for presiding over a meeting of the Society for the Propagation of the Gospel. The Vicar preached his last sermon on the preceding day, the 18th September. The text was the twenty-sixth verse of chapter eleven of the Acts of the Apostles: "The Disciples were first called Christians at Antioch." At this time the gout moved into his internal organs and prevented him taking nourishment. He was attended by Doctors E. J. Furner and Jardine Murray. His old friend, the Rev. James Vaughan, who had been Perpetual Curate of Christ Church since 1838, looked after his spiritual needs. His eldest son, Arthur, was also in attendance, but both his younger sons were abroad at the time. He gradually grew weaker but was conscious to the last and was aware of approaching death. He died peacefully between twelve and one o'clock on Friday the 7th October 1870. He would have completed his seventy-eighth year in nine days' time.

All the Brighton churches were hung with black following his death, and special sermons on the subject of his life were preached on the following Sunday. Both Wagner's wives and his mother's family had been buried in the Michell family vault in St. Nicholas's church. But the Burial Beyond the Metropolis Act, 1853, had prohibited all further burials in the church. His family therefore petitioned the Home Office for special permission to place the Vicar's body in the church, but this was refused. He had therefore to be buried in the Lewes Road cemetery, where his sister had been interred two years previously.

The funeral took place on the 15th October at St. Nicholas's. It was conducted by another old friend, the Rev. Thomas Cooke, who had been Perpetual Curate of St. Peter's since 1828. It must have been one of the grandest funerals ever held in Brighton. The entire clergy from every church in Brighton, most of which had been built during Wagner's incumbency, attended. With them were the Mayor and Councillors of the Borough, the members of the Board of Guardians of the Poor, past and present parish officers, the children of the National Schools and of the Swan Downer School and the inmates of St. Mary's Home. All the shops along the route from St. Nicholas's church to the cemetery were closed, and in all the churches which were passed by the procession the bells were tolled.

The grave was and is in a prominent position in the cemetery near the drive but not in the same section as that of his sister. The tombstone takes the form of a tall red marble cross. A tablet in his memory was also placed on the west wall of St. Nicholas's church. Arthur Wagner also erected a stained glass window in memory of his father in the chancel of St. Paul's church. Seven years after the Vicar's death his old friend Somers Clarke also put up a memorial window to him in the chancel of St. Nicholas's church which is the westernmost window on the north side.

Wagner's will was dated the 24th March 1865 and was witnessed by his friend and solicitor, Somers Clarke, together with one of the latter's clerks named C. H. Stacey. There were also four codicils. The will appointed his three sons as executors. Of the individual legacies, clearly the most important to him was that of £6,000 to his house-keeper, Emma Andrews, on account of her "long, faithful and affectionate services in my family" and "in remembrance of her unremitting attention by night as well as by day during an illness well nigh unto death and to which attention under God's holy and good providence I feel I am indebted for my life".[129] The wording of this particular section of the will was clearly the Vicar's own and not his solicitor's. Moreover in the last codicil made only a week before he died Wagner directed his executors to see that £100 was paid immediately after his death to Emma Andrews for the current expenses of the household—a very modern provision and one most unusual at that date. To the other servants who were in his employment at the time of his death he left nineteen guineas, which represented about two years' wages. To a former servant named Jane Scrase, who had retired and was an inmate of the Percy-Wagner Almshouses he left £100. He also bequeathed £500 to his successor as Vicar for those almshouses and a similar sum to provide an annual treat for the occupants of the Brighton Workhouse.

He left £100 to the Rev. Thomas Cooke, who had been his right-hand man in the parish as Perpetual Curate of St. Peter's church for over 40 years. Another equally old friend was his solicitor, Somers Clarke, who had been Clerk to the Vestry since 1830 and had therefore shared all the Vicar's battles over compulsory church rates. Instead of a legacy to him personally Wagner left £50 to his son of the same name. The latter was an architect who had already worked with Wagner over the rebuilding of the Swan Downer School and the Blind School in Eastern Road. Twenty-five years later he was to add the clerestory to St. Nicholas's church and a few years later the chancel at St. Peter's. Wagner also left £500 to Somers Clarke's daughter, Mary Anne Charlotte Clarke, who was the Mistress of the Upper Gardner Street National Schools.

Amongst his family, Wagner's younger sons, Joshua Watson and Henry Wagner, received £12,500 each. The whole residue, apart from the funds of the testator's two marriage settlements, was left to his eldest son, Arthur Douglas Wagner, for life with remainder to his children and power of appointment between them and, in the event of his having no children, to the testator's younger sons in equal shares with similar cross-remainders between them.

The will was proved in the Lewes Registry on the 7th November 1870 by Arthur and Henry Wagner with power reserved for Joshua Wagner to prove at a later date. The estate was shown at less than £100,000.

Wagner's obituaries for the most part reflected the political and religious opinions of the writers. But most of them stressed his generosity, his eloquence, particularly in making appeals, his kindness, efficiency, good management and punctuality. His only flaw was held to be that he could ill brook opposition and was unforgiving to those who had opposed him in the past. Only the Brighton Herald remained implacable to the last and maintained that he was a man who had missed his vocation. He should have been a military man, for which he was well qualified. A high Tory "iron Duke" was one thing. But an iron Vicar, cast in the same mould, was to this paper a contradiction in terms. But perhaps Wagner was best summed up by the comment made in later life by his youngest son, Henry. In the margin of a copy of Frederick Arnold's "Robertson of Brighton", in which the author was writing of the Vicar's combative nature, his son wrote: "If he had been less masterful, his work would have been less masterly."

Wagner's death was the end of an ecclesiastical epoch in Brighton. His successor and the new Bishop of Chichester reorganised the whole church-apparatus in the town. In 1873 the vast parish was split up and all the chapels of ease in it were given districts or parishes. At the same time the parish church was transferred from St. Nicholas's to St. Peter's. In some ways this has been unfortunate as St. Nicholas's has become something of a backwater, though much the most historic building in Brighton. Since 1870 the town has never again been a "bishopric within a bishopric", with all that this implies, and there has never again been such a dominating ecclesiastical figure there as the Rev. Henry Michell Wagner.

Chapter IV

THE REV. GEORGE WAGNER

THE REV. GEORGE WAGNER was a very different kind of clergyman from his uncle, Henry Michell Wagner. Though he did not survive into the height of the Victorian period, his life and attitudes nevertheless showed the unrelieved piety of a Victorian divine from the full flood of the evangelical movement.

He was born at No. 93 Pall Mall, Westminster, on the 8th January 1818 and baptised at St. James's church, Piccadilly, on the 26th February following. He was the eldest of the two sons and four children of George Henry Malcolm Wagner and Anne Penfold. His father had been apprenticed to an attorney in Brighton but never practised as such. He went at first into the family business but soon withdrew from it and became a country gentleman. To lead such a life he leased the estate of Herstmonceux Place in Sussex.

Herstmonceux Castle was for nearly a hundred years the seat of the Hare family. It was brought to Francis Hare, Bishop of Chichester, about 1727 by his first wife Bethaia, who was the last of the Naylors. The Bishop's son, Robert Hare, was twice married and had children by both wives. His second wife, Sarah Henkel, could not reconcile herself to the idea that the estate was entailed and that her husband's son by his first wife would therefore inherit it. So she conceived the idea that, if the mansion-house could be destroyed, this would break the entail. She therefore employed Samuel Wyatt to steal the bricks from the castle and use them to build a new house nearby which came to be called Herstmonceux Place. She soon found that, not only was her notion quite false, but even that the new house had been built on entailed land. According to her husband's great-grandson, Augustus Hare, in old age she repented of her deed and used to wander round and round the ruins of the castle repeating: "How could I have done such a wicked thing as to pull down this beautiful old place?"[1]

The effect of her action on Herstmonceux Castle was disastrous, and it was not rescued from ruins until after 1910. But in the process she created another masterpiece in Herstmonceux Place. When Georgian architecture was out of fashion Augustus Hare called it "a large but ugly house" which "produces a frightful effect but is exceedingly comfortable within".[2] This is the exact opposite of what we think today. Were the house not now divided into five flats or maisonettes, it would be far too large for a single residence. But it is an exceedingly beautiful Georgian building and one of the best works of Samuel Wyatt.

Robert Hare's son, Francis, sold Herstmonceux Place in 1807 to Thomas Kemp of Barbican House, Lewes, who was one of the Members of Parliament for Lewes. Kemp bought the estate for his son, Thomas Read Kemp, who had married Frances, daughter of the banker, Sir Francis Baring, the year before. Thomas Read Kemp lived at Herstmonceux Place until 1819, when he moved into Brighton and built himself a house there named The Temple. Four years later he began the building of Kemp Town, Brighton. Kemp sold Herstmonceux

Place to the trustees of W. D. Gillon, Member of Parliament for Falkirk, and they leased it to G. H. M. Wagner.

His son, George, was brought up and spent a quiet childhood at the house. He learned there the usual country pursuits but became less of a shot than a rider. His earliest education was entrusted to the Rev. J. C. F. Tufnell, with whom he boarded. There was one other pupil, who was the son of Archbishop Howley. At the age of ten George was sent to Eton where he was in Wilder's house. He remained there eight years. In due course he attained the sixth form and the first cricket eleven. In 1835 he played at Lord's against Winchester and Harrow. He took up beagling and, strangely enough in view of his later life, was also a good boxer.

In 1835 he left Eton and became for nine months a pupil of the Rev. Julius Hare, who had just been presented to the family living of Herstmonceux. It is difficult now to consider Julius Hare dispassionately in view of the relentless severity with which he later treated his nephew, Augustus Hare, and the fiendish cruelties which he allowed his wife, Esther Maurice, sister of the Rev. F. D. Maurice, to impose upon the luckless child. But Hare was undoubtedly a cultured man and had great influence on the clergy in Sussex during the next twenty years, particularly after he became Archdeacon of Lewes in 1840. In fact he had a position in the diocese which was only equalled by that of his fellow Archdeacon, Henry Manning, who was Rector of East Lavington and Graffham and Archdeacon of Chichester. George Wagner's studies with Hare gave him a broad sympathy with the evangelical movement in the Church of England.

The following winter he went to Paris in order to learn French and Italian. Amongst the distinguised people whom he met there were Admiral Sir Sidney Smith, Monsieur Berryer, the French legitimist politician, and Prince Charles de Broglie, formerly Archbishop of Ghent and uncle of the President of the Chamber of Peers in France.

But more significant for his future life was the visit which George Wagner paid in May 1837 to his uncle, Henry Michell Wagner, at the Vicarage in Brighton. There he met the Vicar's curate, the Rev. James Vaughan, who later became the Perpetual Curate of Christ Church, Brighton, and throughout his life was one of H. M. Wagner's closest friends and colleagues. Like Julius Hare, Vaughan belonged to the evangelical movement. Under Vaughan's influence George Wagner experienced a religious conversion which changed his life.

In September he set out with his family to spend the winter in Italy. But at Baden Baden they abandoned the journey on account of cholera in Italy. They settled instead at Neuwied on the Rhine, where they met the Prince of Wied and his aunt, Princess Louisa, who was a friend of Queen Adelaide's. During the winter George learned German and attended the services of the Moravian settlement at Neuwied. He also visited the poor who, according to Wagner's biographer, the Rev. John Nassau Simpkinson, nailed up their windows for the winter and generated an intense heat inside their houses from the stoves with which these were warmed. These visits, Simpkinson alleged, first caused George to suffer from pains in the head and face which gave him much suffering during the next 10 years of his life. But by twentieth century standards the symptoms seem rather psychosomatic. However that may be, Simpkinson says that George did not know what it was to feel well for one whole day thereafter till he went to live in Brighton in 1851.

92

The spring and summer of 1838 were spent at Herstmonceux, and then in October 1838 he went up to Trinity College, Cambridge. He read mathematics and took a first in the first part of his tripos. But he did not find the atmosphere of Trinity College congenial. Though there was no doubt already plenty of piety in the University, it naturally did not dominate undergraduate life. This remained as gay as usual, but George Wagner seems to have been absorbed while there by a gloomy form of evangelical piety. His tutor was the Rev. J. W. Blakesley. He also attached himself to Professor Scholefield and lecturers named Carns and Perry (later Bishop Perry). Julius Hare and Henry Wagner also preached in the University from time to time. George rose at 6 a.m. for prayer, attended chapel twice a day and set aside regular times daily for the study of the Bible and self-examination. He became Honorary Secretary of the local branch of the Society for the Conversion of the Jews.

But he was much troubled while at Cambridge by neuralgic pains in the head and face and in addition suffered from nervous depression. At this time he also became slightly deaf. He wrote to a friend: "It is out of His infinite mercy that God has given me deafness to keep me from an over-love of society—an especial blessing at Cambridge. I would that I were often deafer than I am." [3] It is difficult to know what to make of such unhealthy masochism except that he found Cambridge society uncongenial and wished to take refuge within himself. His biographer suggests that ill health prevented him from being a wrangler. In January 1842 he actually took a pass degree.

During the following spring he went to Marienbad to take the waters and there met the Rev. J. Gould, who was Rector of Burwash in Sussex. He returned via Prague and Dresden. He was ordained in Gloucester cathedral on Trinity Sunday 1842. Through the good offices of Mr. Gould he came to learn of the village of Dallington near Burwash, where a curate was required. The Vicar was non-resident. So George Wagner was able to move into the Vicarage and officiated for the first time in Dallington church on the 24th July 1842.

The population of the parish in 1842 was about 600. According to J. N. Simpkinson they were "not a favourable specimen of the English peasantry". [4] There was still a considerable legacy from the days of smuggling. But there were no Dissenters. The equating of Dissenters with smugglers is an amusing nineteenth century Anglican touch. As a sixth of the inhabitants were children and there was no school or Sunday school Wagner's first task was to form both of these. He set aside two rooms in his house for boys and girls separately and imported from his father's estate a master with the good Sussex name of William Honisett and a mistress from Brighton. The tuition was free, but the elder boys worked for two hours a day in Wagner's garden in lieu of payment. The school-master and two special pupils studied with Wagner himself each evening from seven until nine o'clock.

Later a third school for infants was started. All three classes were subsequently moved under one roof, and a special school building was erected the year after Wagner left Dallington, of which he was invited to lay the foundation stone in July 1849. He also formed an association of school-masters of the neighbouring parishes.

As far as the adults were concerned Wagner visited all his parishioners every six weeks. He started a clothing club, a shoe club for children, and a soup kitchen for the poor. He instituted missionary meetings with preachers from other parishes. All his charitable work was financed out of the fixed allowance which his father gave him. In 1842 Herstmonceux Place had been let to the Chevalier de Bunsen, the Prussian Ambassador. Wagner's family went abroad, and he joined them at Bagni di Lucca during the winter of 1844. On the return journey at Tegernsee, Austria, his father was involved in a carriage accident in which one leg was crippled for life. He spent the following summer with his son at Dallington, before settling at St. Leonard's and during his stay employed a pony carriage to take him about the countryside.

George's mother and sisters sometimes kept house for him. But during the last three years at Dallington he had permanent female companionship. This was a lady named Mrs. Newman. She was of German extraction, had been born at Lisbon, was the widow of an English merchant and had one son, presumably of George's own age. He had made their acquaintance at Cambridge. In 1845 this lady took up her abode in the Vicarage at Dallington. Victorians' exaggerated ideas about propriety would never have permitted such co-habitation unless Mrs. Newman had been at least old enough to have been George's mother. So presumably she was already an elderly lady when he was only 27. Thenceforward she was to play an encouraging and comforting part in his life and remained at the Vicarage for the last three years of his curacy there. During this period his health did not improve. To the pains in his head and face was added backache, and he had to have a high stool fitted into the pulpit on which to rest his seat when preaching.

In 1848 the Vicar of Dallington died. Under the new clerical climate non-residence was no longer tolerated. Therefore the new Vicar, the Rev. R. R. Tatham, needed to have the Vicarage for his own use. George Wagner's connection with the parish consequently ended, and he preached his last sermon there on the 20th November 1848. His work at Dallington had probably been outstanding for a country parish as early as the first decade of Queen Victoria's reign and was a model of a Christian life.

George Wagner's parents had meanwhile settled at No. 77 Marina, St. Leonard's-on-Sea. On leaving Dallington he joined them there for the next three years. Though having no parochial duties, he visited the poor of St. Leonards. After breakfast he read the Bible for an hour every day with his two sisters and he allotted five times a day for private prayer. He took up the study of geology and botany and began to learn Hebrew. He became friendly with Priscilla Maurice, the sister of the evangelical leader, the Rev. F. D. Maurice. During the spring of 1849 he went to London to hear lectures by Archbishop Trench and, while there, got to know Maurice himself and also met Thomas Carlyle and Thomas Erskine of Linlathen.

In the summer of 1851 Wagner took duty for a few months in his native Herstmonceux during Julius Hare's absence. At this time he refused a country living in Sussex offered to him by Lord Chichester, probably on the grounds of ill health. But his health improved during the years at St. Leonards. Then in 1850 he received a more attractive offer.

Queen Victoria visited Brighton for the last time in 1847. The Commissioners of Woods and Forests made preparations to demolish the Royal Pavilion. But the inhabitants of Brighton did not wish to lose this remarkable building. So after a town poll had demanded its retention the Town Commissioners stepped in and agreed to buy the building for £53,000. Since 1824 the original ball-room of the Castle Hotel, designed by John Crunden, had been incorporated in it as the Royal Chapel. The Bishop of Chichester therefore laid claim to this part of the building. It was excepted from the sale, and £3,000 deducted from the sale price. When the Vicar of Brighton, who was George Wagner's uncle, Henry, moved the Brighton Vicarage to Montpelier Road in 1836 his sister, Mary Ann Wagner, who lived with him, had bought a piece of land to the south of the Vicarage, on which she also built a house. She offered the diocese a portion of this land to the south west of her house, on which the Royal Chapel could be re-erected as a church. The offer was accepted and, when erected, the building was known as St. Stephen's church.

The Vicar of Brighton offered the perpetual curacy of the new church to his nephew, George. It says much for the catholicism of Henry Wagner's attitude to church affairs that he should offer this curacy to an adherent of the evangelical movement at exactly the moment in time when the Vicar's own son, Arthur, was beginning to work up the ritualist movement in Brighton and the Vicar himself, under his son's influence, was moving somewhat toward high church procedure. George Wagner was attracted by the bracing air of Brighton and the presence there of both friends and relations. He accepted the curacy and took up residence in Brighton in July 1851. The church was opened on St. James's day in the same month. He took lodgings in a small house nearby. His friend, Mrs. Newman, followed him to Brighton and established herself in lodgings in Temple Street near to his own rooms.

Predictably George Wagner found St. Stephen's church ugly. But this means nothing except that it was not Gothic, which, in 1851, evangelicals and high church men alike considered to be the only style suitable for a Christian church. They looked with scorn upon the Georgian classical preaching-houses of Brighton. This one, having also been the ball-room of a fashionable hotel and the private demesne of a character like George IV, whom they despised, had all the wrong connotations for them. There was no district attached to the church, and indeed the new Vicarage of George's uncle was within a stone's throw of the building. But presumably George Wagner's work among people lay largely within the area near to the church. This district, which is part of the Montpelier and Clifton Hill estate, was new and in fact not wholly finished at that time. It was largely a well-to-do area. His congregation therefore numbered very few poor people. This was a sorrow to him—another form of masochism with which it is difficult for us to sympathise today. Some of the sittings, however, were free, though not as many as he would have liked. Others were rented. Wagner made a point of calling on every person who rented a sitting.

His daily routine began with prayers. He rose early and had finished breakfast by 8 a.m. The next three hours were spent in study. The rest of the morning and the whole of the afternoon (5 hours in all) were given to visiting, with an hour's interval for lunch at one o'clock. He returned home to tea at five. At 7 p.m. there was usually a programme of lectures to be given or institutions to be visited. He took supper at nine and afterwards studied until late in the evening. His one relaxation was his annual holiday in Europe, generally in the mountains.

He at once established a Sunday School. The formation of National Schools was one of the principal interests of his uncle as Vicar of Brighton. On the 5th November 1855 George Wagner started one of these schools for the St. Stephen's district. He himself taught in both the boys' and the girls' section of this. Twice a week he visited the Diocesan Training School for Servants, which was in his area. He became its Honorary Treasurer and rescued its funds from disorder. He started a local branch of the Scripture Readers' Association to assist the clergy. One unusual activity arose out of his former interest in Germany. At that time itinerant street musicians were a great feature of urban life. Most of these were German. As he spoke their language he arranged a special service in German for them at 8 p.m. after they had ceased playing.

But what his contemporaries considered to be George Wagner's principal work in Brighton was the establishment of a Home for Female Penitents. This came about indirectly and gradually. During the summer of 1853, while on holiday in Germany, he visited Pastor Fliedner's establishment for Deaconesses at Kaiserwerth. He formed some idea of starting an English version of this institution but never did so. Then when back in Brighton he happened to see in the street three poor girls who, from their dress and lack of hats, he knew to be prostitutes. He formed the desire to do something for them and their like. He consulted his mentor, James Vaughan, who gave him the wise advice to leave the matter alone as, without the help of a woman, he would never get anywhere.

During the following winter a Mrs. Murray Vicars came to live with an elderly friend of Wagner's in Brighton. She was in origin a Jewess who had been converted to Christianity, had married a missionary and was then a widow. Wagner persuaded her to help and to visit a girl whose address he had. Mrs. Murray Vicars was able to place this girl in a private home. She went on to rescue 23 other unfortunate girls, who were sent, at George Wagner's expense, to institutions in London till these refused to take any more. At about the same time one girl in Brighton died of cholera. Her companions begged Mrs. Murray Vicars to help them. So she hurriedly took a house opposite the Level and later exchanged it for larger premises in Lewes Road. In November 1843 a committee of eight gentlemen was formed to run the Home, of which George Wagner himself was Honorary Secretary. Mrs. Murray Vicars became the resident superintendent with a staff under her of a matron, two or three assistants and a porter.

A vast chasm separates our thinking today from Victorian ideas of charity and good works, and of all subjects the difference in outlook is greatest in the case of prostitution, or what the Victorians called "fallen women". Some of the institutions for the reclamation of prostitutes in the nineteenth century were little better than prisons. In fact some were perhaps worse, as the inmates were subjected to having their hair cut off, which was not enforced in female prisons. Baroness Burdett Coutts alone, under Charles Dickens' wholesome influence, was able to found a bright and cheerful home where the girls were treated as reasonable human beings. It is difficult to judge how the Brighton home rated in character and humanity. At least it avoided the worse excesses of puritanism as the girls were not required to cut their hair. Their dress was described as "studiously plain and modest",[5] and not differing, save in its uniformity, from the normal dress of an indoor servant. Probably the Home was at its best in its earliest days, when it was personally supervised by George Wagner and was quite small. 37 girls were admitted during 1855.

We are told by George Wagner's biographer that very few religious observances were enforced as he shrank from imposing on the inmates "too strict a form of outward penance or constrained devotion".[6] However, the daily routine at once makes plain that it is a matter of opinion what constitutes few and what many observances. The girls rose at 5 or 6 a.m. and immediately had to submit to supervised prayer. While they were dressing a text of scripture was learned by heart in order to "check any tendency to conversation".[7] There were family prayers each morning and evening. The hours of work have not been recorded, but during the day the girls worked in the various departments of the Home: laundry, kitchen or sewing-room. During the sewing sessions a book—no doubt of sermons—was read aloud. The laundry and the sewing room made a contribution to the funds of the Home, but each girl during her stay at the Home made a complete set of wearing apparel which, on leaving, she was allowed to retain "if her conduct had been satisfactory".[8] Suitable intervals for meals and exercise in the garden of the Home were provided. In the evenings the girls were instructed in reading, writing and scripture. The Chaplain and Wagner himself, as Honorary Secretary, attended twice a week.

It was alleged that the girls needed "constant though not excessive employment and strict though not wearisome seclusion".[9] So they were kept night and day under observation and were taught to "acquiesce in this constant surveillance as a necessity imposed upon them for their good; not out of suspicion but as a protection against themselves".[10] One good point was that the mothers of the girls were welcomed to come to tea to visit them and frequently did so. When the girls left some of them returned to their parents' homes, some emigrated, but most went into domestic service and were found places to work. Whatever its limitations, the Home prospered and became much larger after George Wagner's death.

During his first years at Brighton his health greatly improved. But in the summer of 1854 he was too ill to go abroad. So he took a cottage with one of his sisters on the shore of lake Derwentwater. While staying there he met the widows of Wordsworth and Thomas Arnold and Kate Southey, the daughter of the poet. The following summer he went to Dinan and other places in Normandy and Brittany. It was about this time that he developed the cough and other symptoms of the chest affection from which he eventually died.

During the winter of 1856 he had an attack of bronchitis, which incapacitated him for 10 weeks. Following convalescence at St. Leonards he was recommended to seek a warmer climate. So in August, accompanied by both his sisters, Anne and Emily, a female cousin of the Michell family and a man-servant, he travelled across France to Hyères on the riviera. The choice of place was probably made because the Anglican chaplain there was the Rev. W. Clarke who had been a curate at Brighton. The desired improvement did not materialise, and so he moved on further south. Emily Wagner and Miss Michell went home, and he and Annie, as Anne was called in the family, embarked for Malta from Marseilles on the 29th October. They settled at Dunsford's Royal Hotel in the Strada Forni in Valetta.

At first he revived and was able to make outings in a bath-chair along the fortifications. He occasionally saw the Governor and Lady Reade, the Bishop of

Gibraltar and Mrs. Tomlinson and friends named Colonel and Mrs. Adams. In November he was comforted by a week's visit from his uncle, the Vicar of Brighton, who was passing through Malta on his way to Egypt, also in search of warmth to restore his health. But the following winter proved a cold and stormy one in Malta. He was mostly confined to the house. Much of his time was spent in preparing a manual of catechetical instructions to be used by teachers of young children. When his uncle again passed through Malta in January 1857 on his way home George was too weak to derive much benefit from the visit. Dr. Galland, who was attending him, advised Anne Wagner at this time that there was no hope for his patient. The consumption was too advanced. When it came to informing George himself of the situation on the 22nd January his deafness made the communication difficult. The doctor therefore prepared for him in writing a long statement of the circumstances. George at once wrote home to his father, asking him to sell £1,000's worth of securities to give to the Home for Female Penitents, of which £800 was to be used for the purchase of a permanent house and £200 towards the running expenses or for the establishment of similar homes elsewhere. Immediately afterwards he was attacked by bronchitis and diarrhoea but refused all opiates and died on the 10th February 1857. He was only 39. He was buried in the Protestant cemetery at Valetta. On the grave was placed a ledger stone with a simple cross inscribed: "To be with Christ is far better."

During his illness George Wagner had composed a farewell letter to the members of St. Stephen's church, which was printed. This was ostensibly written from St. Leonard's and dated the 23rd July 1856. But from internal evidence it is likely that it was written from Malta after he knew that he had no hope of returning to Brighton.

A sermon in his memory was preached at St. Stephen's church, Brighton, on the 22nd February 1857 by the Rev. Henry Arnold Olivier. His text was: "The Lord gave and the Lord has taken away. Blessed be the name of the Lord." The sermon was printed together with "a few words from a dying pastor to his beloved flock to be read to the congregation after his decease". The congregation erected a memorial to his memory in the church. Contributions were also invited to provide a permanent building for the Home for Female Penitents.

Between our own day, which is wholly secular and largely pagan in outlook, and the extreme piety of the Victorian age there is a wide gap, not only in time but in thought and morality. The Rev. John Nassau Simpkinson in his Memoir of George Wagner, and also in his similar Life of the Rev. Henry Venn Elliott, so piles on the overwhelming piety of his subjects and their world that it produces a reaction of distrust. A rose by any other name would smell as sweet. But if we are told that it is a fragrant, sweet-smelling, odoriferous, melliferous flower, we may perhaps wonder whether there does not linger about its root some whiff of the manure that made it bloom so well. Then too we know from the writings of Augustus Hare, Samuel Butler, Edmund Gosse and others how much children and dependants were made to suffer from the overwhelming piety of Victorian evangelicals. George Wagner had no children or dependants. He was even said to have a particular gift in addressing children. But fortunately there is considerable evidence, less suspect than Simpkinson's Life, to bear witness that George Wagner had an outstanding personality.

Frederick Arnold in his Life of F. W. Robertson, which is not at all written in a white-washing style, says that there was "a singular sweetness and attractiveness in his character" and that "the saintliness and self-sacrifice of his life shone with an almost supernatural beauty". He also quotes Thomas Erskine of Linlathen as saying of George Wagner: "He was one of the most lovable beings I ever met with. In fact I cannot say that I ever met with anyone like him." This was confirmed by Augustus Hare himself who, on account of his over-religious upbringing, had no special liking for clergymen. Hare met George Wagner in youth, when Hare's uncle, Julius, was still alive, and described him then as "a pale aesthetic youth with the character of a medieval saint".[12] He was a great favourite with Hare's mother, with whom he had long religious conversations. Hare went on to say that "he was afterwards a most devoted clergyman, being one of those who really have a vocation, and probably accomplished more practical good in his life than five hundred parish priests taken at random. Of him Chaucer wrote:

'This noble sample to his sheep he gave
That first he wrought and afterwards he taught.' "[13]

Chapter V

THE REV. ARTHUR DOUGLAS WAGNER

ARTHUR DOUGLAS WAGNER was the eldest of the three sons of the Rev. Henry Michell Wagner, Vicar of Brighton, and the only child of the latter's first wife, Elizabeth Harriott Douglas. As we have seen, he was born on the 13th June 1824 in the house of the Douglas family named Park Hill in Windsor. He was christened in Winkfield church near Bracknell on the 6th August following and named after the Duke of Wellington. One of his sponsors was the Duke's elder son, the Marquess of Douro, afterwards second Duke of Wellington.

His mother died when Arthur was five. Following this his paternal grandmother, Anne Elizabeth Wagner, and his unmarried aunt, Mary Ann Wagner, became permanent members of the Vicarage household. So young Arthur must have been brought up by them. His father married again when he was fourteen, but as his step-mother only lived another two years this marriage cannot have had much lasting effect on his life. His grandmother survived for another four years. His aunt remained a member of the Vicarage household until her death in 1868. It is likely that she really took the place of his mother and, when she died, she made him her heir.

Arthur's grandmother records that he was taken to church in Brighton, presumably for the first time, when he was four years old and that he behaved very well.

The first school which he attended was possibly the academy for young gentlemen kept by the Rev. C. W. Fennell at the house in Montpelier Road which immediately adjoined the Vicarage on the north. This had been built by Thomas Read Kemp in 1819 and was called the Temple. In September 1835 Arthur went to Eton. His father took him up personally and introduced him to the Provost, who was still Dr. Goodall, and to Mrs. Goodall. On their way there they went specially to Windsor Castle so that Arthur could be presented to Princess Augusta. At Eton he was placed with Mrs. Kingsley. Later he was in Slingsby's house.

In 1842 he went on to Trinity College, Cambridge, where he read mathematics. He became a scholar in 1845 and took an honours degree in 1846. Whether he found life at Trinity more congenial than his cousin George had done six years earlier we have no means of knowing.

It is evident that from the earliest days it was intended that he should take Holy Orders. This is perhaps reflected in the fact that, when only 16 and not yet confirmed, he was permitted by the Bishop of Chichester to become the godfather of his younger half-brother, Henry, who was born in 1840. Unlike his cousin, George, he did not undergo any special experience of conversion. Neither did he, like many of the Tractarians, progress gradually from low or broad church views to what came to be called a ritualist outlook. He seems from the first to have taken this stand. In this he may have been influenced by Joshua Watson, the father of his step-mother, who had been the leader of the high church movement in the previous generation, and was a powerful influence in the Wagner household.

St. Paul's church, West Street, Brighton, was the fourth Brighton church to be erected by Arthur's father, Henry Michell Wagner. In building this the Vicar had in mind from the first that his son should be its first Perpetual Curate. But when the church was opened in 1848 Arthur Wagner had not yet been ordained. H. Hamilton Maughan in his "Wagner of Brighton" says that "some difficulties" had arisen with regard to his ordination. What these were we cannot say. Almost certainly they did not denote a crisis of faith. It is also unlikely that he felt unable to subscribe to the thirty nine articles. More probably it was nothing more than that, because he had not read divinity at Cambridge, he had not yet had time to complete the necessary studies required for ordination. However, whatever the difficulties were, they were resolved shortly afterwards, and Arthur was ordained deacon in 1848 and priest in 1849.

St. Paul's was administered from the parish church by the curates of St. Nicholas's for the first two years. Then in 1850 the Vicar presented his son to the perpetual curacy. This he held until 1873, three years after his father's death. In that year the Bishop of Chichester, Dr. Richard Durnford, and the succeeding Vicar of Brighton, the Rev. John Hannah, subdivided the then huge parish of Brighton. St. Paul's was given a district and became a parish church. Arthur Wagner exchanged the title of Perpetual Curate for that of Vicar and held this position until his death in 1902. He was thus in charge of St. Paul's church for 52 years, thereby surpassing his father's record of 46 years as a Brighton incumbent.

When St. Paul's was opened in 1848 the building was unfinished, and all the windows were glazed with plain glass. The embellishment and completion of the church were the work of Arthur Wagner, first as Perpetual Curate and later as Vicar. Most of the fittings were designed with the church by R. C. Carpenter: for instance the pulpit and the rood-screen in its original form. The latter was a simple partition of medieval character, painted by S. Bell, who also executed the fresco of Christ in Majesty above the chancel arch. About 1861 Wagner called in G. F. Bodley to give advice, and Bodley designed the additions to the screen of a traceried canopy and a rood with flanking figures. The work on the screen was actually carried out by one of Bodley's pupils named Ingram. He was assisted in this by the Rev. C. E. Roe, who was then one of the curates at the church and later became Vicar of St. Mary's, Buxted. Roe also painted the pictures of St. Paul and of the Madonna above the altars in the north and south aisles respectively. The figures of the rood above the main chancel screen are the work of McCulloch of Kennington. Bodley was also responsible for the painting of the roof and the murals in the chancel. He was further commissioned to design a reredos but for this purpose he recommended a then little-known artist named Edward Burne-Jones, who later lived for many years at Rottingdean. Burne-Jones produced a triptych, of which the central panel represented the Adoration of the Magi and the flanking panels the Virgin Mary and the Angel of the Annunciation. One of the Magi is a portrait of William Morris. Later this triptych was remounted as a single long panel to form an altar-piece. It is now on loan to Brighton Museum.

The brass lectern was the gift of a private benefactor who stipulated that it should cost £1,000. It was the work of James Powell of Powell and Sons of White Friars, London. Much of the stained glass was designed for Wagner by Pugin in

1848. It was executed by Hardman. The finest window is the Jesse tree in the east wall of the chancel. The colours of this were later toned down by C. E. Roe and now give the effect almost of medieval glass. At the time of Bodley's work some windows by C. E. Kempe were inserted. One of these, representing Saint Edmund and Edward the Confessor, was given by Arthur Wagner in memory of his father and another in memory of his mother, whom he had hardly known.

In addition to internal embellishments, Bodley also added a narthex at the west end of the church. This joined the long passage on the south side of the nave to the fishermen's reading-room, which became a vestry.

But it was not until after his father's death in 1870 that Arthur Wagner was able to complete the church by building its tower. For advice over this he turned, not to Bodley, but to Richard Herbert Carpenter, the son of the original architect. The first proposal had been to build a tower and spire of stone to the north of the chancel. But the foundations laid for this had been weakened by the construction of the organ-chamber. The collapse of the spire of Chichester cathedral in 1861 had made Wagner doubtful whether it would be safe to build a stone spire so close to West Street. Carpenter was apparently satisfied that there was no risk in this, but Wagner still had misgivings and so instructed him to redesign and erect a timber version of the spire, which took the form of an octagonal lantern with a short spire. The work was carried out between October 1873 and February 1875 by George Cheesman & Co., who had built the main body of the church. The cost was £3,120 10s. 4d. and was wholly borne by Arthur Wagner. This and the embellishments of the church brought its total cost up to at least £16,000. In 1873 when St. Paul's was given its own parish and Arthur Wagner became its Vicar he used the occasion as the opportunity to abolish all pew-rents. Henceforward all the seats in St. Paul's were free.

A number of notable high church clergymen came to St. Paul's to preach for Arthur Wagner. Amongst these were Henry Manning, when he was Rector of Graffham and East Lavington in Sussex and Archdeacon of Chichester, and John Keble. Edward Pusey remained a life-long friend though he never preached at St. Paul's. Arthur Wagner was only 21 when John Henry Newman went over to Rome. But he remained in touch with Newman after Newman's conversion and was actually present in Rome in 1879 when Newman was made a Cardinal.

In 1855 to help with the running of St. Paul's church Arthur Wagner founded a religious sisterhood in the Church of England: the Community of the Blessed Virgin Mary, and established this at Nos. 3 and 4 Queen's Square nearby. Their functions were to care for the fabric of St. Paul's, to help with the Sunday school, to carry out district visiting and possibly to assist in the reclamation of prostitutes, though this last part of their work was not much developed until a later date. The formation of such a sisterhood was an action which, in the ultra-Protestant climate of the time, was only too likely to cause controversy. A religious community suggested sinister undertones of Roman Catholic convents on the continent where reluctant girls had been immured to escape the attentions of unwelcome lovers. Moreover the Sisters wore a veil and a kind of religious habit. So they were conspicuous as they went about the streets and as a result were frequently insulted.

At about the same time (1854) Arthur Wagner's cousin, the Rev. George Wagner, Perpetual Curate of St. Stephen's church, Montpelier Place, had started a small home for Female Penitents in a house in Lewes Road. When George Wagner died of tuberculosis in 1857 Arthur took over this home and moved it to two houses in Wykeham Terrace, adjoining Queen's Square. The Sisters of the Community expanded their activities to cover such rescue work. At that time they could take in 13 inmates. St. Mary's House, as it came to be called, eventually occupied eight houses in Queen's Square (Nos. 1-6, 10 and 11) and nine houses in Wykeham Terrace (Nos. 1-5 and 8-11). The sinister connotation attached to the sisterhood at that period gave rise to the legend that the houses in the two streets were connected by an underground passage. Any such connection was totally unnecessary as the two sets of houses adjoined each other back to back and so could communicate internally.

In 1857 Catherine Ann Gream was appointed Lady Superior of the Home. She came into public notice at the time of Constance Kent's trial, when she gave evidence before the magistrates at Trowbridge. But not much is known about her. Yseult Bridges in her book "Saint With Red Hands?" made her into a sinister figure and alleged that when both the inmates and the staff of St. Mary's Home were summoned to an interview with her they were expected to address her kneeling. If this was so, it is strange that so kindly a man as Arthur Wagner should have introduced such a harsh rule into his community. But Mrs. Bridges was most unreliable in what she said about Wagner himself, and so perhaps this alleged ruling, which was mentioned by her alone, was apocryphal.

St. Mary's Home rapidly increased its activities. The number of female penitents received there at one time rose from 13 to 30. The girls came from all over the country. There was also a dispensary for the poor of St. Paul's parish, which supplied 800 medicines a year, an infirmary or home for aged women, and an orphanage in three separate sections: infants, boys and girls. The boys formed the choir of St. Paul's church while they were there and were trained for a trade when they left. The girls went into domestic service. There was a district visiting association, with a room set aside for the relief of the poor. Six hundred blankets were distributed on loan during the winter. Coal and clothing clubs were organised. There was a needlework society and a bible class. At a paying level boarders were taken for £25 a year. There was a middle class day-school for the children of tradesmen. The establishment was staffed entirely by the Sisters and other lady volunteers. But the whole cost of running it, other than the fees received, was borne by Arthur Wagner.

The penitentiary for reclaiming prostitutes was probably conducted on much the same stern lines as George Wagner's home in Lewes Road had been. The girls were employed in laundry and needlework. They were expected to earn a certain number of marks per day, and, if they did not do so, were deprived of their ration of sugar or butter. During Lent only dry bread was provided for breakfast. As a result there were many casualties. Girls often ran away or were expelled for bad conduct. Others, however, made a success of it and were placed in good homes or emigrated.

The total charitable effect of St. Mary's Home during the second half of the nineteenth century, when the only charity available was in private hands, must have been considerable: probably the most effective single unit in the town. After Arthur Wagner had taken a summer house at Buxted he started a branch of the community there, which was known as St. Margaret's Cottage. By the end of the

103

century it was clear that St. Mary's Home had outgrown its cramped quarters in the very small houses of Queen's Square and Wykeham Terrace. But nothing could be done during the last years of Arthur's life owing to his illness. Ten years after his death the question of finance must have been stabilised, and both communities moved to much more spacious premises in an isolated site in Falmer Road behind Rottingdean. The new building was designed by F. T. Cawthorn. St. Mary's Home remained in operation on that site until recent years.

From the moment of Arthur Wagner's presentation as Perpetual Curate of St. Paul's church in 1850 he was the pioneer of the Tractarian movement or "Puseyism" as it was called. J. H. Newman in one of his books acknowledged St. Paul's as being one of the first churches in England to adopt the revived catholic ritual and teaching. From 1850 onwards the services there began to be conducted with a degree of ritual that had never before been seen in the town. All Souls' church in Eastern Road had had a surpliced choir when the Rev. G. B. Langdon had been its Perpetual Curate from 1834 to 1844 or 1845, but this had lapsed after Langdon had been transferred to Oving. Wagner instituted such a choir at St. Paul's which, as late as 1865, was the only surpliced choir in Brighton. It sang Gregorian music. This led to the erection of posters on houses in West Street proclaiming such absurdities as "Morning opera at St. Paul's".

Then there were the strange figures of the Sisters of St. Mary's Home, who looked after the fabric of the church and were seen coming and going in the streets in their unfamiliar dress or uniform. Inside the church were such unusual fittings as altar lights and a sedilia. But strangest and least acceptable of all visual effects was a complete set of Eucharistic vestments, which was perhaps the first such set to be used in a Church of England church since the reformation. Its use was, however, discontinued at a later date for a short time. Incense was never used at this time at St. Paul's. But the whole service of Holy Communion was conducted in a manner that was suspicious to the Protestant mind.

Throughout the eighteen fifties there were constant complaints in the local press about the proceedings in the church. Most of these related to the officiation of the Rev. William Gresley or the Rev. Henry de Romestin, rather than that of Arthur Wagner himself. Romestin was actually suspended by the Bishop of Chichester, Dr. A. T. Gilbert, from officiating further in his diocese. Perhaps the best example of the complaints made at this time to the Bishop is a letter written on the 21st October 1861 by the Rev. D. Tucker, Rector of Sandon in Hertfordshire. He informed the Bishop that at 7 a.m. on the 9th October, hearing the bell of St. Paul's tolling, he had attended a service of "Holy Eucharist" there. The celebrating priest was accompanied by an assistant and eight veiled females. The priest wore a red scarf, stood to the north of the altar, made copious genuflections and held up both the wafer-bread and the chalice in silence, as if for adoration, which clearly implied a belief in the corporal presence. Tucker wrote to ask whether or not the Bishop approved of such practices. The Bishop's reply of the 24th October in his own handwriting was most tactfully worded. He asked his correspondent whether he had actually seen the elements distributed and, if so, what words were used in the process. If Mr. Tucker replied to this letter with the information requested his reply has not survived.

Altogether the ritual used at St. Paul's was probably very moderate. It was certainly surpassed in other Brighton churches which were the offspring of St.

Paul's, such as St. Michael's and All Angels, St. James's and St. Bartholomew's. The hostility probably sprang from two separate causes. The first of these was unfamiliarity. In the eighteen fifties ritualism of any kind was entirely new and therefore suspicious. This was probably what Arthur Wagner's father, the Vicar of Brighton, had in mind when he preached—perhaps rather reluctantly—at St. Paul's for his son and took as his text: "Lord have mercy upon my son for he is lunatic and sore vexed." This incident is related in almost all accounts of Arthur Wagner's life. So one hopes that it is not apocryphal. But it has not been possible to establish an exact date for it. It is perhaps doubtful whether Arthur would have appreciated the reference as, according to one account of his character, he was rather lacking in humour.[1]

The other and much more important cause of hostility to St. Paul's and all its works was a deep distrust of the Roman Catholic Church, which had not been dispelled by more than a hundred years of comparative religious tranquillity. This was in fact greatly resuscitated by the so-called papal aggression in 1850, when the Pope redivided Great Britain into Roman Catholic dioceses that had not been used since the reformation. The reaction to this measure throughout the country was quite unreasonable and in fact hysterical. But it followed a series of conversions of prominent people to Roman Catholicism as the result of the Oxford movement. It is very difficult for us today to understand the violence of the feeling on both sides over these subjects at the time. Life long friends ceased to have any communication with each other after one of them had been converted to the Church of Rome.

St. Paul's and all that it stood for produced a similar reaction. The ritual used there was considered bad enough by extreme Protestants. But much worse was a hidden practice which did not at first come to light. Confession was from the beginning practised at St. Paul's but very discreetly. The confessional-boxes were not in the church itself but in an enclosed yard to the north of the church, to which the public was not admitted. The existence of the practice was, however, brought into the open by the most famous incident of Arthur Wagner's life, the trial of Constance Kent for the murder of her half-brother, Francis Savill Kent— one of the most famous murders of the nineteenth century in England.

Samuel Savill Kent, the father of both children, was a man of unattractive reputation. He had started life in his father's carpet factory and had then been a partner in a firm of dry-salters in London Wall. But about 1832 he had given up business and had become a Sub-Inspector of Factories in the west of England. Here he occupied a series of quite elaborate manor houses which were probably well beyond his means. His salary was £800 a year. Consequently he had the reputation of being always pressed for money. He was twice married. By his first wife, Mary Ann Windus, he had ten children, of whom five died in infancy. One son was aged 23. About 1840 he engaged a governess for his two elder daughters. This lady, Mary Drewe Pratt, very soon acquired a dominant position in the household. She first became Samuel Kent's mistress and then established herself as the mistress of the house. Samuel Kent lived with her openly in one part of the house, and his wife was relegated to another part. The wife was in fact so totally disparaged by the governess that, after Mary Ann Kent's death, it was even suggested that she was insane, which was not the case. The situation in the household soon came to be known locally, with the result that the Kents were constantly obliged to move and always chose rather remote houses, where they had little relations with their neighbours. In 1852 Mary Ann Kent died, aged 44. A year later Samuel Kent married Mary Drewe Pratt and proceeded to have five children by her.

In 1860 they were living at a handsome house of three storeys and 20 rooms which had been built in 1790. It was then called Road Hill House, Wiltshire, and lay between Trowbridge and Frome. The village is now known as Rode and is in Somerset. There the family continued to lead an isolated life. Samuel Kent was not on good terms with the adjoining villagers and had the reputation of being a martinet in his household. A constant succession of domestic servants came and went in the house, and it was rumoured that many of them received unwelcome attentions from Samuel Kent.

In 1860 the household consisted of Mr. and Mrs. Kent, his two elder daughters, Mary Ann Alice and Elizabeth, aged 28 and 27 respectively, his third daughter, Constance Emily, aged 16; his son, William Savill, aged 15, who were all his first family; and three children of his second wife: Mary Amelia Savill, aged 5; Francis Savill, aged three years and 10 months; and the baby, Eveline Savill, aged 20 months. Mrs. Kent's last two children had not then been born. The resident staff were Elizabeth Gough, the nursery-governess, aged 28; Sarah Kerslake, the cook; and Sarah Cox, the housemaid. In addition an assistant nursemaid, a charwoman, a groom-gardener, an odd-jobs boy and a casual labourer came to work daily at the house. The four children of the first marriage slept on the second floor. Of the second family, the elder daughter slept with her parents on the first floor and the two others shared the adjoining room with the nursery-governess.

At 5 a.m. on the morning of Saturday the 30th June 1860 the boy, Francis Savill Kent, aged nearly four, was found missing from his cot in the nursery-governess's room. When the grounds of the house were searched his body was found in a large privy near the back door. He had been stabbed in the chest, and his throat cut from ear to ear. But the medical evidence was later to suggest that the cause of death was suffocation and that these wounds had been inflicted after death had occurred.

The inquest, the police investigations and the proceedings before the magistrates were all conducted with the maximum inefficiency and irregularity. They give an appalling idea of the investigation of crime and the administration of justice in a rural area in mid-Victorian England. The police were much hampered by the absence of any adequate motive for anyone in the household to have committed such a murder. The most that they could discover was a general idea that there was some ill-feeling or jealousy between the offspring of the two marriages.

As no progress was made locally the magistrates asked the Home Office to send down a detective officer. Inspector Jonathan Whicher of Scotland Yard was despatched. From the first his suspicions fell on Constance as the only member of the family who could have had any motive for killing the child and the only one against whom there was any evidence at all. So on the 19th July he procured a warrant for her arrest. But when she appeared before the Trowbridge magistrates no evidence could be produced against her other than that one of her three nightdresses was missing and that one of her school-mates testified to the fact that she had no love for her step-mother. This was insufficient to secure a committal. But the magistrates acted with characteristic hesitancy in that they did not discharge her but only released her on her father's recognisance for £200. So she was left with the charge hanging over her head.

The conditional discharge of Constance Kent was greeted with general approval. Samuel Kent was so unpopular locally that public opinion had decided that he was the murderer and that the various inadequacies of the investigation and legal procedures up to date were attempts to protect him from an accusation. This feeling totally disregarded the fact that there was no evidence against Samuel Kent, other than some rather suspicious movements on the morning when the murder was discovered, and that he had no motive for killing the child as he had been very fond of the boy. The inefficient Wiltshire police greeted the discomfiture of the Inspector from Scotland Yard with considerable satisfaction but, when left on their own again, had no alternative solution to offer. They therefore fell back on an investigator's last resort: propinquity. To the question: "Who had the greatest opportunity to kill Francis Savill Kent?" there could be only one answer: the nursery-governess, Elizabeth Gough, whose room the boy shared. So on the 28th September the police took our a warrant for her arrest.

At the second hearing before the Trowbridge magistrates the police made a better showing than they had done in the case of Constance Kent as they were represented by counsel on this occasion. But as there was even less evidence against Elizabeth Gough than there had been against Constance Kent the magistrates were unable to commit her. But again they acted with humbling hesitation. They merely released her on the recognisance of £100 paid by her uncle. So there were now two people with a suspicion of guilt hanging over their heads.

Public opinion was still very uneasy, and a view widely held was that, as the original inquest had been so inadequate, it should be re-opened. The Attorney General was therefore induced to present a motion to the Court of Queen's Bench calling on the Coroner, George Sylvester, to show why the original inquest should not be quashed. The case was heard on the 30th January 1861 before Lord Chief Justice Cockburn, Mr. Justice Compton, Mr. Justice Hills and Mr. Justice Wightman. The court held that there had been no judicial misconduct at the inquest but only an error judgment in not calling Samuel Kent as a witness and that this did not justify the court in re-opening the matter.

There for over four years the matter rested, with the problem unsolved. Elizabeth Gough at her own wish left the Kent household in order to avoid the unpleasant atmosphere with which they were surrounded. She returned to her own family in Isleworth but was not able to obtain another job. She maintained herself as a sempstress until she married in 1866. The Kents themselves left Road Hill House and moved, first to Weston-super-Mare and later to Llangollen in north Wales. Constance was sent to a finishing school at Dinan in Brittany kept by a Mademoiselle de la Tour. But she did not escape gossip there and at her own request was removed to the Couvent de la Sagesse in the same town. She remained there for nearly two years. During this time she acquired a liking for convent life and began to show an extreme tenderness for young children. However, it was not thought that she could stay there for ever. So a friend of hers — the name has not been recorded — wrote to Arthur Wagner and asked him whether

Constance could go to St. Mary's Home in Brighton. He agreed to take here there as a paying-guest, and she arrived in Queen's Square on the 10th August 1863.

She was known as Emilie Kent—the French version of her second name which she had used in France—and worked as a nurse, looking after the small children in the orphanage. She remained at St. Mary's Home for 21 months. Wagner afterwards described her conduct there as uniformly good and that she was always truthful and ready to do anything that he asked her to do. At first she had little religious feeling but soon found that everything at St. Mary's Home revolved around the service of Holy Communion, or the Holy Eucharist as they would have called it. From this she was excluded as she had never been confirmed. Arthur Wagner therefore prepared her for confirmation, probably in the spring of 1864. She also had many conversations with the Lady Superior, Catherine Ann Gream, on the subject of sin. As we have seen, auricular confession was at that time practised at St. Paul's church, to which St. Mary's Home was attached. So Constance formed the habit of making a confession to Arthur Wagner.

On the 6th February she came of age and inherited the sum of £1,000 from her mother. She drew £800 of this sum out of the bank and offered it to Wagner for use in the various charities in which he was involved. He refused to accept it. She then took batches of notes and stuffed them into collecting boxes at St. Paul's church. Wagner, suspecting whence the notes came, retrieved them and placed them for safe custody in the London and County Bank. They were eventually, by agreement with her, handed over to Constance's father to be used for the good of the family.

In Holy Week 1865 and probably soon after Wagner had refused to accept her £800 Constance made her specific confession to him that it was she who had murdered her half-brother. At the end of her mother's life she had come to realise and resent the acute suffering that the mother was experiencing at the hands of her supplanter, Mary Drewe Pratt. After the mother's death the interloper, now the second Mrs. Kent, had continued to disparage and belittle her predecessor on every occasion. Constance had treasured all this in her heart with increasing resentment. She came to hate her step-mother and to wish to be revenged on her. She first thought of poisoning her but then decided that a more appropriate punishment would be to make her suffer as her own mother had suffered. So she resolved to kill Mary Drewe Kent's favourite child. Having confessed this story of revenge to Arthur Wagner Constance went on to say that she had determined to give herself up to the authorities.

When this confession was later made public both Wagner and the Lady Superior of St. Mary's Home, Catherine Ann Gream, were reviled for having, it was said, pressurised Constance into surrendering to the law. As far as Miss Gream was concerned Wagner, in a letter to *The Times* after Constance's trial, certified that Miss Gream had never at any time had the slightest suspicion of Constance's guilt or had ever had any conversation with her on the subject of the murder until after Wagner had specially informed Miss Gream of Constance's guilt at the latter's request. In his own case Wagner repeatedly denied that he had used any influence upon Constance either to confess to him in the first place or to surrender to justice. This latter was her own fixed intention from the moment of her confession. He did, however, add that he had concurred in the proposal to surrender herself and had not opposed this. Therefore he had incurred some responsibility in the matter. Here the stern Victorian idea of justice casts a tall shadow. But the motivation came solely from Constance's own feelings, and these stemmed from the religious atmosphere which she had absorbed in St. Mary's Home for the past 21 months and possibly in the French convent during the two years preceding this.

Wagner had a slight personal acquaintance with Gladstone, who always worshipped at St. Paul's church when he stayed in Brighton. Gladstone was then Chancellor of the Exchequer. So at Constance's insistence Wagner communicated with the Home Secretary, Sir George Grey, through Gladstone. He travelled to London to put the case before the Home Secretary personally. Sir George was most reluctant to take any action and in fact refused to make the first move. Constance, however, persisted in her intention. So on Tuesday the 25th April 1865 she and Miss Gream travelled to London in one railway carriage and Arthur Wagner in another for Constance to give herself up. Wagner went first to the Home Office and then accompanied the others to the Bow Street Police Station. There they saw the Chief Magistrate, Sir Thomas Henry, who had had no previous knowledge of the matter. Constance handed him a written statement, drawn up and signed by herself in which she stated that alone and unaided she had committed the murder. No-one knew of her intention beforehand or of her guilt afterwards, and no-one had assisted her in committing the crime or in evading discovery afterwards.

In the later detailed confession that she was to make after her conviction Constance stated that she had taken the child, still sleeping, from his cot, had carried him downstairs to the privy, had there cut his throat and then stabbed him in the chest. But despite these details, it is almost certain that the child was suffocated by a blanket before any wound was inflicted on him. The details in any case were not included in the confession handed by Constance to Sir Thomas Henry on the 25th April. He also took a deposition from Wagner concerning Constance's confession which, Wagner said, had been entirely her own act. She was cautioned by Sir Thomas that she need not sign her statement if she did not wish to do so, but she nevertheless signed it. A warrant was then issued for her arrest. As the crime had been committed in Wiltshire Constance had to be sent back to that county. Wagner accompanied her to Paddington station and Miss Gream as far as Trowbridge Police Station. She appeared before the Trowbridge magistrates—for the second time—on the following morning.

Immediately the circumstances of Constance's arrest became public a Protestant furore arose on the subject of confession and all that this led to. Wagner and Miss Gream were as much blamed for their part in circumstances as suspicious as confession as if they had actually committed the murder themselves. Gladstone was one of the few people to retain a sense of proportion. Writing to Wagner two months later (the 25th July 1865) he said: "I must take this opportunity of recording my sense of the extraordinary injustice with which you have recently been treated in regard to the case. Having conferred a real service on society, you have been dealt with by a large portion of the Press as if you were yourself a criminal. You have borne and will bear this with a strength proceeding from within and from above. But society is not intentionally unjust, and commonly comes round after a while in such cases. After a while it must come to be recognised that in the faithful discharge of your pastoral office you have conferred a service on your country."[2]

Constance Kent's preliminary examination before the Trowbridge magistrates took place on the 5th May. All the old evidence of the previous examinations was repeated. The new witnesses were Miss Gream and Arthur Wagner. Miss Gream proved a hopeless witness. She began by trying to establish a position of privilege on the grounds that during the last 21 months she had acted as the prisoner's mother and so could not be expected to reveal what passed in confidential conversations between them. But she was too inexperienced under cross-examination to be able to maintain this standpoint. She went on to reveal many things that Constance had told her about the murder after the witness had been informed of Constance's guilt by Wagner. But she rambled on to such an extent and contradicted herself so much that eventually the court was entirely confused.

Wagner was made of much sterner stuff. He began by trying to read a prepared statement to the effect that, as he had acted as Constance's confessor for the past 17 or 18 months, he would decline to reveal any information about what passed between them during her confessions. The Magistrates refused to allow him to make this statement before he gave his evidence, but he skilfully managed to interweave it into his answers. During his evidence he did refuse to reply to two not very material questions put to him by the Chairman of the Magistrates, and the Chairman, being a layman and an amateur, did not persist. These refusals were greeted by an outbreak of hissing in court, which was sternly repressed by the police.

It was until recently very difficult to know why, other than for the principle of the matter, Wagner was so determined not to reveal any of the subject matter of his conversations with Constance Kent about the murder when her general guilt had been publicly acknowledged and he could therefore not say anything to her hurt. But her latest biographer (Bernard Taylor in his book "Cruelly Murdered") thinks that Constance's admission of guilt was most carefully worded by her in order to conceal suspicious circumstances relating to her father. These did not involve him in any criminality as to the murder. Indeed he was extremely fond of his son. But Mr. Taylor thinks that at the time of the murder Samuel Kent was carrying on an affair with the nursery-governess, Elizabeth Gough, and that at the actual time of the murder on the night of the 29th–30th June 1860 she and Samuel Kent were closeted together in the adjoining spare-room and that when Constance removed the child from his cot Elizabeth Gough was missing from the room. When the latter returned to it she would have noticed that the child was absent and have informed Mr. Kent. He was not able to give the alarm as this would have revealed his own amatory intrigue. So he immediately searched the grounds of the house with a dark lantern, found the dead body of his son in the privy with a stab wound in the chest and himself added the throat wound so that the murder might have the appearance of having been committed by someone outside the household, which indeed he consistently maintained to have been the case throughout all the investigations. It was therefore to shield Samuel Kent from a revelation of these circumstances that it was essential for the sanctity of the confessional to be upheld.

Immediately the evidence before the magistrates was reported in the press and particularly the fact that Wagner had refused to answer two questions put to him by the Magistrates a fresh outburst of ultra-Protestant fury arose. A police guard had to be placed on the Brighton Vicarage, where Arthur Wagner lived, and and St. Mary's Home in Queen's Square.

Questions on the subject were asked in both the Houses of Lords and Commons. In the Lords the Earl of Westmeath asked whether Wagner should have been allowed to decline to answer questions put to him by the Magistrates and whether the Government would introduce a bill to prevent such persons as Wagner from officiating as clergymen of the Church of England. The Lord Chancellor, Lord Westbury, replied that the law was quite clear on the first point. It did not permit any clergyman, even a priest of the Roman Catholic Church, to refuse to answer a question which was put to him on oath in court on the grounds that, to do so, would be a breach of a confidence made to him in confession. There was therefore no doubt that Wagner had been under an obligation to answer the questions put to him by the Magistrates if these had been insisted on. In reply to the second question Lord Granville, Lord President of the Council, said that no measure on the subject was under the consideration of Her Majesty's ministers.

In the House of Commons the attack was made by the Member of Parliament for Peterborough named George Hammond Whalley, who was well-known for the violence of his anti-Catholic views. He also probably had some connection with Brighton, as he was married there. He first asked the Home Secretary, Sir George Grey, the same questions as Lord Westmeath had done in the House of Lords and received roughly the same answers. But a fortnight later he returned to the charge and moved for a select committee to enquire into the mode in which services were conducted at St. Paul's church, Brighton, and especially that part of the service which was called sacramental confession. Sir George Grey replied that it would be most inexpedient to appoint such a commission. He went on to reiterate that "the law of the country does not recognise any privilege by which a clergyman is entitled to withhold any evidence in courts of law which may be material to the interests of justice".[3] In the Trowbridge case the Magistrates did not allow Wagner to withhold any evidence that they thought essential, and if the same witness should refuse to answer any such question when he came to give evidence at the Assizes no doubt the trial judge would know what action to take.

By this reply Wagner was clearly warned that, if at the later High Court trial he was to refuse to answer any question put to him, he could risk being imprisoned for contempt of court. This would not have deterred him in the least. He would cheerfully have gone to prison for the sake of such a principle. As it happened the issue never arose. Probably at this time he preached a sermon at St. Paul's on the text: "Whoever hateth his brother is a murderer, and you know that no murderer hath eternal life abiding in him."

The extreme prejudice of the ultra-Protestant party was well demonstrated by G. H. Whalley's speech in the House of Commons at this time. He mentioned on the strength of rumour in Brighton another girl named Scovell, the daughter of a Church of England clergyman, who, he alleged, had come under Wagner's influence and had been an inmate of St. Mary's Home at Brighton. While there, she had made a will, bequeathing £8,000 to the Home. She had then been sent by the authorities of the Home to attend fever cases elsewhere and, as a result, had herself caught the fever and had died. "It had been essential for the purposes of Mr. Wagner and his coadjutors to get rid of her".[4] This accusation, if it had not been made in the privileged context of the House of Commons, was undoubtedly libellous as it attributed to Wagner a clear intention to murder this girl. Wagner therefore wrote to *The Times* the next day to contradict the whole assertion. No-one named Scovell had ever been an inmate of St. Mary's Home and no-one of any kind had ever left the Home any money. He had a distant acquaintance with the girl in question, but the Lady Superior of the Home, Catherine Ann Gream, had never set eyes on her.

It subsequently transpired that the Home in question was St. Margaret's Home at East Grinstead, of which the permanent building, designed by G. E. Street, was begun that same year (1865) and the clergyman under whose influence Miss Scovell was alleged to have come was Dr. J. M. Neale, the Warden of the Sackville College at East Grinstead, who was responsible for the establishment of St. Margaret's Home. These facts would probably have induced a normal person to put forward an apology for a wholly slanderous accusation, as indeed the *Morning Post* pointed out, but not G. H. Whalley. He merely wrote another letter to *The Times*, trying to make out that the nature of the circumstances was still the same, though he made no apology for having given the wrong names. At the public meeting in Brighton which he attended on the 26th May he even asserted in his speech that "every man who preached at St. Paul's church practised the very incarnation of lying".[5] He also induced the same meeting to pass a resolution which stated (inter alia) that Arthur Wagner's letter to *The Times* was "another instance of the unscrupulous mendacity with which they (Puseyite Fraternities and Sisterhoods) systematically prosecute their objects".[6] Of his own mendacity there was no admission at all.

This meeting was the second prong of the attack against St. Paul's and everything connected with it. Paul Foskett, Chairman of the Central Protestant Association, called on the Mayor of Brighton, Councillor J. L. Brigden, and deposited with him a requisition signed by 159 people urging the Mayor to summon a meeting to petition Parliament against the "base and degrading confessional practices carried on contrary to the spirit and character of the Protestant Reformed Church by the traitors nominally within her pale".[7] The Mayor, who was a parishioner of St. Nicholas's church, after consultation with the Town Clerk, very wisely declined to call such a meeting—to the great indignation of Paul Foskett.

The latter therefore proceeded to arrange a public meeting himself. This was held in the Town Hall on the 26th May. Foskett himself took the chair and the principal speaker was George Hammond Whalley, M.P. No-one of any special prominence in public life in Brighton attended. But one brave dissident tried to make his voice heard. This was the Rev. Thomas Walter Perry, Curate at St. Michael and All Angels, Brighton, which was a church founded on the principles of St. Paul's but which had taken ritualist ceremonies much farther. Two years later Perry was to be a member of the Royal Commission which enquired into the question of rubrics, orders and directions for regulating public working in the Church of England. At Foskett's meeting he was not able to make much headway because the Chairman very soon tried to stop him speaking. When Perry persisted Foskett asked the meeting to signify whether they wished to continue hearing him or not, whereupon the meeting overwhelmingly voted against hearing him further.

A very long resolution was then passed to be submitted to Parliament, which declared that priestly confession and absolution were (inter alia) "contrary to the spirit of the Church of England, a violation of privacy and the sanctity of domestic life, an infringement of personal liberty, a fruitful source of immorality, pernicious to priest and people, utterly useless for good, grossly corrupting those who make it and extremely pernicious to those who receive it".[8] A second resolution took the form of a vote of thanks to G. H. Whalley for "bringing to light the practice of Puseyite Fraternities and Sisterhoods in this town".[9] After the resolution had been passed T. W. Perry tried to speak again. On being denied a hearing he sprang on the table in order to try and make himself heard. The table was then tipped up and he was set upon, his clothes torn and his hat destroyed. He managed to make his escape through an anteroom and the magistrates' entrance to the Town Hall, where the police secured a cab to take him home.

The violence of the ultra-Protestant party did not, however, stop there. Two days later (Sunday the 28th May) at 5 p.m. Arthur Wagner was walking up the south side of North Street, when he was set upon by two drunken ruffians. His attention was first called to them by hooting on the other side of the road. William Brazier, a sweep aged 32, then crossed the road, seized Wagner by the arms and swore at him. Wagner was carrying a walking-stick. So he struck Brazier across the legs with this, whereupon Brazier knocked him down. Another sweep aged 19 named James Hersey then also came across the road and adopted a fighting attitude. At this point Sir Thomas Barrett Lennard of No. 7 Lewes Crescent, Brighton, who had been walking a few paces in front of Wagner but was not known to him, turned back and intervened: he struck Hersey in the face, while Wagner was able to pick himself up. Wagner and Sir Thomas then endeavoured to make their escape up North Street. But the two assailants followed them uttering taunts, hit Sir Thomas in the face and knocked him down. At this point a police constable named Field intervened and called on a passer-by named George Harmer, who, as it happened, had formerly been a member of the police, to assist him. They managed to arrest Brazier and Hersey, though not before Hersey had again kicked Sir Thomas in the face. A third sweep named Henry Chatfield, aged 21, subsequently tried to secure the release of Brazier and Hersey but only succeeded in getting himself arrested with them.

The three assailants were brought before the magistrates the next day and were charged with drunkenness and assault. Sir Thomas Barrett Lennard appeared in court with a black eye and his face damaged. Arthur Wagner's solicitor, Somers Clarke, said that his client had no wish for the men to be sent to prison but only brought the action to prevent further breaches of the peace. However, the Magistrates took a serious view of the case and gave Brazier and Hersey the maximum sentence available to them, namely one month's hard labour. Chatfield, who had only been involved in the end of the fray, was fined £1 with costs.

Whether this assault was a spontaneous outburst of two drunken men at the sight of a well-known citizen whom they knew to be unpopular at the moment or whether they were a hired gang it is now impossible to say, but such a rascally crew as the Central Protestant Association were certainly capable of hiring ruffians to beat up a high church clergyman of whom they disapproved.

This was not the only time that Arthur Wagner was the subject of public violence. All his obituaries record that he was also once shot at in the streets, but they do not give the year when this occurred. The assailant was, however, apprehended and sentenced to imprisonment for one year. Wagner sought out his wife and made her an allowance while her husband was in prison. It is not recorded whether he made any similar gesture in the case of the sweeps, such as paying Henry Chatfield's fine so that he did not have to go to prison. But it would have been quite characteristic of Wagner to have done so.

At about the same time as this assault by the sweeps St. Mary's Home was also in trouble. The Sisters were frequently insulted in the street on account of their dress. But in this instance two girls named Emma Jane Broadbridge and Harriet Delves, who were laundresses, caused a disturbance outside the Home. Both had been inmates in the penitentiary at one time. They were not prostitutes but had been sent there by their parents because the parents had not been able to control them at home. While there they had behaved badly, had been disciplined and as a result took themselves off. They started to hang around the houses in Queen's Square, shouting insults at the inmates and throwing oranges and apples through the open windows. The Lady Superior, Catherine Ann Gream, brought an action for breach of the peace against them. She and one of the Sisters named Louisa Kirby gave evidence before the magistrates. Both girls were bound over to keep the peace for 6 months. Characteristically Paul Foskett acted as security for Emma Jane Broadbridge, who was under age. This fact does much to substantiate the view that these disturbances from which Arthur Wagner and his associates suffered were not unplanned.

Whether or not this was so, the violence of the ultra-Protestant party over-reached itself on these occasions and disgusted all but the most bigoted section of the community. *The Times*, *The Morning Post*, "The Brighton Herald" and "The Brighton Gazette" all had leading articles, pointing out that G. H. Whalley and Paul Foskett were doing the Protestant cause no good. *The Times* in fact on the 26th May quoted Whalley himself as having said that he had unearthed cases in which Protestants had been locked up in religious institutions as the result of which they had lost their intellect. The paper went on to say: "One is almost inclined to surmise that Mr. Whalley had at some time in his life been locked up in a religious institution." Confession may have been unacceptable, but assaulting a respected citizen was much more so. So the local outcry faded away.

We must now return to Constance Kent. On the 21st July 1865 she came up for trial at the Salisbury Assizes before Mr. Justice Willes. He was later described by Lord Chief Justice Coleridge as "the greatest and *largest* lawyer I ever knew . . . and so really considerable a man".[10] Coleridge had good cause to know for in 1865 he was only John Duke Coleridge Q.C. and was briefed as Constance Kent's counsel at this trial. John Karslake Q.C. acted for the Crown.

A reply to a question in Parliament given by a Lord Chancellor or a Minister is only a ministerial statement made in good faith of what the minister concerned considers the law to be at that time. It is not the same thing as a judicial ruling given in court. The Lord Chancellor's and the Home Secretary's statements were therefore not binding on Mr. Justice Willes. It so happens that we have a fascinating insight into the minds of the three principal lawyers concerned in this trial

114

as to what their intentions were before the trial opened. This is contained in a letter written on the 6th April 1890 by Lord Chief Justice Coleridge, as he then was, to William Gladstone. This was printed in Yseult Bridges' book "Saint with Red Hands?" This tells us that Sir James Willes had made up his mind that he would have to hold one way or the other as to the sanctity of confession. "He took infinite pains to be right and he was interested because the point since the Reformation had never been decided. There were strong dicta of strong Judges— Lord Ellenborough, Lord Wynford and Alderton—that they would never allow Counsel to ask a clergyman the question. On the other hand Hill, a good lawyer and a good man *but* a strong Ulster Protestant had said that "there was no *legal* privilege in a clergyman".[11]

Willes, however, had satisfied himself that "there was a legal privilege in a priest to withhold what passed in confession. Confession, he said, is made for the purpose of absolution. Absolution is a judicial act, the priest in absolving acts is a Judge and no Judge is ever obliged to state his reasons for his judicial determination".[12] Willes had therefore decided that, if Karslake (the prosecuting counsel) asked Wagner questions about matters that were the subject of Constance's confession to Wagner and Coleridge objected to such questions being put to the witness, the Judge would uphold Coleridge's objection. However, Karslake also had been turning the matter over in his mind before the trial and had resolved not to put such questions to Wagner. He even told his opponent, Coleridge, that he did not propose to press the witness on this point. Coleridge knew that he could rely on Karslake's assurance but had resolved that, if he did not keep it, he (Coleridge) would not object to the question being put but would comment on it in his closing speech to the jury.

In relating in 1890 these past feelings Lord Chief Justice Coleridge added that he doubted whether the English Judges would have upheld Mr. Justice Willes's ruling, had he made one, on the privilege of confession. One can only echo the doubt, both for 1865 and today. Since then the law has not been altered or made clearer. In the abstract it remains the law that no right of privilege exists for the subject of a religious confession. But judges have been consistently reluctant to force a clergyman to answer such a question against his will. If this was so in 1865 when Roman Catholicism was still considered discreditable and Anglo-Catholicism had hardly emerged into recognised existence, it must be much more the case now when both these branches of the Christian faith are completely acceptable. It is therefore most unlikely that a judge would today compel a clergyman of any faith to answer such a question against his will or commit him to prison for contempt of court if he declined to do so, unless the point was absolutely vital as to the guilt or innocence of the accused. So Arthur Wagner can be held to have struck a blow for this idea of privilege which was not without its effect on the spirit in which the law is administered.

In Constance Kent's case the issue in the end never came to the point as she pleaded guilty, and so no witnesses were called. Her legal advisers tried hard to induce her to enter a plea of not guilty. They told her that, if she did so, she would almost certainly be acquitted, despite her own confession. But having formed the view that the only way for her was through the path of suffering and atonement, she was adamant in pleading guilty. At the present time a plea of guilty is not accepted in murder trials and, if an accused purports to enter one, this is automatically converted into a plea of not guilty. But that was not the case in 1865.

At the trial therefore no evidence was given. Her own counsel could only make a short statement to the effect that she had not been driven to her action by unkind treatment at home and that she only was responsible for her act. Any suspicions that had fallen on her father and others were unfounded. The Judge had no option but to pass sentence of death. In doing so he hinted as far as he was permitted to do in the circumstances at the Crown's prerogative of mercy being exercised. In his short speech he was so overcome by emotion that he was twice forced to pause in order to choke back a sob.

Wagner at once wrote to Gladstone to plead for mercy to be shown. In reply Gladstone claimed unfamiliarity with the rules guiding the executive in juris- prudence. He said he could do no more than pass Wagner's letter on to Sir George Grey, the Home Secretary, and state to him "anything that may occur to me as likely to support it".[13] Wagner then applied to Sir George Grey for an interview which was refused. He therefore wrote to Sir George to say that he was satisfied of Constance's real repentance—a religious argument that is not likely to have made much appeal to a politician. "She felt it a duty she owed God, to make at the cost of her life, what reparation she could to her father and others, for the unjust suspicions under which they had so long laboured."[14] Fortunately for Constance she had a more powerful advocate in Mr. Justice Willes, who at once recommended the Home Secretary to commute the death sentence on account of Constance's age at the time of the murder (sixteen) and the fact that she had been detected and convicted solely through her own confession. Her family and others also signed a petition to the Queen. As the result Sir George Grey con- sulted the cabinet, where no doubt Gladstone was able to speak in favour of mercy, and on the 25th July it was announced that the sentence had been commuted to penal servitude for life. Had Constance been convicted in 1860 at the time of the crime, she could not have been sentenced to death.

Wagner did not rest content with the commutation of the sentence. On the 16th August he wrote again to Gladstone to ask whether Gladstone thought anything could be done to get the sentence modified. Rather characteristically he wrote that he cared comparatively little for "the temporal part of her punish- ment, believing that it will do her no harm, nay, that patiently borne, it will deepen the grace of repentance in her heart".[15] But spiritually imprisonment would be almost worse than death because it would cut her "from some of the means of Grace to which she had been accustomed and from the use of many spiritual books which may be of great benefit to her soul, exposed as she is likely to be as life advances and with such sad antecedents, to great internal temptations".[16] He therefore suggested that, after a temporary imprisonment, she might be sent "with a ticket of leave or in any other way"[17] to be in his care at St. Mary's Home in Brighton, where she would be almost as shut out of the world as in a prison but accessible to the religious privileges to which she was accustomed, i.e. confession and Holy Communion. That such a plea could be made at all was only due to Wagner's unworldly nature. Naturally it was not entertained and produced only a formal reply from the Under Secretary at the Home Office, Horatio Waddington, which was forwarded by Gladstone.

Throughout Constance's imprisonment Wagner kept in touch with her. He visited her several times as did Catherine Gream until her death in 1873. She was at first confined at Millbank prison, later at Parkhurst in the Isle of Wight, then at Woking and finally at Fulham. She worked at first in the laundry and then in the infirmary. But while in Parkhurst she created a series of mosaic pavements which could be removed and re-erected in sections. These can still be seen today in the private chapel of the Bishop of Chichester's Palace at Chichester, in the parish church at East Grinstead, in St. Peter's church, Portland, and in St. Paul's cathedral. But perhaps the saddest part of her prison term was that, owing to the nature of her crime, she was never accepted by her fellow prisoners, despite the fact that most of them were a somewhat degraded band of people. She eventually became the servant of the Matron at Fulham.

The first attempt to secure Constance's release was made by her brother, William Savill Kent, in 1872. He forwarded the petition to the Home Office through the then Attorney General, who was none other than Constance's own Counsel, by then Sir John Coleridge. Another attempt was made in 1875 by Bishop Webb, then Bishop of Bloemfontein, who—possibly prompted by Arthur Wagner—was anxious to take her out to South Africa as a laundry matron of a religious establishment. But the Home Secretary, Sir Richard Cross, thought this too soon for her release. Up till 1864 the average time served in prison by a prisoner sentenced for life was 15 years. A further remission of three years could be earned by good conduct. With a casualness that amounted to cruelty Constance was informed when she first came into prison that she might look forward to such treatment. But actually in 1864 the period had been lengthened to 20 years, though some exceptions were still made. When she applied for release herself, she came up against this ruling. The 12 years elapsed in 1877. So she made her first petition for release, without success. The same thing happened in 1878.

In 1880, when the fifteen years were up, Wagner appealed to Gladstone—by that time Prime Minister. In forwarding Wagner's letter to the Home Secretary, Sir William Harcourt, Gladstone made a greater recommendation of Wagner than he did of Constance's case. He spoke of his merits as a well-known high churchman in Brighton, who had conferred a benefit on society when the police had laboured unsuccessfully to detect the perpetrator of a crime. His testimonial, however, actually wronged Wagner as well as he said that Wagner had "induced her to make the confession to the ministers of public justice",[18] which was not the case. Harcourt, however, was implacable. He again refused in 1881, 1882 and 1883. In all these cases he simply wrote on the file "Nil", as if determined to give himself the least trouble that the English language could afford. Constance had to wait for the elapse of the full period of 20 years before she could secure her release. In 1883 Bishop Webb, by then, Bishop of Grahamstown, tried again. But his party had to sail without Constance. She made another attempt in 1884, but it was not until the following year that her seventh and last petition was successful. On the 18th July 1885 she was finally released. Wagner went to Fulham prison in a cab to fetch her and took her by train to his country house, St. Mary's at Buxted, where she could be looked after by the Sisters of St. Mary's Home, Brighton, in their country retreat known as St. Margaret's Cottage, Buxted.

When Constance Kent left prison in 1885 she was 41 years old. Amazingly enough she was to live for nearly another 60 years. Her step-mother had died in

1866, her father in 1872. The member of her family with whom she had always been closest was her full brother, William Savill Kent. He had emigrated to Australia and had changed his name to Kent-Savill. He returned to England in 1886, possibly for the special purpose of collecting Constance. At any rate when he returned there she travelled with him. In Australia she adopted the name of Ruth Emilie Kaye. An appeal for nursing help during a typhoid epidemic at Melbourne decided her to take up nursing as a profession. She qualified at the age of 48 in 1892. In due course she became a matron and in 1910 acquired her own nursing-home at Maitland in New South Wales. She did not retire from this until she was eighty eight. She celebrated her hundredth birthday at Maitland on the 6th February 1944 and died two months later.

In the course that she had chosen for herself from 1865 onwards, through 20 years of prison suffering and 42 years of nursing service there is no doubt that she had achieved a full atonement and peace of mind. To use an old-fashioned phrase, she had saved her soul. There is equally little doubt that she had been set on this course by Arthur Wagner and without his help in the first place would never have achieved this release of spirit.

The story of Constance Kent and everything to which this led has taken us a long way away from the narrative of the churches in Brighton which were built by Arthur Wagner. We must now return to this.

As we have seen, St. Paul's, West Street, was in effect Arthur Wagner's first and parent church, though its original construction was due to his father. It had several offspring which were entirely Arthur's work. The first of these was St. Mary and St. Mary Magdalene's, Bread Street. This was built in a poor quarter of the original town. It was opened in 1862. It was a small and very simple Gothic building designed by G. F. Bodley, whose father had been a Brighton doctor. Almost its only feature was the timbered roof with tie-beams and arched braces. The windows had no tracery. The church cost only £2,500, which was wholly borne by Arthur Wagner. It was never consecrated and was administered from St. Paul's by curates. It gradually lost its parishioners as the area around it became more and more commercial and was finally demolished about 1950.

Wagner's next venture was in another poor district north west of Queen's Park. One of his hidden charities was to advance small sums of money to modest builders to erect houses for poor people. For the most part these were builders in such a small way that they could not enter into financial commitments and needed to be paid every week. Some of the recipients may not even have been builders at all but may have been the prospective tenants themselves who were thus subsidised to build their own homes. The sums involved were occasionally as little as £7 and on one occasion as much as £150. But normally they were between £20 and £40 a week in each instance. Two little receipt books of these weekly transactions have survived. We do not know exactly what transpired when the houses were complete. Presumably the occupants remained Wagner's tenants and paid him a small weekly rent. Some of the streets in which these operations were undertaken were Islingword Road, Islingword Place, Park Road, and Whichelo Place.

It was to serve the houses in this district that Wagner built the church of the Annunciation of Our Lady, Washington Street. This was opened at the festival of the Annunciation on the 15th August 1864. Like St. Mary and St. Mary

Magdalene's it was served by curates from St. Paul's until it was given its own parish in 1881. It was not consecrated until 1884. The original church was a very simple building faced with flints but with only one elevation exposed. It was not the work of a London architect but was designed by a local surveyor named William Dancy who lived in Montpelier Street. Originally almost the only feature of the building was the west window, which is liturgically the east window as the church is orientated the wrong way round. This is a triple lancet without tracery showing the Annunciation. It was inserted in 1865 in memory of Elizabeth Austin Attree, the wife of Thomas Attree, whose house, the Attree Villa in Queen's Park, was very close to the church. The central light was designed by Dante Gabriel Rossetti and the flanking lights by Edward Burne-Jones. The window was made in William Morris's factory.

The church of the Annunciation prospered, and in 1881 its enlargement was proposed. Wagner was prepared to demolish it and start again with a more ambitious church. But the clergy and congregation of the Annunciation were attached to their little building. So instead aisles were added, and the original portion refurbished. The work was entrusted to another Brighton architect, Edmund Scott, who is renowned for his much more famous Brighton church, St. Bartholomew's. This had already been built for Arthur Wagner in the preceding decade. In his new work at the Annunciation Scott followed rather closely the model of Bodley's St. Mary and St. Mary Magdalene's, Bread Street, but he is said to have been also influenced by St. Mary's Hospital at Chichester. The chief feature of both the main building and the aisles is a timbered roof with heavy square columns and tie-beams with arched braces. The south (liturgical north) chapel was built in memory of John Keble and Edward Pusey. The reconstruction probably cost about £5,000.

Further work was undertaken in 1892, when Scott's partner, F. T. Cawthorn, added the tower at the south east corner and the memorial room or vestry at the north east corner. At the same time the east (liturgical west) window was inserted. This had started life as the east window of St. Nicholas's church, which had been put into that church by R. C. Carpenter during his restoration of 1853. It was removed from there when the roof was heightened by Somers Clarke in the same year, 1892. The Vicarage adjoining the church of the Annunciation on the north was added 6 years later.

Arthur Wagner's father, the Vicar of Brighton, died on the 7th October 1870. He had therefore to make way for the new Vicar, the Rev. John Hannah, at the Vicarage. So he moved to the next house, Belvedere, which had been built about 30 years before by his aunt, Mary Ann Wagner, and left to him in her will in 1868. There he lived for the remaining 32 years of his life. Two unmarried cousins came to keep house for him. These were the daughters of his father's sister, Anna Maria Wagner, who had married the Rev. Thomas Coombe. The elder cousin, Elizabeth Chassereau Coombe, died on the 26th November 1891 and is buried in the Lewes Road cemetery at Brighton. The younger cousin, Fanny Coombe, outlived Arthur by 23 years. His life at Belvedere was simple if not ascetic. Friday was a fast day—though this forbearance did not prevent Arthur becoming very stout at the end of his life. His only luxuries were books and manuscripts, some of which he occasionally gave as presents to visiting clergymen. At his death his library comprised 12,000 volumes. The sale took three days. The catalogue described the library as comprising: "Manuscripts, choice early printed books, 1480–1589, fine editions of ecclesiastical histories, writings of the early fathers of the church, histories of church acts and councils, first editions of old and modern theological works, early sermons by Pusey, Newman, Manning, etc., a large collection of tracts and pamphlets, fine illustrated topographical works, a set of beautiful lithographs of pictures in the Munich gallery, various specimens of choice binding, and numerous standard works of history, biography, travel and general subjects." It is a pity that there is no record of the prices that these books fetched.

On the 2nd March 1871 the Judicial Committee of the Privy Council gave judgment in the case of Hibbert versus Purchas relating to St. James's chapel, Brighton. The court was composed of the Lord Chancellor, Lord Hatherley; Lord Chelmsford; Archbishop Thomson of York; and Bishop Jackson of London. All but two of the charges were given against Purchas. The court held that there was no evidence that he had ever consecrated water or that he had ever worn a biretta, though he had held one in his hand. But the use of Eucharistic vestments, incense, wafer-bread, a ceremonially mixed chalice, altar lights and the eastward position at Holy Communion were all declared to be illegal. Purchas was inhibited from using them, was suspended from officiating for one year and condemned to pay the costs of the action amounting to £2,096 14s. 10d.

Arthur Wagner had expressed no opinion about the Purchas affair as long as his father was alive. But when the judgment of the Privy Council was given he was unable to keep silence any longer. He wrote a letter to *The Times* in 1872 which was quoted in Sawyer's "The Churches of Brighton". He said that members of the Church of England were bound to submit to the judgment of the Church when this was expressed through its own free synods. But it was quite another matter in the case of what he called an "irresponsible" secular court of justice. He could not admit that such a body had the right to determine for all time the doctrines and worship of the Church. If its clergy were "too apathetic or too cowardly to stand up in defence of the truth of God and their own spiritual liberties then the Church Association—a vocal evangelical body—would have done much to prove that the Church of England is a mere creedless Act of Parliament church steeped in the most loathsome Erastianism".

Purchas himself received the verdict of the Privy Council with complete equanimity. He not only continued to conduct services with exactly the same ritual as before but told his congregation that no secular court had any power to suspend him from office. Moreover, if he was arrested, he had arranged with another clergyman to take his place and to continue officiating at St. James's. He also refrained from paying the costs given against him. When the court tried to distrain against his goods in order to obtain payment it was found that he had made over everything which he possessed to his wife. The congregation of St. James's at this stage appealed to the new Bishop of Chichester, Dr. Richard Durnford, to protect Purchas from persecution. The Bishop replied on the 1st April 1872 that he had no power to shelter Purchas from the sentence of the court. "It is a subject of much regret to me that matters have been pushed to an extremity which would not have been reached had my advice been listened to".[19]

Purchas's defiance of the court caused his opponents to apply to the Privy Council to deprive him of his Perpetual Curacy for disobedience. He was summoned to appear before the Court in June 1872, when it would consider whether he should be so deprived or condemned for contempt of court. He did not, however, appear and in fact preached a sermon in open contempt of the Privy Council. How long this process of defiance might have gone on it is not possible to say. But on the 18th October 1872 John Purchas suddenly died of congestion of the lungs, aged only 49. Two thousand people attended his funeral in the Brighton cemetery. His successor, the Rev. J. J. Mallenby, restored more conventional services at St. James's, and thus the whole dispute there came to an end.

But the Purchas judgment was of much wider significance than in Brighton alone, particularly to supporters of the high church movement. Tractarians would not have had much sympathy with Purchas's original contention that St. James's chapel was his private property and that therefore he could do what he liked within it, as they did not approve of the existence of proprietary chapels. But as soon as the judgment of the court had been given the position became quite different. It was their consistent view throughout the Oxford movement that matters of doctrine and worship could only be determined by a synod within the Church of England, and therefore they could not recognise a pronouncement of a secular court on such subjects.

Arthur Wagner felt so strongly on this point that in 1874 he wrote and published an open letter addressed to the Archbishop of Canterbury, Dr. Archibald Campbell Tait, that he called "Christ or Caesar?" The Public Worship Regulation Act had been passed that year. In some ways that was an improvement of the situation as far as high churchmen were concerned, as, under that Act, it was no longer possible for proceedings such as had been brought against John Purchas to be started without the consent of the bishop of the diocese. But Wagner seems to have viewed the Act with very bitter feelings. He had already crossed swords with the Archbishop of Canterbury when Dr. Tait had stated that most of the clergy of the Church of England thought of Holy Orders as "a mere sort of decent form".[20] Wagner considered this to be an astounding statement and in a sermon stated in no uncertain terms that, in his view, Holy Orders were "the gift of God's Holy Spirit"[21] and that the priesthood was "the mouthpiece as it were of the mystical Body of Christ".[22] On the occasion which provoked the publication of Wagner's open letter the Archbishop had made an accusation against certain clergy of "lawlessness". "Christ or Caesar?" was intended as a reply to this plea. Wagner did not mince matters in the least. He began by saying that the Archbishop was himself the chief offender in this line, as he had taken no steps to obtain from the Church of England in her synods any clear exposition of the Church's mind. He added: "Were I writing for mere controversy's sake, I might say that, of all Archbishops who have ever sat on the throne of Canterbury, no-one except perhaps Archbishop Cranmer, has so little right as Your Grace to complain of lawlessness in others; unless indeed you maintain that what is wrong in a Priest is right in an Archbishop." He pointed out that the Judicial Committee of the Privy Council was an ecclesiastical court created during the nineteenth century by Parliament without any pretence of asking the sanction of the Church in its corporate capacity. He and those who supported the high church movement could not accept the jurisdiction of such a court in ecclesiastical causes. The Gorham judgment of 1850 was still unrepealed. There had been several other judgments that were also unacceptable, and now there was the Purchas judgment.

121

He went on to give fifteen reasons for disobeying on principle the ecclesiastical judgments of the Judicial Committee of Her Majesty's Privy Council. This body had already denied (inter alia) the following truths: baptismal regeneration (the Gorham judgment); the inspiration of the whole word of God; and the eternal punishment of the wicked. He and those of his colleagues who shared his views would prefer "even expulsion from the Establishment, supposing that Your Grace intends to push matters to extremities, than an enforced submission to the decision of the court".

The Archbishop of Canterbury seems to have taken no notice of the letter. But the new Bishop of Chichester, Dr. Richard Durnford, who had only taken office in 1870, thought that the letter could not go without a reply. He was by no means unsympathetic to high churchmen. In his first charges to the clergy of the diocese he had stated that, in his view, there was room for confession within the Church of England, provided that this was the exception rather than the rule. He was not opposed to the use of vestments within reason and in the sermons which he preached for Arthur Wagner at the opening of St. Bartholomew's and St. Martin's churches in 1874 and 1875 respectively he supported Wagner over the arrangement of the churches and the nature of the services there. But he thought that Wagner's letter to the Archbishop had gone too far and had greatly exaggerated the position.

The Bishop's "Reply to a Letter of the Rev. Arthur Douglas Wagner entitled 'Christ or Caesar?'" was published in 1877. He thought that the publication of such a letter was not, in his opinion "the course a Minister of Christ of mature years and experience and holding a most responsible place in the Church ought deliberately to adopt". The ecclesiastical courts did not make the law. They only interpreted it. The Gorham judgment had enhanced the Grace of Baptism and had only pronounced that Gorham's views, which were peculiar to himself, were not so contrary to the official teaching of the Church as to disqualify him from the Ministry. The courts had never pronounced on matters of dogma, and Wagner was free to hold whatever views he liked. If he thought that the Public Worship Regulation Act should be repealed, Wagner was at liberty to work to that end. What he was not at liberty to do was to say that "This is, in my judgment, an unrighteous law, and I will not obey it."

The Bishop went on to say that he was by temper and experience a tolerant man but he had no sympathy with men "who push matters to extremity because they are forbidden to carry on the service of God exactly as their own private judgment and opinion may incline them". Wagner's comparison of the clergymen who had been suspended from preaching under the Act with the Christian martyrs of old was wholly false as the offending clergymen of 1877 were only concerned with relatively trivial matters such as the garments which they wore. He added that if Wagner was put to trouble it would be "not for your teaching but for an obstinate adherence to the use of ornaments, decorations and attitudes confessedly indifferent—that is not commanded by the Holy Scriptures, nor involving the truth of Christ".

At about the same time the Bishop of Chichester expressed himself rather more forcefully about Wagner in a private letter. Edward Pusey had written to the Bishop on Wagner's behalf. The Bishop replied on the 2nd September 1877 to the effect that "Mr. Wagner does not conceal that circumstances may compel him to make his submission to Rome. One of his curates has gone over to Rome, after writing a book which foreshadowed his change of creed. The arguments brought forward in that book exceedingly resemble those used by Mr. Wagner himself. Roman doctrine and even modern Roman decrees do not either repel or alarm him. I cannot regard his future course but with the greatest uneasiness. But he cannot say that I have ever shown any 'animus' against him or treated him with unfairness or unkindness."[23] But this was a second-hand view of someone who regarded Wagner as a difficult and even troublesome figure. There is no direct evidence from Wagner himself that he ever contemplated leaving the Church of England of his own accord. Two years later the Bishop wrote to Wagner himself to say that, when two members of the clergy at St. Bartholomew's went over to Rome, he could have wished that Wagner had issued a public statement disowning them and their action. But it was not in Arthur Wagner's nature to take such an action.

He never had to face disciplinary action by higher authority himself even though he went so far as to invite several high church clergymen to join his staff at St. Paul's who had, under the Public Worship Regulation Act, been inhibited from officiating elsewhere, and two of them at least accepted the invitation. But the Archbishop of Canterbury certainly never "pushed matters to extremities", as Wagner had written to him. Neither did the Bishop of Chichester. In fact within limits the Bishop always supported him, though clearly considering him to be a rather unreasonable man.

The Purchas judgment had condemned the wearing of Eucharistic vestments, which had always been used at St. Paul's. Wagner continued their use there for the rest of his life in a discreet way until they came to be accepted. He was himself restrained from making an official break by his ingrained loyalty to the Church of England, which was even greater than his indignation at the interference of the civil courts. It was as if his ancestry of three generations in the Church of England, his father's 46 years' ministry and his own 52 years gave him an insurmountable obedience which could not be broken except by compulsion from outside, which fortunately was not forthcoming.

As the Purchas affair ended the question of confession at St. Paul's again broke into dispute. This had two causes, one local and one national. The local cause was the discovery in 1873 of a notice-board at the church to the effect that confessions were heard there regularly, though this had been the current practice for over 20 years. The national cause was the presentation to Convocation of a petition signed by 483 clergy of the Church of England in favour of confession. The result was a public meeting at the Dome in Brighton on the 4th December 1873. The Chair was taken by Henry Moor, one of the Members of Parliament for Brighton, who strangely enough was one of the few Members for Brighton to receive the support of the Rev. H. M. Wagner. The chief speakers were the Rev. J. Bardsley, Rector of Stepney, the Rev. E. B. Elliott, who was Vicar of St. Mark's church, Brighton, and Canon Babington. A resolution was passed without opposition to the effect that attempts to introduce into the Church of England the Roman doctrine of sacramental and auricular confession were a serious danger to that Church. The meeting pledged itself to resist the introduction of practices which were "contrary to God's word"[24] and urged the Archbishop of Canterbury and the Bishop of Chichester to adopt measures to arrest such dangerous practices which already existed in Sussex and stemmed from St. Paul's church at Brighton.

Arthur Wagner replied with the publication of a little book called "Questions for Self-examination for the special use of Children", in which he justified his views on the subject. This pamphlet moved the ultra-Protestant party to fury, and they at once denounced it to the Bishop of Chichester, Dr. Richard Durnford, but without success. The Bishop wrote Wagner a long reasoned letter in which he said that he did not think that these "questions" went "beyond the very letter and teaching of Holy Scriptures" and that the passage complained of "does not justify the condemnation which has been passed upon it, nor the imputations which have been cast upon the clergy who distributed the tract".[25] This episcopal pronouncement effectively silenced Wagner's critics in this instance. Gradually the evangelical world had to get used to the idea that such practices as confession had come to stay and had captured certain sections of the Church of England. By the time of Arthur Wagner's death in 1902 their existence was accepted by all but the most rabid Protestants.

During his father's life Arthur Wagner had already built two churches and spent a considerable amount of money in charitable works, though there is little record of this. But his father's death made him a relatively rich man as tenant for life under the Vicar's will. The acquisition of this money enabled him to embark upon the two biggest enterprises of his life: the building of St. Bartholomew's and St. Martin's churches.

St. Bartholomew's, Ann Street, was the first of these. Arthur Wagner already had some connection with the district as in 1868 he had built a school for 400 children in Providence Place to the west of the London Road and a temporary church to the west of this. This could hold 350 people and was a simple brick building somewhat similar to the churches of St. Mary and St. Mary Magdalene and the Annunciation which he had just built a few years before. His father's death enabled him to think of something grander to replace the temporary church. R. C. Carpenter had died in 1855. For some reason or other Wagner did not choose Bodley to design his new church but turned instead to an architect who was then quite unknown: Edmund Scott, who had come to Brighton from London in 1853 and was then practising at No. 26A Regency Square. He and his later partner, F. T. Cawthorn, were from then onwards to have a considerable connection with Arthur Wagner and his charities.

Scott's first plan received municipal approval as early as the 7th June 1871. It was for a building considerably different from the church that was actually erected. Even this project had been modified from Scott's first thoughts and had been amended on the drawing itself. The first plan showed a very narrow and immensely long building with no break along the Providence Place elevation between it and the school and 322 feet in length for the two together. It seems likely that Scott had made an informal consultation with the Borough Surveyor, who had advised him against making the church and school continuous. Scott therefore amended his plan to reduce the length of the church from thirteen to eleven and a half bays and to provide a space or court-yard between the church and the school. This church would have been only 46 feet wide. Between it and the houses on the west (Nos. 49–57 London Street) would have been a long but very narrow triangular space which was to have been devoted to a vestibule and no less than four vestries behind this to the north.

But the chief difference between the first plan and the church as erected was in the respective heights of the buildings. The first project showed only a height of 41 feet 9 inches to the wall-plate, which was just under half the height actually built. Strangely enough Arthur Wagner seems not to have been in the least concerned about the correct liturgical orientation of churches, and nearly all the churches erected by him have unorthodox orientations. St. Bartholomew's was no exception. The south (liturgical west) elevation of the first project would have been very plain. There was to have been a round window, as was actually built. But the only other feature of the front would have been a central pair of door-ways with curved trefoil-shaped heads set in a tall pointed arch and flanked by buttresses. The east (liturgical south) elevation was not inspiring. There would have been three tiers of windows: paired lancets on the ground floor, casements of two tiers of two lights on the next level and of two tiers of three lights above that.

The foundation stone was laid on the 8th February 1872. The contractors were Stenning & Co. of Brighton. Wagner must have changed his mind soon after the work was begun. Edmund Scott's second plans were submitted to the town on the 16th September 1873. There is no information to show why Wagner had second thoughts, but he presumably wanted something grander. The new proposal used the whole site between Providence Place and the houses in London Street. So the building as erected was 59, instead of 46, feet wide. It was also 90, instead of just under 42, feet high to the wall-plate and 135 feet to the ridge of the roof. This makes the roof higher than that of Westminster Abbey. It is probably the tallest church in England. The length without the school to the north is 170 feet.

Arthur Wagner's aim was to produce the maximum of magnificence at the minimum of cost. St. Peter's, which dated from his father's time and had been built of stone, had cost £20,000. He therefore chose to build St. Bartholomew's in brick. The cost proved to be £18,000. He used to say, in reference to the church's great height, that, measured by the standard of cubic feet of air space, it was the cheapest church ever built in England. The style was early Italian Gothic, but Scott was probably influenced by the work of James Brooks and G. F. Bodley in England. Instead of the eleven and a half bays of the first plan the church comprises nine wider bays with no division between the nave and chancel. It is likely that the church, as it now stands, is incomplete. Sawyer's "The Churches of Brighton" stated that it was intended to have transepts. The Brighton Gazette of the 10th September 1874, when reporting on the opening ceremony, spoke of proposals for an apsidal chancel and a "pretty spire". But Scott's deposited drawings do not show any such proposals. Transepts were manifestly impossible as the church is flush with Providence Place on the east (liturgical south) side. If Wagner ever intended to have an apsidal chancel it is likely that the plans were abandoned when, presumably on the advice of the municipal authorities, Scott reduced the length of the first project by one and a half bays and left a space between the church and the pre-existing school. But the north (liturgical east) end of the church appears unfinished. So at least three plans have been made to complete the building, one by Henry Wilson in 1906 and another by Sir Giles Gilbert Scott in 1924.

It is the great height of the church which gives St. Bartholomew's its stunning effect. In 1874 only the triforium windows could be seen above the surrounding small houses. But today the full majesty is revealed from far off. The design of the main elevations is extremely plain: only a series of lancet windows at two levels set between a rhythm of brick buttresses. The south (liturgical west) front has the large rose window (25 feet in diameter) which was common to both schemes. But below it is a row of four small lancets, a statue of St. Bartholomew in a niche with a canopy over it and a wide but single round-headed doorway.

No sooner had the great height of the building become apparent than a storm of protest arose. It was christened "Noah's ark", "the barn", "Wagner's folly" and such names. The occupants of Nos. 49–57 London Street on the west side of the church claimed that the great height of the building caused their chimneys to smoke and their fires to cease drawing. One cannot help thinking that this claim was very dubious and that they were unduly conscious of the fact that Arthur Wagner was a rich man, was notoriously generous and had built many small houses in Brighton for poor people. If so, their calculations proved well-based. Wagner proceeded to buy up all the houses in question and reduce their rents.

The local uproar caused Brighton Council to reconsider the question of the church. At a meeting on the 14th October 1873 the Works Committee reported that if the original plans had shown the great height that was now revealed they would have required more open space to be left behind the building. But the Council had not resolved that the height should be reduced. It was therefore impossible to provide more open space. So no further objection could be made. In other words they were saying that, when the plans were submitted, they had not realised how high the building would look when completed. Councillors Reeves and Booth proposed that the plans should be approved, but this was rejected by 21 votes to 13.

Arthur Wagner seems to have paid no attention to this reversal of permission and proceeded to complete the church as designed. According to H. Hamilton Maughan's book on "Some Brighton Churches" the Council at a later date went on to consider whether they should prosecute Wagner for breaking the by-laws in making the building two feet higher than the plans had shown but decided by 20 votes to 11 that a fine of forty shillings and costs would make little impression on a man who had just spent £18,000 on building the church. Adverse criticism, however, continued in full measure after the church was opened. Sawyer says that reproaches were dealt out with unstinted liberality upon all connected with the church: "the founder, the architect, the Bishop of the Diocese who opened it, the clergy present at the opening, the building in every detail, the Town Council who permitted its erection, the bell calling the worshippers to service, the services themselves, in a word upon everything".[26] One of the absurd rumours that circulated was to the effect that the church contained a spiral staircase of 175 steps which led to 58 dark cells, each 11 feet by 4½ feet wide and situated on three separate levels. What were they for? it was asked. Clearly something sinister. The rumour must presumably have referred to the portions of the double triforium that passed through the main pillars of the church. But, however great the criticisms, Arthur Wagner cared for none of these things.

The interior of St. Bartholomew's derives much of its great effect from the fact that it is all seen at one glance. There is no division between chancel and

126

nave, and there are no aisles. But the pointed arches between the brick pillars form side-chapels with a triforium over. When first built the interior must have seemed rather stark as most of the features which make it so magnificent today were designed by Henry Wilson, a pupil of F. D. Sedding, at a later date and inserted either at the very end of Arthur Wagner's life or after his death. Almost the only original fittings are the altar, painted by S. Bell, and above it at triforium level the great cross 20 feet high which was outlined on encaustic tiles with the incised figure of Christ upon the Cross. Between this and the altar was originally a huge dossal of fabric, said to have been designed by G. E. Street, and shaped like a large triptych with the centre panel higher than the flanking ones and surmounted by a canopy bearing the words "Sanctus, Sanctus, Sanctus". The great Byzantine baldachino, the silver tabernacle and the candlesticks by Henry Wilson were added in 1899–1900, the mosaics by F. Hamilton Jackson in 1911 and the altar cross by McCulloch of Kennington in 1912. The original pulpit was of stained wood, standing on open legs and with a flat sounding board over it. In 1906 it was replaced by Wilson's magnificent marble version of today. Wilson also designed the altar in the Lady Chapel in 1902, the gallery in 1906 and the baptistry in 1908. The sixteen windows were to have contained stained glass designed by Walter Tower, the partner of C. E. Kempe, but only four were ever completed.

The church was opened by licence on the 18th September 1874. The seats were all free and could normally accommodate 1,500 people. Three Eucharists were celebrated that morning. For the third service at 11 a.m., at which the Bishop of Chichester, Dr. Richard Durnford, preached, 2,000 people were present. Many had no doubt come out of curiosity to see such a strange building and others out of a hostile desire to criticise. The Bishop preached a most tactful sermon. After pointing out that the church had been built entirely for the poor with no rented pews, he said: "I look around me and I see nothing that our Church forbids or that might justly be charged with superstition."[27] A representation of Christ crucified he could not consider to be such. The Purchas judgment was then no doubt fresh in everyone's minds. He therefore added that if superstitious objects should creep in later "the courts are open. I for my part shall be prepared to do my duty".[28] He went on to ask the pointed questions whether, because St. Bartholomew's did not resemble other churches "is it therefore to be an object of suspicion? Is it the part of Christians to spy out another's liberty and to spy it out so that it may be narrowed?"[29]

The Rev. Alfred Payne, who was one of the curates at St. Paul's, became the first priest in charge of St. Bartholomew's. The church continued to be administered from St. Paul's for another six years and was largely financed throughout this period by Arthur Wagner, though there was an endowment of £150 a year from the Ecclesiastical Commissioners. St. Bartholomew's did not become a parish church until 1881. The first Vicar was the Rev. T. W. C. Collis, who ministered there until 1895. The church was not consecrated until 1887. The Bishop of Chichester, Dr. Richard Durnford, had expressed the hope ten years earlier that it would be offered for consecration "when it was freed from debt and could obtain a definite district".[30] But this did not happen until 1887.

The second of Arthur Wagner's great ventures was St. Martin's church. At the end of H. M. Wagner's life the Vicar had intended to build another church in Brighton and had set aside £3,000 of his own money for the purpose. But he had not made up his mind what site to choose. In his last years he felt himself too frail to embark on another such church venture and so consulted the Bishop of Chichester, Dr. A. T. Gilbert. The Bishop advised him to appoint a building committee. This he did. The principal members of it were his life-long friends and colleagues, both of whom had originally been his curates, the Rev. Thomas Cooke, Perpetual Curate of St. Peter's, and the Rev. James Vaughan, Perpetual Curate of Christ Church. But nothing had been done by them at the time of H. M. Wagner's death in 1870.

When this occurred the money which he had set aside naturally passed to the Vicar's heirs as part of his estate. But his three sons decided that they wished this money to be used for the purpose intended by their father. They therefore offered the building committee a choice of a gift of £3,000 to be used by the committee towards the cost of erecting any church that it might decide to build anywhere in Brighton, or for the Wagners themselves to accept the full financial responsibility for building in their father's memory a church of a character and on a site chosen by them. The committee very naturally chose the second option as being very much the more handsome offer.

The Wagners chose a site in Lewes Road immediately to the north of Elm Grove with which Arthur was already connected. The area had been part of Ireland's Gardens. About 1855 the Conservative Land Society had begun to develop part of it as the Round Hill estate. Their architect, George Morgan, had enquired from Henry Michell Wagner, as Vicar of Brighton, whether he would favour the erection of a new church there if a site for the purpose was provided. The Vicar evidently mistrusted the financial intentions of the company and gave them no encouragement. So nothing materialised at that time. But he did mention that he knew someone who might contribute towards such a project. This may have been an anonymous reference to his son, as about 10 years later Arthur Wagner began to take a hand in the development of this area. In much the same way as he did around Islingword Road he began to pay modest builders small sums each week to erect for poor families houses which cost not more than £120 each. In the two areas he may have built as many as 400 such houses. The names of St. Paul's Street and St. Mary Magdalene's Street record his association with the district. But he was also active in streets with more secular names such as Caledonian Street, Franklin Road, Lewes Road itself and Upper Lewes Road. In 1867 to meet the spiritual needs of this district he opened a temporary chapel in what is now St. Martin's Street. When he and his brothers decided to erect a church in memory of their father they resolved to replace this temporary chapel by a permanent and worthy building. The temporary chapel then became the parish school.

In choosing an architect the brothers did not turn to one of those most favoured by the Tractarians such as G. F. Bodley or G. E. Street but almost certainly consulted in their minds what might have been their father's preference in the matter. One of his life-long friends had been Somers Clarke, the Clerk to the Brighton Vestry. The Vicar in his will had left small legacies to both Somers Clarke's son and daughter. The son of the same name was an architect who had been a pupil of Sir Gilbert Scott and was then in partnership with J. T. Micklethwaite. He was later to become Surveyor to the fabric of St. Paul's cathedral and architect to Chichester cathedral. He had already executed work in

Brighton in the Blind School in Eastern Road and the new Swan Downer School in Dyke Road, with both of which H. M. Wagner had been connected. Somers Clarke was later to add a clerestory to St. Nicholas's and a chancel to St. Peter's churches. It was to him that the brothers Wagner turned for their new St. Martin's.

A contract for its erection was signed on the 10th October 1872 with Jabez Reynolds, a builder who had been responsible for erecting much of Cliftonville, Hove. The cost was to be £11,398. The construction took two and a half years. The church was Somers Clarke's first major work. His later buildings were not to surpass it in quality. It was and still is Brighton's largest church. It is built of brick and externally is rather an austere essay in thirteenth century Gothic. It was originally intended to have a belfry or tower with a saddle-back roof at the north (liturgical east) end, but this was never built.

The magnificence of the interior comes therefore as somewhat of a surprise. Entered as it is from the baptistry platform at the south (liturgical west) end, which is five steps above the level of the rest of the church, its full spaciousness is visible at a glance as there is no division between the nave and the chancel. Of all the Brighton churches which existed in Arthur Wagner's day, whether built by him or not, St. Martin's probably had then the finest interior, since the greatest internal features of St. Bartholomew's date from after Wagner's death. In this St. Martin's derives great advantage from the fact that all the internal fittings were designed by Somers Clarke himself and were executed under his supervision. The reredos contains 20 pictures and 69 statues and was constructed by J. E. Knox. The statues were carved at Oberammergau in the workshop of Josef Mayr (a former "Christus" in the passion play). It is said that three of them are likenesses of the Rev. Henry Michell Wagner, his grandfather, the Rev. Henry Michell, who was also Vicar of Brighton, and his father-in-law, Joshua Watson. But if so, they are too small in scale and too high up in position to be identifiable. The gallery on the east (liturgical south) side of the chancel, opposite the organ was intended to accommodate members of the band during military services as St. Martin's was the nearest church to Preston Barracks, where a cavalry regiment was then always quartered.

The pulpit was not erected until 1880. It was inspired by the Sacrament House in the church of St. Sebald in Nuremberg. It is higher than the bishop's throne at Exeter cathedral, which is said to be its nearest equivalent in England. The wood for the inlaid floor was brought back from the Mount of Olives by the late Vicar's son, Henry, on one of his journeys. At the south (liturgical west) end of the church is the font. The canopy of this, which echoes the pulpit, was also designed by Somers Clarke but was not erected until 1907. The font itself is of Sussex marble and is inlaid with other marbles brought back by Henry Wagner from Cairo, Rome and Pompeii.

On the north wall is a tablet with a Latin inscription which records that the church was erected in memory of the Rev. Henry Michell Wagner. His son, Henry, also gave the east window in memory of his own mother, whom he had never known, and his aunt, Mary Ann Wagner, who had brought him up. This window was designed by James Powell of Powell & Sons, White Friars, London.

The church was consecrated by the Bishop of Chichester, Dr. Richard Durnford, on the 1st May 1875. The full seating capacity of 1,500 was engaged and nearly 2,000 attended the confirmation service on the following day. As in the case of St. Bartholomew's, many came out of curiosity in order to see what they thought was going to be another mysterious ritualist church and some, no doubt, out of actual malice and in a spirit of disapproval. The Bishop in as tactful a sermon as he had given at St. Bartholomew's the year before answered their questions and re-assured their doubts. He said in effect that it was a free world full of diversity and there was room for diversity within the law in ecclesiastical affairs. The rich had always been free to build what churches they fancied. But this was a church wholly built for the poor with no rented pews. He said: "We (the Clergy) ask not to be denied the liberty allowed to us, for surely it was never intended that all congregations of the Church of England should be confined to one fixed unvarying groove?"[31] He went on to refer specifically to the choral services which so annoyed the anti-ritualist party. "If we choose to use more music than elsewhere, let us not be condemned."[32]

The first incumbent was the Rev. Robert Ingham, who became a full Vicar in October 1875, when St. Martin's was allotted a parish. The Bishop in his sermon said that Ingham had laid down "what, in his judgment, is most in edification in accordance with the plain directions of our reformed Church. These he will follow".[33] This in fact Ingham did. The church never had ritualist services and never excited any trouble.

Arthur Wagner's last Brighton church was the church of the Transfiguration, as it was at first to be called, or the church of the Resurrection, as it came to be known, in Russell Street. This was built in 1876-7. It seems strange now that he should build another church so close to St. Paul's—little more than 100 yards away. But the tradition is that the fishermen, for whom St. Paul's church had been built by his father, had perhaps been awed by the size and grandeur of that building or by the fashionable nature of its congregation and had never frequented it in any numbers. Wagner hoped that, if he built them a small and simpler church of their own nearby, they would be attracted to it.

He had no sooner started work on the church than he ran into trouble. The owner of the adjoining brewery objected to a building of the height proposed and successfully claimed the right of ancient lights. Undaunted, Wagner resolved that, if he could not build above ground, he would do so below it. So he had the land excavated and built the church partly below ground level, so that it was approached down 32 steps. As a result it may have cost at least £12,000. The architect was Richard Herbert Carpenter, the son of R. C. Carpenter. The exterior was a plain brick box of one storey above ground in virtually no style, but internally the building had Gothic aisles.

A second difficulty arose over the consecration. Wagner had a fixed objection to the consecration of churches. He even went so far as to describe consecration to the Bishop of Chichester, Dr. Richard Durnford, as a "farce". This objection was rooted in an idea of the Tractarians that the consecration of Church of England churches gave an opening for the State to intervene in their affairs. Dr. Pusey, in writing to the Bishop of Chichester on the subject, went so far as to say that consecration gave the Dissenters the opportunity to use churches of the Established Church. The Bishop could not forget that St. Bartholomew's had been licensed but not consecrated. So he refused to provide a licence for the opening of the new church if it was not also consecrated. Wagner enlisted the support of Dr. Pusey, who had known him for 40 years, since he was a boy. Pusey wrote to tell the Bishop that Wagner was "in great sorrow and depression"[34] because the church had not been opened. The Bishop replied that "Mr. Wagner expects that concessions should be made to his own feelings or apprehensions. But he forgets that some concessions on his part may also be expected."[35] In this case Wagner must have made the necessary concession as the church was opened in 1878. It never succeeded in attracting the fishermen, and 10 years after Wagner's death the building was converted into a wholesale meat store. It was finally demolished in 1966.

After the church of the Resurrection Wagner built one other church. But this was not in Brighton. Three years after his father's death he took a small house in the country. This was a modest early nineteenth century stuccoed building named Totease House, Buxted. It stood and still stands on the western fringe of the village almost adjoining the railway line. On his visits there during the summer Wagner found that the old parish church of St. Margaret's was about a mile away to the south west in the grounds of Buxted Park. So he decided to build at his own expense a new church for the parishioners nearer to the centre of the village.

He first erected a school-room, which served as a temporary church for two years. St. Mary's, Buxted, was begun in 1885 and consecrated by the Bishop of Chichester, Dr. Richard Durnford, on the 11th June 1887. It was designed by the Brighton architects who had already produced two churches in Brighton for Arthur Wagner: Edmund Scott and F. T. Cawthorn. It is a simple essay in Perpendicular Gothic, faced with the traditional Sussex materials of flints. The principal feature comprises the tower and spire at the west end of the south chapel. Inside, the building is of the utmost simplicity, with a barrel-vaulted roof and no division between the chancel and the nave. The cross of the hanging Rood was designed by the Rev. C. E. Roe, who was at that time one of Wagner's curates at St. Paul's but subsequently became Vicar of St. Mary's, Buxted. The church was also decorated originally by several pictures that were brought there from St. Paul's, Brighton, but have since been removed. The original altar-piece has also been altered. The stained glass windows are the work of Charles Eamer Kempe but were mostly inserted at a later date in memory of the early Vicars (the Rev. Edmund Francis Mackreth, 1885–1890, and the Rev. John Baghot De la Bere, 1890–1908).

When not in residence at Totease House, Buxted, Arthur Wagner placed the house at the disposal of the Sisters of the Community of the Blessed Virgin Mary, which he had founded in 1855 in connection with St. Paul's, Brighton. He intended it to form a sort of rest-house for them. But in 1878 he built them special premises of their own at the end of Church Road, Buxted. This was called St. Margaret's Cottage. Five years later he erected on the adjoining land in Church Road a new house for himself named St. Mary's, with a private chapel to be shared between himself and the Community. There the Sisters remained until they moved to much larger premises in Falmer Road, Rottingdean, Brighton, in 1912. Both the Buxted buildings still exist. St. Mary's House has become a childrens' home which was run, first by the Sisters of the Wantage Community, and now by the Gilthallion Trust.

In 1896 Arthur Wagner was only 72. But he had become infirm and mentally incapable of doing business. In that year a crisis occurred in relation to St. Mary's Home, Queen's Square, when the local authority required new drainage to be

131

installed which would cost £383 0s. 0d. The year before Wagner had made over the Home to trustees, of whom he was one. But the other trustees considered themselves to be what they called "dry" trustees, that is to say that they had accepted office on the understanding that they would not be responsible for the financial liabilities of the Home but only for its general administration. Wagner himself had always provided the funds required. They turned therefore to his solicitor, Charles Alfred Woolley of Fitzhugh, Woolley, Baines and Woolley of No. 3 Pavilion Parade, Brighton. Woolley undertook to see Wagner in order to point out to him the difficulties in connection with the church and the parish. But the interview proved unsatisfactory. Woolley therefore advised one of the trustees named R. Ball Dodson of No. 1 Vicarage Gardens, Montpelier Road, Brighton, who was a church-warden of St. Paul's, to make an informal approach to the Bishop of Chichester, which he did.

The Bishop, Dr. William Wilberforce, had only been appointed to office the year before and had never met Arthur Wagner. But he seems to have accepted without question the representations that were made to him by Ball Dodson and to have concluded that it was time for Wagner to give up his office. He therefore called on him but did not find Wagner at home. On the 28th April he wrote him as tactful a letter as possible. He began by saying that "not only all Brighton, but the whole church knows of the energy, the self-sacrifice, the wonderful generosity and the large measure of success, which have marked the whole of your work at Brighton: and as well that you are the second generation who have, under God, been enabled to do such great things in the service of the Master".[36] He went on to say that, from the representations that had been made to him, it seemed that the time had come "when you might willingly resign the charge of the Parish of St. Paul's into the hands of a younger man, who would be better qualified by reason of health and strength for carrying on the work so nobly performed by yourself for so many years",[37] and that he, as the bishop of the diocese, was the proper person to make this suggestion. He did so on the understanding that Wagner would remain where he was, in his own house, and that he should help "by your counsel and presence in the work which you have loved so well".[38] Here the Bishop rather revealed his ignorance of the circumstances as Wagner's house "Belvedere" had never at any time been the Vicarage of St. Paul's, and therefore there could be no question of his leaving the house. The Bishop concluded by asking him to think the matter over and let him know his decision.

No reply was received. So the Bishop wrote again on the 23rd May. We do not know what occurred subsequently. But whether or not any answer was sent to the Bishop's communications, the reply in effect was that Wagner declined to relinquish his charge, and in fact he remained Vicar of St. Paul's until his death six years later. The church continued to be administered by his curates, of whom he had about five or six. Meanwhile he lived on in complete retirement at Belvedere, where his cousin, Fanny Coombe, looked after him. He could occasionally be seen in the Brighton streets in an elderly victoria drawn by an old white unclipped horse and driven by an aged coachman in shabby livery.

He quietly declined in physical and mental strength and died at Belvedere at 5 a.m. on Tuesday the 14th January 1902, aged 77. His body was attired in full eucharistic vestments, the chasuble being the one which he had worn when he first preached at St. Paul's. On the lid of the coffin was a brass cross and the inscription "Arthur Douglas Wagner, Priest, died the 14th January 1902, aged 77 . . . Jesu mercy." The coffin was taken to St. Paul's church on the evening of Friday the 17th January, and those who had been intimately associated with him, who were presumably the Sisters of St. Mary's Home, kept watch over it during the night. Early on the following day, Saturday the 18th January, several celebrations of the Holy Eucharist were held, not only at St. Paul's but also at St. Mary and St. Mary Magdalene's, at the Annunciation, the Resurrection, St. Bartholomew's and St. Martin's. A requiem mass at St. Paul's followed, at 10 a.m. This was conducted by the priest in charge, the Rev. E. F. Courtney, who had been one of Arthur Wagner's curates. The ritual was simple, and there was no incense. Gregorian music was sung by St. Paul's choir. The chief mourners were Fanny Coombe and Arthur's only surviving half-brother, Henry. The church was so crowded that many people had to stand or kneel. There was also a great crowd in the street outside. Equally large congregations attended the similar requiem masses at the other churches associated with Arthur Wagner. The interment was at the Lewes Road cemetery in the grave already occupied by his cousin, Elizabeth Chassereau Coombe, and next to that of his aunt, Mary Ann Wagner, who had brought him up. About 3,000 people collected round the grave. The service was taken by the Rev. John Baghot de la Bere, the Vicar of St. Mary's, Buxted. A plain stone cross stands on the grave inscribed only with the dates of his birth and death and the words "Jesu mercy". His cousin and housekeeper, Fanny Coombe, was buried in the same grave 23 years later. A memorial tablet was placed in the chancel of St. Paul's church. This shows a bas-relief portrait of Arthur Wagner, dressed in the vestments which he had introduced into the church and which caused so much controversy.

Arthur Wagner's will was dated the 9th October 1894 and was made by Charles Alfred Woolley of Fitzhugh, Woolley, Baines and Woolley of No. 3 Pavilion Parade, Brighton, who acted as one of the executors. For some years Arthur had dedicated certain portions of his estate to "the ecclesiastical charities" of the churches with which he had been connected (St. Paul's, the Annunciation, St. Mary and St. Mary Magdalene's, the Resurrection, St. Bartholomew's and St. Martin's); also, St. Mary's Home. In order to continue their work after his death he had made over certain money to them and expressed his intention in his will of making further grants for the same purpose. He confirmed these grants in his will and asked his residuary legatee to make good any deficiency in them that might arise. His elder half-brother, Joshua Watson Wagner, having predeceased him, under the terms of their father's will the property of which Arthur was the tenant for life passed to his other half-brother, Henry Wagner. This he was not free to leave. But the remainder of his property he bequeathed to his unmarried first cousin, Fanny Coombe. The will was proved by Fanny Coombe and C. A. Woolley at Lewes registry on the 4th April 1902. The estate amounted to £49,907 15s. 6d.

The most phenomenal thing about Arthur Wagner was his remarkable generosity. His father had noted in a private letter-book towards the end of his life that he had given £3,327 for the building of churches in Brighton and his family another £2,236. Arthur's gifts far exceeded these sums. He must have spent at least £60,000 in building churches alone. One booklet on St.

Bartholomew's, "A Story of the Last Fifty Years", puts the total at as much as £70,000. But in either case such a sum was not the whole story. When built, the churches had to be administered and almost the whole cost of running the six Brighton churches for which Arthur Wagner was responsible fell on him. At St. Paul's he maintained five or six curates at his own expense to administer his five other Brighton churches until these became independent parish churches in the eighteen eighties. In the accounts for St. Paul's for the year 1901-2, during which year Arthur Wagner died, it was noted that he had subsidised the church funds to the tune of £800 a year, plus an extra amount of £150 towards the expenses of St. Paul's school. It is likely that his contributions to St. Bartholomew's and St. Martin's at least, if not to his other three Brighton churches, amounted to similar sums.[39] St. Mary's Home was probably the most expensive of all to maintain as almost the whole expenditure of this fell on Arthur Wagner. This amounted to £2,500 a year in 1865 and no doubt was more 30 years later. Towards the end of his life he made over capital funds to trustees to provide for these ecclesiastical charities after his death.

To these sums must be added about £40,000 spent in building 400 modest houses for poor people. Finally there was charity to individuals which was almost certainly in proportion to his institutional gifts. It is said that every Saturday morning a crowd of poor and aged people gathered in the vestibule of St. Paul's church to receive their weekly allowance. He also relieved distressed gentlefolk and small tradesmen who were in financial difficulties. Such gifts were not confined to members of the Church of England. On one occasion he called on a parishioner who had long been ill and asked if he could render him any assistance. The man's wife replied that he was not a member of Wagner's congregation but a Dissenter. To this Wagner rejoined that he did not wish to interfere with the sick man spiritually but would like to minister to his temporal needs.

It seems almost as if, in Arthur Wagner's case, the old biblical adjuration to give away one tenth of one's income was stood on its head and he may possibly have given away nine tenths of his income and have lived himself on the remaining tenth. One of his obituaries even suggested that he might have beggared himself, had his activities not been curbed by his illness during the last years of his life.

Apart from his generosity Arthur Wagner was a great contrast to his father. The least combative of men, he probably never had a personal quarrel with any-one in his life. He spent his whole career returning good for evil and seeking to love those who persecuted him in a way his father would not have understood. But at least in his early life his views were so unpopular and the practices to which they gave rise so in advance of their time that they generated controversies that made his father's quarrels seem what they were: parochial. This produced a difference in relations between the two Wagners and their ecclesiastical superiors. H. M. Wagner was, throughout his incumbency, on excellent terms with the five successive Bishops of Chichester under whom he served. This was due to his great ecclesiastical tolerance and his traditional approach to authority. Arthur Wagner was a less easy man to deal with in such circumstances. Most of his working life was spent under two Bishops. Only one of these, Dr. Richard Durnford (1870-1895), has left any record of what he thought about Wagner. But from letters to and about Arthur Wagner it is clear that the Bishop considered him to be a difficult man who liked his way and that he involved the Bishop in many controversies that the Bishop would have liked to avoid. In these the Bishop supported him to a great extent but would not go beyond a certain point and said so.

Where Henry and Arthur Wagner were alike was in the way in which they appeared to be completely impervious to the criticism and unpopularity which they aroused. Just as Henry Michell Wagner had made his way completely unmoved through a howling mob at the hustings after he had voted publicly against the popular Radical candidate, so Arthur Wagner showed no sign of being aware of the extreme dismay to which his ritualist practices at St. Paul's and the much more extreme ones elsewhere gave rise in Brighton and beyond.

Perhaps in the latter's case this was due to his remoteness. He always remained a lonely and austere figure, somewhat out of touch with the world. He took no part in public life other than his church work and never made a speech at a civic meeting. He avoided publicity of any kind and led as retiring a life as possible. As a result he was a rather unworldly figure. Even his curates stood somewhat in awe of him, though more in wonder than in fear. His friends were perhaps more inspired by loyalty and respect than by affection. The fact that he did not marry did not help to lessen the distance between him and other people. R. V. Ballard, who knew him at the end of his life, records that he presented all confirmation candidates at St. Paul's with a copy of "The Treasury of Devotion" by Canon Carter, together with a small sacred French print and a larger picture of two angels,[40] but that he had no means of communicating with young people. His life was too austere, even ascetic. He disapproved of such things as dancing and, Ballard thought, probably had little sense of humour. But he was not in the least intolerant. He always retained the kindest feelings for those who were distressed by the ritual and doctrinal changes introduced into the Church of England by the Oxford movement.

More remarkable was his attitude to the Church of Rome. As early as 1855 he was thinking in terms of reunion. Although this was only 5 years after the so-called papal aggression, when feeling against Roman Catholicism was still running high, he could distinguish a "kinder and gentler feeling towards Christians of other lands which has now, thanks to God, set in among us".[41] Those of less benevolent outlook at the time might have found difficulty in discerning this generosity of feeling in 1855. But he went on to express the wish that these sentiments might "flow in a stronger and stronger stream each successive year till He who Alone 'maketh men to be of one mind in a house' and Who prayed that all His Disciples 'might be One as He and the Father are One' 'may restore to distracted Christendom the precious but long-lost Gift of visible Christian Unity'."[42]

Unlike his father, Arthur Wagner was not a good preacher. He usually chose theological subjects which were too learned for his congregation. Moreover his delivery was not good. He had a weak high-pitched voice which did not carry well. He spoke from a prepared manuscript and, owing to short sight, held his notes too near his face. He did, however, publish one slim volume of sermons, which is now a rare book. This was issued in 1855 and was called "Parochial Sermons bearing on Subjects of the Day". They were all delivered at St. Paul's church and included many of the subjects which were to be of importance to Wagner at a later date in his controversies with the Archbishop of Canterbury,

Dr. A. J. Tait, over doctrinal matters and judgments of the Judicial Committee of the Privy Council. These were "Holy Orders, a Mystery of the Kingdom of Heaven"; "The Holy Eucharist, the Chief Act of Christian Worship"; "The Eternity of Future Punishment"; and "The Blessedness of the Virgin Mary".

In all this work and thought Arthur Wagner was an early pioneer of the high church movement, which first translated the principles of the Tractarians into practice. His achievement was that his work has lasted and has grown to a much greater scale. It is true that the two least important of his Brighton churches have been demolished, and St. Mary's Home no longer exists in Brighton. But St. Paul's, the church of the Annunciation, St. Bartholomew's and St. Martin's, Brighton, and St. Mary's at Buxted, still flourish. The high church movement has not only been accepted but has come to be one of the principal sources of life in the Church of England, whereas the fanatical evangelicalism which so vehemently sought to persecute Wagner in his lifetime has little following today outside Northern Ireland. In Brighton the name Wagner is still in good repute and, though the nature of its associations may be now rather blurred, the work of Arthur Wagner is now probably better remembered than that of his father and the result of his ministry in the town is the more lasting of the two.

Chapter VI

HENRY WAGNER

HENRY WAGNER (1840-1926) was more robust both in body and mind than his elder brother Joshua. His personal circumstances and the times he lived in made him a wealthy, charitable, industrious amateur, an outstanding genealogist and art collector, who never married or followed a profession. He was sent in 1851 to Rugby, partly, it seems likely, because of Joshua's unhappiness at Eton and their father's feeling, perhaps justified, that Eton was not then at its best. One suspects, however, that Henry, loyal Rugbeian though he always was, a little regretted Eton.

A letter book of Henry Michell Wagner, the Vicar of Brighton, for the years 1857 to 1859 preserves copies of correspondence about Henry's future, mainly between his father and the Rev. Dr. Edward Meyrick Goulburn (1819-1897) tutor and dean of Merton College, Oxford, from 1843 to 1845 and head master of Rugby from 1849 to 1857, and with Goulburn's very different successor, the Rev. Dr. Frederick Temple (1821-1904), head master of Rugby from 1858 to 1869, then Bishop of Exeter till 1885 and Archbishop of Canterbury until his death. William Temple, Archbishop of Canterbury from 1942 to 1944 was his son.

The correspondence begins with a letter of 3 November 1857 from Mary Ann Wagner to Goulburn conveying her brother's thanks "for the trouble you have taken in regard to a College for Henry. He will be quite satisfied to have him at Exeter, Merton or Christchurch. Please however understand that by my placing that Exeter is not the first nor is Christchurch the last, because he is not acquainted with the particulars of these Colleges intimately so as to enable him to judge which is the most desirable. University is, like Balliol, filled beyond 1859, and were it not so, it would seem—amongst the young ones—to have the reputation of being an expensive College—'somewhat fast'—which neither his father nor Henry would desire; while Balliol, on the other hand, being 'open', and consequently having the very best scholars of all the public schools, would present such a formidable amount of competition as probably. to leave Henry 'no where in the race.' "

Dr. Goulburn replies from School House, Rugby (4 November) "My dear Miss Wagner, How can you consult a former Fellow and tutor of Merton upon the question whether any other College is superior to Merton? Of course, none is, and I am all for Henry going up and standing for a Postmastership there, which I think he is very likely to get, next year, if not this. Shall I go and get the Warden to put his name down for October 1859? Exeter is also a very good College. I do not hear great things of Ch.Ch. just at present."

The Postmasters at Merton are equivalent to scholars at other Colleges. In a later letter (12 July 1858) Dr. Goulburn says that "the singular name—Postmaster—is a corruption of 'Portionista', in allusion to the daily commons, which, as members of the House, they received under the old Monastic system."

On 10 November 1857, back at Rugby from Oxford, he writes "My dear Vicar, I called on the Warden of Merton yesterday and sued for a vacancy for Harry in two years time. The Warden complained of the number of his applications, but I know that *if he likes* he can grant your application as you desire. At last I induced him to put down Henry's name for *Easter Term*, 1859. This he did in my presence but said it was not absolutely certain he would then have room for him. He added that a line to the Warden from the Vicar 'might have the effect of further rivetting the engagement in his memory'."

On 5 July 1858 the Vicar wrote again to the Warden, R. Bullock-Marsham, to ask the position and was told that Henry's name was on his list for a chance vacancy in Michaelmas 1859 or later or he could be a candidate for a Postmastership in June 1859. Goulburn, consulted, wrote on 12 July 1858, "I think our course with Henry is pretty clear. Let him by all means stand for the Postmastership in the June of next year. The position is a very nice and distinguished one, and yet the competition is not *very* formidable. . . . If he fails, he will doubtless acquit himself very creditably, and in that case I have little doubt that, after his promise of a chance vacancy for Easter 1859, the Warden will receive him. Should the worst come to the worst and rooms not be offered to him before January 1860, it would no doubt be well to send him to a Tutor in the interim. Even then, Henry will not be too late for College. Academic life is now postponed by young men generally to a much later period than it used to be."

On the 5th of August 1858 the Vicar writes to the new Head Master, Dr. Temple, to ask if Henry, now 18, may remain at Rugby till Christmas. "There is difficulty in finding rooms for him in College, but even in the absence of such difficulty it would be my desire that my son should remain unto the utmost limit at Rugby." On 20 August, having had no answer, the Vicar wrote again. On the 21st Temple replied, "Rev. & dear Sir, You were right in supposing that I did not answer your letter because I thought it better to see your son first. The fact is that I am a little unwilling to give a promise so long beforehand, without taking the opportunity of impressing on him that a boy who remains longer at school than is usual ought to be more than usually attentive to school duties. Age imposes responsibility and the tone of a school is very seriously affected by the character and bearing of those who remain till they are really young men. Your son has won my regard; I believe him to be pureminded and truthful, with a very real sense of religion, but he is still somewhat childish and does not, I think, see as clearly as he should the great importance of a very strong sense of duty. I have every now and then to find fault with his lessons: he is approaching an age when it ought to be no longer necessary to speak on such a subject at all. I should in fact be glad to consent to his staying, if he shows a corresponding growth in manliness of character. I like him and I think well of him, but he must not stand still. I will not mention the subject to him if you do not wish it. yours faithfully, F. Temple."

The Vicar wrote a serious letter conveying the sense of this to Henry and one to Temple thanking him warmly. Henry also took it seriously, but Temple's next report on him, for the Half-Year ending Christmas 1858, saw no improvement. "*Wagner* is very defective in power of concentrating his attention, and wastes half his time and labour by allowing his mind to wander from what he is doing. . . . I am obliged perpetually to remind him not to whisper to his neighbour . . . He is a high-minded and conscientious youth and most desirous to do his duty; and most useful in my House in maintaining proper discipline and discouraging whatever is wrong. I do not think that he is at all aware how much this habit of inattention comes in his way."

Among the Vicar's friends was the vastly wealthy and charitable Miss Angela Burdett-Coutts (1814–1906), who in 1871 was created Baroness Burdett-Coutts. On the 12th of January 1859 the Vicar wrote to Dr. Temple that Henry was then staying with her at Torquay, but that on his return in a few days' time he would not fail "to impress upon his mind how wrong, nay how sinful, the inattention is, and the failure to profit by those rare advantages which he has under your auspices". He wrote Henry a long letter with extracts from earlier school reports by Goulburn and other masters, including Edward White Benson (1829–1896, Archbishop of Canterbury 1882), who wrote "He never does his best; he is quiet and well-ordered, but has fallen into a listless manner."

Henry answered on 23 January from Meadfoot House, "I can only say, and say with truth, though I know that appearances are against me, and that you don't believe it, that I have worked hard during the last half-year, not at my German alone but at my Classics also. Miss Coutts", he went on, "has been kind enough to ask, besides Joshua, an old school-fellow of mine whom she met at Rugby and likes very much, Sandford by name, who is now at Christ Church; just as he comes here, I can't leave him, a comparative stranger on their hands, or I should only be too glad to run home at once. Your letter has taken away all enjoyment of this. I can do my two hours here, and when I get home I'll work from morning till Night." Two days later he wrote again with further promises of amendment.

The friend was Ernest Gray Sandford (1839–1910), later Archdeacon of Exeter (*Burke's Landed Gentry*, 1972, p. 792), whose son Daniel (1882–1972), the friend and adviser of Emperor Haile Selassie of Ethiopia, was Henry Wagner's godson.

On the 2nd March 1859 the Warden of Merton wrote that he was unexpectedly able to offer a vacancy after Easter and requested Henry's attendance on the 23rd for the College examination. The Vicar regretted this curtailment of Henry's time at Rugby but decided that the chance could not be missed. Henry accordingly went up in May 1859, with an allowance of £200 per annum from his father, the same as his brother Joshua's.

While he was at Merton, from 1859 to 1862, his lifelong bent as a devoted and discriminating art collector came to the fore. He brought home from a visit to Italy a handsome marble mantlepiece of Venetian Gothic design, on which he had had carved his own arms, those of the University and those of the College. This he had fixed in his rooms at Merton without first seeking the permission of the College, for which he was nearly sent down. The authorities, however, relented and the mantlepiece remains in the rooms to this day.

He also commissioned two watercolour drawings of the room; one showing it without figures, the other (from the opposite end) with the figures (from coloured photographs) of himself and several friends. The latter was given by O. H. Wagner to the College and hangs in the room which it depicts. O. H. W. also gave the College an album of H.W.'s of signed photographs of his Oxford friends. In later years, as each died, Henry painted in a cross with the date and mounted on the opposite page a *Times* or other obituary notice.

Apparently at Miss Burdett-Coutts' suggestion the Vicar wrote on Henry's behalf to Sir Charles George Young, Garter King of Arms, to ask about the possibilities of an appointment at the College of Arms. The reply was kind but not encouraging and the matter was not pursued. The correspondence shows, however, that Henry had already the keen interest in genealogy, which lasted all his life. There is further evidence of this in a notebook entitled "Genealogical 'Notes & Queries' June 1862", in which he has made many entries of family and genealogical interest. At first his enquiries were concentrated upon families linked with his own. But a call paid on his distant cousin the architect William Milford Teulon, (p. 7, *supra*) in 1863 made him aware of the French Hospital of La Providence, the Huguenot almshouse, of which in 1865 he became a director[1] and so led to his interesting himself in the genealogies of the Huguenot refugee families in general. During the ensuing half century research into these took up much of his time. Articles and pedigrees by him dealing with them appeared in the *Transactions of the Huguenot Society*, the *Genealogist* and *Miscellanea Genealogica et Heraldica*. His extensive manuscript collections on these subjects were eventually given to the French Hospital whose directors have deposited them in the Goldsmiths' Library of University College, London. They are described in the Huguenot Society's *Proceedings* Vol. XIII 1926, No. 3.

The history of his own family is dealt with in a manuscript volume entitled:

The Family Book of Numbers

or

Family Memoranda

showing the descendants of the

Great-Grandfathers

of

Henry Michell Wagner

recorded by his son, H.W., F.S.A., up to 1892.

---

                                                         parentavit
Ejusdem filius min. nat. S.A.S. hunc librum   addidit

De te ipso res agitur.
Indocte discant et ament meminisse periti!
Scribuntur haec in generatione altera.   Os. C II. 18.

This enumeration shows in 1892–3
Of Melchior Wagner 133 descendants, *exclusive* of the Anthony Wagners, c. 30.
of Henry Godde   38 descendants, exclusive of the 65+30 Wagners, &c.
of John Michell   165 descendants, exclusive of the Wagners.
of Francis Reade   3 descendants, exclusive of the Michells, &c.

339
The thread that binds them is mine own.

For a' that, and a' that
All man to man the world o'er
Shall brothers be for a' that.

Novos parans amicos, ne obliviscere veterum.

Finding something through the whole
Beating — like a human soul.
Nascentes morimur finisque ab origine pendet.
For Family Circulation only.

1892.

γενεα πορεύεται καὶ γενεα ἔρχεταί

Che sara sara.

He further set out in tabular pedigree form the genealogies of these and other connected families, with full copies of monumental inscriptions on pages added to a specially bound and interleaved copy of *County Genealogies—Pedigrees of the Families in the County of Sussex;... By William Berry, Fifteen Years Registering Clerk in the College of Arms, London, ... 1830*: namely those of Webb, Pigot, Godde, Ashcroft, Harrison, Michell, Wagner, Coombe, Kershaw, Cumberbatch, Penfold, Paillet, Chassereau, Scrase, Byne and Bolney. Without his preservation, collection and recording of material the present book could not have been written. These interests were combined with his art collecting in his bringing together of family portraits, oils, drawings, miniatures and silhouettes, which over the years were given, sold or bequeathed to him by relations and others.

In 1875 he was elected a Fellow of the Society of Antiquaries. Forty years later it gave him pleasure to learn that a young cousin (A.R.W.), then seven years old was evincing the same spontaneous interest in genealogy and this he encouraged by the gift of his copy of H. B. George's *Genealogical Tables*. As a genealogist he was precise, scholarly and critical. His interests were wide and his knowledge of the Huguenot families, especially, was profound.

Henry Wagner had another interest, which he pursued with passion for half a century—mountain climbing in Switzerland. This was already well developed when a diary begins in which he recorded in some detail certain holidays he took abroad between 1868 and 1877. Between 2nd September and the 4th of October 1868 he was climbing in Switzerland. Between the 26th of July and 4th of October 1869 he was first climbing and walking in Switzerland and then travelling in north Italy, Bavaria and Austria. In 1870 and 1871 he records the bare fact of Alpine holidays without detail. In 1873 he gives a brief but interesting account of a visit to Oberammergau—evidently not his first—where the Passion Play, the people and the products of their craftsmanship became a great interest of his life; and in 1877 he narrates at some length travels mainly in Switzerland between the 5th of June and the 1st of October.

1868 gives the liveliest picture of his climbing, its discomforts, struggles and rewards. On the 2nd of September between Lausanne and Sion he "turned the talk in the train on the Matterhorn—the carriage knew all about the *3* ascents—there has been a 3rd by Mons. Thiolly(?) of Geneva from Zermatt down, on the Breuil side, & he himself told my informant the affair had cost him £500. They spoke strongly & rudely on Elliott's going and leaving only 100 F. to pay his 2 guides—& all joined in, insisting on the risk of life & that it deserved more—& it was no good representing the views of "*ce* Mons. Elliott". Slept with widely open windows, preferring the risk from malaria, to that from the drain-stinks, filling the house."

Next day he "Met several pleasant young fellows at breakfast, & h^d. there has just been a *4th* ascent of the Matterhorn by a party of 4." The discomforts, poor food and excessive charges at some inns contrast with admirable service at others. Henry suffered a good deal at times from fatigue, headaches and indigestion, but was never out of action for long. At St Luc there was a "thoroughly good little inn—good dinner, grapes, & muscat wine at F.1.50. *very* moderate withal, tho' not equalling Kandersteg, Frütigen or Chateau d'Oex." At the Col de Forclaz on the 16th of September, however, "I was heavily legged at the little Inn for a cold meat lunch—& the man, tho' I tipped him, was barely civil. Two French parties there joined with me in complaining of the wateriness of the wine—to wh. mine Host cooly replied that that was all that the Comte de Cambacéres had had to drink, save a petit verre de Kirsch, & yet it was said he lost his life through having drunk too much!"

Later on the 25th September he "lunched at Hotel de Mt Blanc—where I slept ages ago, when with Miss Coutts.[2] Found the Chatillons, mine host & hostess, very pleasant people. He pointed me out on the Col de Voza, or thereabouts, the chalets of Mr Urquhart (of Hummums celebrity)[3] his beau frère, Major Poole". There were interesting encounters. On the 7th of September "long pleasant talk with an Eton Master—one of the reformers—Oscar Browning. He proposing to go over the Lys Joch tomorrow to Gressonay. On the twelfth, after climbing Monte Rosa he found at the hotel Prince Arthur (1850–1942, third son of Queen Victoria, Duke of Connaught 1874), who "with Col. Elphinstone & Major Harrison dined at 6 at the table d'hote. Col. E. (who *15 years* since was up both the Jungfrau & Monte Rosa) wished to hear about guides, as Prince A. wished to go—and I lent them my Ball." On the 13th "The Chaplain never having come, Mr. Clayton did a short service—& asked me to hand the plate. Prince A. gave gold, & we got 71 F. for the Obergesteln fire."

Next day "En route, I was overtaken by 4 ladies in a chair, who were greatly alarmed at the 'precipices' & roughness of the road—& saw a constant need for walking little stretches—tho' the descent & ascents of their conveyance were not easy to manage sans a ladder—and they claimed my constant aid—but I reaped the reward of merit, in getting my 'knap' carried to St. Nicolaus—which I made by 2.30, being very thankful for my lunch, after my 7 o'cl. breakfast. Talking of the Simplon the young lady of the quartette begged me to try and assure the 3 old girls, her mother & aunts, that there were no dangers on that road—but I found I was talking to the winds. There was much talk of the outrages committed lately on travellers above Visp (who had rashly helped themselves to the grapes overhanging the road) by the watchers of the vineyards set by the Commune, who levied a blackmail on their own account. Prince A.'s party had been attacked & the story going was that the Queen had signified she shd. withdraw her subscr$^{n.}$ to the Fund at Visp for the injuries caused by the inundation unless these men were punished & checked."

It was after he came down from Oxford in 1862 and before the climbing diary started in 1868 that Henry was for about a year, apparently in 1865-6, Assistant Secretary to "a kind old friend", the very rich and philanthropic Miss Angela Burdett-Coutts (1814–1906), largely concerned with the administration of her extensive charities. For a part of the same year he also acted as secretary "to a very notable man, Sir James Brooke, Rajah of Sarawak" (1803–1868),[4] of whose friendship with Miss Burdett-Coutts, and her companion Mrs. Brown, Edna Healey has written in her recent life of the former.[5]

A close friendship with Miss Coutts (created Baroness Burdett-Coutts in 1871), continued until 1881, when her marriage, aged 66, to W. L. Ashmead Burdett-Coutts-Bartlett, aged 27, caused a breach with some of her old friends. Henry always remained attached to her and preserved letters and presents from her, but saw little of her thereafter.

For nearly fifty years he lived at 13 Half Moon Street, Piccadilly. When he came to live in London he soon formed the habit of attending Christie's, Sotheby's and other sale rooms. His detailed catalogue of his collections shows that he was buying as early as 1866 and by the time that he gave up the house it was so filled with them, and especially the pictures, that not only were the walls covered but pictures were screwed onto the doors. Besides the house in Half Moon Street he had a house at Brighton, 7 Belvedere Terrace, one of those built by his aunt Mary Ann Wagner on the plot of ground adjoining the new Vicarage. After his brother Arthur's death in 1902 he took upon himself the financial and personal burden of completing and supporting the family church and other charities in Brighton, especially St. Martin's Church. In 1921, his health failing, he settled at Brighton and decided to dispose of 13 Half Moon Street and most of his collections there. This, however, could not be done quickly. He had been a great preserver of letters and papers and his cousin O. H. Wagner (p. 158) spent many hours over three or four years sorting, destroying and making other arrangements as instructed.

The National Gallery, to which H.W. had made gifts since 1912, were given a choice of his pictures and in 1924 took twelve. The Alpine Club, of which he had lived to be the oldest member, was given watercolours by Elijah Walton. After this, on the 16th and 22nd of January 1925, most of his remaining pictures, drawings and armorial porcelain were sold at Christie's, fetching about four times what he had paid for them. This gratified him as an endorsement of his taste. In 1978 Mr. James Byam Shaw was so kind as to look through his catalogue of his collections and set down for me the following opinion:

Notes on Catalogues of the Collections of
Henry Wagner (1840–1926).

* * * *

I. *Paintings*

(a) *Presented to the National Gallery between 1912 and 1924.* These give a good idea of the character & quality of H.W.'s picture-collection. There are 13

Italians, four early Flemish and one German. They are all small, and include four fragments of one altarpiece. All the Italians are 14–15 c. Wagner's taste seems to have been rather like that of Walter Savage Landor—to judge from the collection left to Christ Church, Oxford, by Landor's nieces. But I think he was more selective than Landor—only one of the pictures given to the N.G. (no. 2863, now catalogued as a near-contemporary copy of Benozzo Gozzoli) is recorded in Davies's catalogue (Early Italian Schools) as in bad condition.

Of the Italians, the most important are the predella-piece of the *Deposition*, and three other fragments of the S. Croce altar-piece by Ugolino da Siena (nos. 3375–8), of which other fragments were already in the N.G. The *Deposition* is particularly fine, but has been lately cleaned. Apart from these, the most valuable gift (by modern standards) was the exquisite little *Elsheimer* on copper. The *Baptism of Christ*—A smaller painting by E., part of a small altar-piece in the Frankfurt Gallery fetched over £50,000 lately in a Sale at Bonham's in London.

With the other paintings given to the N.G. in 1919 was a mosaic fragment, described as 12th c. Roman, which has been on loan to the V. & A. since 1953. It was published in *Burlington Magazine* XXXV, 1919, p. 72.

(b) *Paintings sold from his Collection, 1925.* There was one more painting in the N.G., which was sold by H. W. in 1925 and was presented by Lord Rothermere in 1926—*The Baptism of Christ* (N.G. n. 4208), formerly called Cavallini, now catalogued as Florentine School, 2nd half XIV c. (Davies cat., 1961 ed., p. 192).

Other paintings that sound interesting, but were sold in 1925, were attributed to *Taddeo di Bartolo* (catalogue p. 2) and *Michael Pacher* (cat. p. 13).

Wagner evidently bought at many of the best sales in England—the Ugolino fragments and the *Baptism of Christ* (see above) came from the Rev. John Fuller Russell sale 1885; he also bought at the sales of Wynn Ellis 1876, C. S. Bale 1881 and Charles Butler 1911—all very well known collectors. He does not seem to have given high prices—the highest I have noticed is 195 gns. for the so-called *Benozzo* (N.G. no 2863) at the William Graham Sale (also a famous collection), 1886.

II. *Drawings*

Whereas the paintings in the collection seem to have been nearly all early—the Italians at any rate—the drawings were of all schools and dates. Many of these, according to Sotheby's sale catalogue of 12 Dec. 1928, had the marks of famous collections: Lely, Richardson, Marietta, Reynolds, Spencer, Lawrence etc.— drawings by or attributed to Parmigianino, Claude, Murillo, Guercino, van Dyck. That they did not fetch high prices in that sale does not necessarily mean that they were not by the artists named—high prices for drawings were not common in 1928.

I should like to trace the early Florentine, *Burial of the Virgin* which fetched £62 in that sale. Other interesting-sounding drawings in the collection are:

Cat. p. 57. Dragon and Lizard, attr. to *Dürer*—There is a photograph of this in the Witt Library—it looks good, but more than half a century later than Dürer somewhat in the manner of J. de Gheyn II.

Cat. p. 71. Drawing (portraits of ladies) by *Ottavio Leoni*, bought 1866 for 14s. 0d., sold 1925 for 28 gns. much sought after nowadays.

Cat. p. 74b. *Raphael* Angels & Sibyl.

Cat. no. 206. *G. Terbor*. Portrait of Constantine Huygens.

Among the drawings are many of the XIX c., from Wilkie onwards—Sir Charles Eastlake, G. F. Robson, John Leech, Richard Doyle and many modern Sussex artists—also some Germans of the same time.—All very popular nowadays. I have hardly traced any of the drawings sold—But the fine Head of a Man by *Lorenzo Lotto* which was bought from the collection by Archibald Russell, and sold at the Russell sale for a high price, is now in the Seilern Collection; see catalogue of *Italian Paintings & Drawings at 56 Princes Gate*, 1959, no. 90 and Pl. XLVII.

(Count Antoine Seilern, the collector, died on July 6 this year, and his collection, which is a very fine one, is bequeathed to the Courtauld Institute of Art. I have written his obituary notice for the November *Burlington Mag.*).

III. *Other Works of Art*

I am hardly qualified to judge these from the catalogue descriptions, but it is evident that Henry Wagner was a compulsive collector of every sort of "antique"—wood-carvings, ivories, cameos, ceramics, enamels, glass, gems, everything that collectors value. The miniatures sound interesting particularly. There seems to have been a complete (?) collection of *Arundel Prints* collected again, nowadays, but these, I gather, were dispersed. I expect some of the early photographs would also be exhibitors pieces.

J.B.S.
Sept. 1978.

*   *   *   *

Henry Wagner died at Brighton in 1926 and many thousands who remembered the benefactions of his family came to witness his funeral. All his life he had lived very simply giving much of his large income to charities and leaving £40,000 to charities in his will.

In his later years he had by stages in effect adopted as a son his cousin Orlando Henry Wagner (1867–1956), the great-grandson of his great-uncle Anthony Wagner. The next chapter will say something of the breach between the two branches of the family and how it came to be healed. In the last decade of his life, especially, Henry leant ever more heavily on Orlando, making him the agent of his wide charitable interests in Brighton and elsewhere and the prop of his old age in countless ways.

Chapter VII

THE LATER WAGNERS

WITH THE DEATH of Malcolm Wagner in 1933 the male line of Melchior Henry Wagner (1749–1811) expired and the only remaining Wagner male progeny of Melchior (1685–1764), who came to England about 1709, were the descendants of Anthony Wagner (1770–1847), M.H.W.'s youngest brother. Between him and the widow and children of M.H.W. there was a breach of relations for what Henry Wagner thought "not insufficient reasons",[1] but he gives only hints of what these were. In a margin of a pedigree, written probably in his Oxford days, and so expressing, perhaps, parental discouragement of genealogical enquiries in that direction, he noted: "N.B. for a warning against any renewal of acquaintance with the above-mentioned portion of our kith and kin, that my great-uncle, Anthony W., having behaved ill in many various ways—(having amongst other misdemeanours, got into his possession the family plate, sold it entirely, and appropriated the proceeds—and at length insulted his widowed sister-in-law, my grandmother, was (altho' he got his portion of the inheritance from my great-grandfather) cut by his family *in toto*, after wh. he further evinced his low tastes by marrying a woman of the humblest class, and of no education—one of his daughters I believe to have married a respectable Ironmonger, named Williamson, in London: the others probably to have done *less* well for themselves."

When H.W. wrote this he did not know that some half century later he himself would virtually adopt as a son one of this despised great-uncle's descendants. It is a pity we have only one side of the story, which bears some traces of exaggeration. The "ironmonger", for example, was a Civil Engineer. Clearly, however, there had been deep animosity.

Elsewhere H.W. wrote that Anthony's sister, Mary Wagner (1774–1852, p. 17) "had conceived a prejudice" against her sister in law, Mrs. M. H. Wagner, "probably owing to the representations of her brother Anthony, with whom she had been thick". But on the death of their mother, Mrs. George Wagner, in 1808, "she, like the rest of the family, broke with him, and she then shewed his letters, wh. were very bad & *untrue*" to her brother Melchior Henry and his wife. "At the reading of the will, when it came out that Mrs. G. Wagner had only left", Mrs. M. H. Wagner "the Family Bible—that wh. now lies in the Drawing-room—having no doubt been primed by Anthony, who apparently thought others like himself, to believe that my grandmother [Mrs. M.H.W.] wld take care to have a hand in the making of the will, she was much astonished—and not being accustomed to mince matters, said to her brother before the assembled family 'Anthony, you shd. have left the Bible to yourself, for you had much more need of it than Mrs. Wagner—'.[2] Whatever had gone before, this scene in itself might cause some want of cordiality. Anthony Wagner and his family make only brief appearances in Mrs. M. H. Wagner's diary. On 26 November 1828 in London she "Met Mr. Anthony Wagner", but whether by accident or arrangement is not said. On 5 January 1827 in Pall Mall "Mr. J. Anderson & Thomas Wagner & Mr. Hughes called". On 19 May 1829 at Brighton "Mr. A.W.'s 2 sons were here". On 26 May 1830 she "Wrote 6 letters in behalf of Nephew Anth^y" and on 11 Nov. 1830 she had a "lre from Mr. A. Wagner—on the subject of Br. George giving up the living: Mary was so good as to answer it—". On 20 January 1831, having come to Pall Mall in a coach from George Wagner's at Fulham, she "Went in a Coach to Palmers, & left Fulham acc^t book, my acct book & Drummonds book for inspection of Sister John, Miss M. & Mrs. A. Wagner to whom Mr. P. sent Circulars to inspect the books on Monday next.—Went from them to Br & Sister John & passed the day there most agreeably. Br. J. thro' Marg't presented Mary & me with a book; Mr. M. Attree Mr. T. Wagner & Nephew's Eardley & Mr. Best call'd whilst we were there.—Did not get home from Fulham 'till ½ past 10". This must refer to a joint family financial arrangement for the benefit of the Rev. George Wagner, the Rector of Mursley, resident not there but in Elysium Row, Fulham, one, it would seem, of those mildly incompetent, amiable characters, for whom others have to put themselves out and forget for the moment their mutual animosities. On 8 August 1831 there was a "lre from Henry, wrote on one from Br. Anthony, satisfactory with respect to Br. G's affairs". On 19 June 1834 Mrs. Wagner "Wrote 10 lrs to solicit Office of Secretary to St. Ann's Society Schools Brixton Hill & Aldersgate for Mr. Thos. Wagner".

Anthony Wagner was twenty years younger than his brother Melchior and had been at Westminster School from 1779 to 1786. On the 19th of April 1791 he was admitted a member of Staple Inn and an attorney at law in Chancery. At this time he was living with his parents in Duke Street (p. 12). On the 9th of April 1799 he was again admitted to Staple Inn. Just a month after his mother's death in 1808, being then aged 37, he married at St. George's, Hanover Square— "beneath him", according to Henry Wagner[3]—Sarah Harby (1783-1838), who came from Stathern, Leicestershire, a parish in the Duke of Rutland's neighbourhood, where the poet George Crabbe was curate in 1785. Her father's occupation has not been traced, but her grandfathers were a blacksmith and a hemp-dresser and her more remote ancestors husbandmen and yeomen. In the nineteenth century Harbys probably akin to her were in service at Belvoir Castle. Malcolm Wagner had a notion that her father Thomas Harby kept tea gardens— which has the right disreputable flavour for the period.

Anthony Wagner lived for many years and practised as an attorney at 35 Grosvenor Row, as a tenant of the Grosvenor Estate, in what is now a part of the Pimlico Road. He was a member of the original committee of the British and Foreign Bible Society from 1804 to 1809 and his name appears as such next to that of William Wilberforce on a table which used to be visible just inside the door of the Society's building in Queen Victoria Street. He was a collector on the Society's headquarters staff for 27 years. He was also a sidesman at St. George's, Hanover Square. Besides a son and a daughter who died in infancy Anthony and Sarah Wagner had five sons and two daughters. Anthony Mitchell Wagner (1808-1839), the eldest, was a Doctor of Medicine, surgeon and apothecary of Lincoln's Inn and 4 Bishop's Court, Chancery Lane. In H.W.'s words he "was respectable but died young". A letter from him to his father dated 28 November 1838 and letters from him and about him to his brother Melchior dated in 1839 were lent to Sir Anthony Wagner by the Stepney Borough Library in March 1961.

Feby 18th 1839

Dear Melchior

If Mr. Sampson should be coming to Chelsea as I think you said was likely ask him to be good enough to bring me two or three poppy heads and a little Gum Arabic.

I enclose you the rec^{t.} It appears there are three quarters rent due from Pocock up to Christmas last. I think I mentioned to you on a former occasion I had a Clothes Brush realy new which is not to be left at the Dispensary and some other things. As the Postman has been here about the Letter I wrote to you containing the Proxies If you have not destroyed it be good enough to send it by Mr. Sampson or other [words indecipherable crossed out] opportunity.

Believe me

Your Affectionate Sister
(Signed) E. L. WAGNER
for A. M. Wagner &c.

[Endorsed on back]

Mr. Wagner
at Price's
48 Chancery Lane.

A letter from E.L.W. for A.W. Junr. respectg. Pococks Rent Stepney house 3 quars. due at Xmas 1838.

[In different hand and ink—Letter Acknowledg £5. Novr. 28 1838].

from Doctor at Hastings   Wednesday 28 November
Dear Father,

Nine or ten days having elapsed since I wrote you, I suppose you will expect to hear of some advancement towards recovery: I believe I do improve but it is certainly very slowly. This is another wet day and I cannot in consequence stir out— it is very stormy, & the sea roars with great violence: yesterday the chimney smoked so as almost to suffocate one—they say all the houses in Hastings are so annoyed. There are certainly nuisances enough of all descriptions in Hastings and it is a most wretched place to live in especially alone. I think of returning to Town on Monday or Tuesday week but have not quite made up my mind—it may be before: I shall however write to Melchior before I return though you will most likely not hear from me again whilst I remain here. I am sorry to say the power of reading improves very little with me and my feet continue to swell. The weather has been unfavourable and I have not known what to do with myself so that I have tried to sleep in the day & have sometimes gone to bed soon after nine o'Clock & remained there 12 hours, which may not have done me any good—but I could not do otherwise. I have not seen Mr. Wallace about since Betsey left Hastings—I don't know if he has returned to London or whether he is confined to the house. Hastings is said to be very full; there are certainly sometimes a great many people about. I don't know what I shall do with regard to the Dispensary; they seem to be dissatisfied at my absence—being quite out of the way of all news I dont know whether they have taken any steps for the election of a Secretary or not—however I shall be at the next committee unless I am worse: indeed if it were not for that I should not come up to Town. What I shall do about getting away again will be a matter of difficulty for I shall not be fit to remain in Town by that time: but I suppose I must wait & let things take their course.

Thursday Morning 29th.—I resume my pen not having finished last night in time for the post—I have received this morning a letter from Melchior enclosing £5 0s. 0d./4 which he desired to have acknowledged: I need not send him a separate Letter for that purpose if you will be good enough to tell him it arrived safely. He says the weather has been very severe with you—we have not had any frost, though the winds have been high: this house shook last night which was very stormy—the waves breaking over the parade (they say) and a hundred yards of the new parade at St. Leonards having been quite carried away. The fishing boats are all in—two boats expected from London with goods for the Tradesmen are said to be seen in the Channel but cannot get in. Believe me to remain

Yours very affectionately
(Signed A. M. WAGNER)

[Endorsed on back]
A. Wagner Esqr
35 Grosvenor Row,
Pimlico,
LONDON.

Pray remember me to Brothers & Sisters—Tell Betsy this weather will fatten the shell-fish on the Rocks which she was so fond of. a chimney or two down though Hastings is so sheltered a place. I think I have already mentioned that I shall write to Melchior before I return—unless I hear from Town I shall not probably write any other letters except that to him next week perhaps.

Dear Melchior;

I lose not a moment in writing you. I have just engaged a lodging No. 4 Parade —returning to the Swan Hotel when I write I was accosted by a Lady who said she had met me at Mr. Shinn's, she knew my name & I was glad to learn from her that Tom Shinn was better & about to resume Business—but after all confound ye if I know who she was.

I believe the woman's name is Balls where I have taken Lodgings. This Hotel is a very miserable one to what it used to be: if ever you travel don't put up here.

As to myself I [sic] my Cold is very severe & my cough has not allowed me to sleep at night—my condition is truly miserable the violence of the cough caused my heart to go all wrong and beside preventing me sleeping at night hinders other people in the adjoining Rooms: so that in the middle of the night the [sic] set to thumping the wall in positive Rage—how can I help it? it is not my fault— if any are to blame my family are they.

When you write me you can perhaps enclose me an acct. of the auction in a frank if Mr. Taylor can oblige me by procuring one—else it must cost a parcel which should be got from the borough (not from Piccadilly)—if by frank care should be taken not to exceed the weight, else the M.P. franking has to pay.— I don't wish anyone to be possessed of my address here unless Mr. Thedden asks for it, of course your father will be made acquainted with it by yourself—or if Mr. Sampson wishes let him know but give strict charge not to publish it—I can't afford so many postages as I had last time to pay. Powel's letters alone cost me near 10s. 0d. Tell him you will enclose his letter if he wants to know where to send & then direct it to me if of sufficient importance. If you could let me have the second list of things to be sold before auction takes place I could mark out what should be retained if anything is worthy of distinction. My compts. to Powel Taylor Sampson & other friends—the latter will render you any aid he can I have no doubt. Remember me to my Father & sisters & to yourself—you may also to Wm. but he is a very selfish lump of Earth (so will I be in future) if you write to Alexr. advise him homewards tell him I think he is much to blame not to return from a place where the dangers are not seen by those who inhabit it— but are visible to those at a distance. You will not forget my Boxes to Chelsea except one to your own place—Pictures & prints to Pollocks as well as some parcels of family Physic^n Reports & what loose Books may need place—I forgot to give Mr. Sampson some french Books I promised him but must select some from the bought in lots when I return. I think I gave you a list of debits to me including Powell 19s. 6d. & burn for waste paper 2s. 6d. I dare say I have much more to write on but I am quite confused & bewildered I cannot think of any more.

Believe me then yours very truly,
(Signed) A. M. WAGNER.

Endorsed on back

19 January   No. 1
Melchior Wagner Esquire,
Chancery Chambers
Quality Court
(London)   Chancery Lane.

Letter from the Doctor at Hastings [in different writing & ink]

Directing Goods to be sent to Chelsea & pollocks &c. &c.
19 Jany. 1839.

There were some bills to go to the next meeting of the committ. or any other meeting of Governors. Mr. Sampson will attend to that if you mention it—& he will also pay my Bill at Apothecaries Hall if you give him the Cash a very few shillings—the samallest bill on their Books I'll be bound for't. The bill will be sent in—My writing desk should go to Chelsea & be taken great care of for it contains papers of very great consequence & all my accounts of any importance besides other things.

In his will (proved P.C.C. 4 April 1839) he made a bequest to John James Powell (1809–1890), a fellow surgeon, whose sister Catherine had in 1834 married his brother Thomas.

This Thomas Jepson Wagner (1810–1864) and his brother Melchior George (1812–1873) were both attorneys though Melchior never practised. Both were

[in pencil] I did not mean to leave my honey behind. You need not sent till I write again unless you get a frank.

said by Mollie Wagner (p. 153) to have been in love with Catherine Powell and her marriage to Thomas led to a quarrel between them. Melchior was prosperous and settling in Jersey, at the Maisonette la Chasse, St. Helier, eventually married (privately, it seems) about 1864 his housekeeper, Harriett Ann May. She after his death married again, becoming Mrs. Edward Helsham. On her death about 1905 what she had was divided between Melchior's nephews and nieces excepting the children of Thomas.

Catherine Powell's ancestry was not without interest. Her great-grandfather James Powell (1708-1777) came from Devynock near Brecon to Jesus College, Oxford, and taking holy orders became in 1739 Rector of Church Lawford, Warwickshire, where his son and namesake later succeeded him. Through his mother Sarah Williams, of the Abercamlais family, the elder James had descents from both the native and the Norman descended gentry of Brecknock and ultimately from Welsh princes, including Owen Glendower.[4] His own marriage to Letitia Wilcox of Brandon and Wolston, Warwickshire, brought in further interesting descents.

Anthony and Sarah Wagner had two younger sons who married and left issue, Alexander Hewgill Wagner (1814-1886) and William Alfred Wagner (1817-1890), two daughters who both, oddly married husbands with alliterative names[5] Welburn Wilkes Williamson (1818-?) and William Wallyer Walkyier, a postmaster, by whom they left issue, and a son and daughter who died young, John (1817-18) and Mary Wilhelmina (1824-6).

The godparents of children often give some indication of the parents' family and social links and standing. Those of Anthony Wagner's children include his sister Louisa (1810 and 1818), his brother the Rev. George W. (1812), his wife Sarah (1824), his son Anthony Mitchell Wagner (1824), relations of his wife, John Mitchell (1809 and 1816), Alexander Mitchell (1809, 1814 and 1816), Margaret Mitchell (1809), Mrs. Mitchell (1814, 1816 and 1822), Mrs. Elizabeth Mitchell (1824), Hannah Harby (1812 and 1819) and friends Thomas Whipham (1810), the Rev. Graham Jepson (1810), Culpepper Conant, Esq., of Mortlake (1812), the Rev. Francis Hewgill (1814), William Alfred Gould, Esq. (1818), Benjamin Shinn, Esq. (1818), Mrs. Shinn (1819), William Skeat, Esq. (1819), John Fisher, Esq. (1822) and Mrs. Carter (1822). The eldest son, Anthony Mitchell Wagner, was born at Kennington (possibly his mother's home), the next seven children at Chelsea (Grosvenor Row) and the youngest at Brighton. John, who died young in 1818, was buried at All Saints, Hastings. Mary Wilhelmina in 1826, Sarah (Harby) Wagner in 1838 and the eldest son Anthony Mitchell in 1839 were buried at South Audley Street Chapel. Thomas in 1834, Sarah in 1841 and Elizabeth in 1844 were married at St. George's Hanover Square. The elder son in law, Welburn Wilkes Williamson, the engineer or "ironmonger", was born in 1818 at New Malton, Yorkshire, of a family from Beverley and Hull. The birthplaces of his children show him (or his wife) in 1841 at his father in law's, 35 Grosvenor Row, and in 1843 and 1849 at No. 31, hard by. In 1845 and 1847 he must have been working on the construction of the Great Western Railway, for children were born at the Knapp, Minchinhampton, and High Street, New Swindon, respectively. Four more children were born successively in 1852, 1854, 1856 and 1858, at Camden Town, 2 High Street, Bloomsbury and Watford, and the last two at 133 High Holborn. At least one son and three daughters left children, who seem to have remained in the middle class. A daughter Charlotte Antonia (b. 1856) married her cousin Edward Williamson and a Scotland Yard detective, Maurice Moser, after whose death she was in business as a 'detective expert' at 37 and 38 Strand and sent Henry Wagner her card. Her younger sister Ada Catherine Wilhelmina (b. 1863) later married the cousin Edward Williamson and had a daughter, Edna Ada (b. 1900). In the 1920's O. H. Wagner (1867–1956) repaired the tomb of Anthony Wagner (1770–1847) in Fulham church yard, whereupon he received a letter from Edna Williamson, of whose existence he had been unaware, explaining that she too was Anthony's great-granddaughter, was living with her father at 16 Edenhurst Avenue, Hurlingham, and possessed portraits of Anthony Wagner (1770–1847) and his son Anthony Mitchell Wagner (1808–1839). These she ultimately bequeathed to him (see also p. 154).

Anthony's other married daughter, Elizabeth Louisa Walkyier, who lived at Sandown Isle of Wight, had four sons and six daughters, some of whom left descendants, two named alliteratively and respectively Wallyer Wagner Walkyier and William Wagner Walkyier (b. 1894). One daughter with her husband settled in Sardinia, another in Western Australia. One grandson, a chemist, lived in Hackney in 1940.

Of Anthony Wagner's sons the most obscure fate is that of the youngest, William Alfred (1818–1890) of whom kinsmen, who had more or less vague knowledge of his brother and sisters and their offspring, had absolutely no tradition. He married Julia Maria Field and was a wood engraver. He was living at 5 White Hart Row, St. Pancras when their son, Anthony Thomas, was born on the 14th of October 1847, and died at 6 Cressingham Road, Lewisham, on the 5th of December 1890. His widow appeared among the beneficiaries on the death of Mrs. Helsham, the widow of Melchior George Wagner. She died at Dartford, Kent on the 3rd of May 1911.

To discover, if possible, the fate of the son Anthony Thomas Wagner a search was made in 1931 at Somerset House in the General Register of Deaths. This brought to light a record of the death at Dartford, Kent, on the 19th of January 1927 of one Anthony Wagner, aged 79, general labourer of 14 London Road, Crayford, who seemed in all probability to be the same man. The information had been given by certificate from Mr. H. B. Sewell, Coroner for Kent, who had held an inquest on the 24th of January. Mr. Sewell replied as follows to a letter of enquiry:

"I have looked up my record of the Inquest held by me on the above named deceased whose age was given as 79 years and his address 14 London Road Crayford. The deceased was found dying in the street and he was identified by William Churchill, a Boot Repairer of the same address, with whom the deceased lodged. Mr. Churchill stated he had known deceased about 14 years and that he had no relatives."

A letter to Mr. Churchill brought no reply. One is reminded of a passage in one of George Gissing's novels (*The Town Traveller*, 2nd ed. 1898, pp. 47–8):[6]

"I couldn't help thinking to-day what a strange assembly there would be if all a man's relatives came to his funeral. Nearly all of us must have such lots of distant connections that we know nothing about . . . It's a theory of mine . . . that every one of us, however poor, has some wealthy relative, if he could only be found. I mean a relative within reasonable limits, not a cousin fifty times removed. That's one of the charms of London to me. A little old man used to cobble my boots for me a few years ago in Ball's Pond Road. He had an idea that one of his brothers, who went out to New Zealand and was no more heard of, had made a great fortune; said he'd dreamt about it again and again, and couldn't get rid of the fancy. Well, now, the house in which he lived took fire, and the poor old chap was burnt in his bed, and so his name got into the newspapers. A day or two after I heard that his brother—the one he spoke of—had been living for some years scarcely a mile away, at Stoke Newington—a man rolling in money, and director of the British and Colonial Bank."

Anthony Thomas Wagner (if it were he) had a rich second cousin Henry Wagner, who had died in April 1926, a first cousin in Cardiff (Ada Richardson), who survived him, and a first cousin once removed, Orlando Wagner, living within a few miles of him. None of them had known of his existence.

Next in age of the sons of Anthony Wagner (1770-1847) above William Alfred was Alexander Hewgill Wagner (1814-1886), who, like his eldest brother A.M.W., studied medicine. He was about to leave for study in Germany, when he heard of William Lyon Mackenzie's rebellion in Canada in 1837. Moved by this he went to Canada in 1838 and was working in a store in London, Ontario, when in 1855 he was able to purchase for $500 the postmastership of Windsor, Ontario, which he held for many years and in which his daughter Mary Antonia (1855-1945) followed him. He had married in 1846 Isabel Sarah Cousins, a Roman Catholic (of Scottish descent), and his children were brought up in that faith.

Between 1927 and 1944 Mollie Wagner (Mary Antonia) wrote many letters to English cousins, whom she never met, O.H.W. and A.R.W. Though she never left North America, she was attached through life to her English family and origins and thus became a channel of information and tradition between kinsmen unknown to one another. Her letters are unstudied but vigorously expressive of a strongly individual personality. Her grandfather Anthony Wagner (1770-1847), she wrote (25 June 1929), "was a terrible cross old man, he would not allow them out without his permission so they had a hard time of it". His son (her father) Alexander Hewgill Wagner (1814-1886), "a very silent independent man", quarrelled with his father and emigrated probably largely for that reason. He was on affectionate terms with his mother (Sarah, née Harby) and inherited something on her death, but nothing from his father. After his father's death A.H.W. visited England, with his wife, who was then told by her husband's sisters Sarah Williamson and Bessie Walkyier family tales "of all the trouble, never learned from him". When A.H.W. and his wife returned to Canada, his sisters kept up correspondence, but Bessie Walkyier later had family troubles and dropped it. Sarah Williamson, however, went on writing till her death in 1875.

She too, however, had written less often than she would have wished. Mollie preserved and eventually sent to O.H.W. this letter from her to her brother.

High Holborn
Febry 1st 1873.

My dear Alex.

...I am sorry to have to inform you of the death of poor Melchoir [sic]. He resided at Jersey of later years—& as I suppose he has told you he got married at Jersey—Therefore he has left a widow—to whom he leaves everything for life & then to his brothers and sisters—Mr. Williamson & myself went to Jersey but were to[o] late to see him alive through the bad weather but we stayed to the funeral. We were the only relatives there. I thought Mr. Cowlard would inform all his relations—but I find he did not write to my brother William so probably he has not written to you.

I must also tell you of the death of Mr Walkyier. He died last summer & I suppose poor Bessie has not written to tell you. She has a grown up son capable of managing for her.

I have not been able to write as often as I would have wished of late years—but will do so in future. I have had a great deal of trouble in my family so that must be my excuse.

My dear Brother
Yours affectionately
S. WILLIAMSON

Write soon.

He did, and kept a draft.

1 March '73

My dear Sarah,

I received your kind letter yesterday. It brings the melancholy news of the death of poor Melchior, as also that of poor Walkyier. I was not aware that Mel was married but that being the case, he did perfectly right in leaving his property to his widow.
You talk about troubles. I hope you will never have to go through a quarter of what I have had to do.

Your affectionate brother
A.H.W.

P.S. Mrs Wagner or Fid, or perhaps both will write to you after you answer this.

Shortly after this A.H.W. had an unexpected letter on black edged paper from his 17 year old niece Charlotte Antonia Williamson (later Mrs Moser).

High Holborn
London Mar. 29th.

My dear Uncle

Perhaps you may be rather surprised at receiving a letter from one who when you were in London was one of the very VERY little "Ws" or perhaps was not in existence at all—however as I have since that time grown into ONE of the BIG Ws I trust there will be no precosicty [sic] in my addressing a letter to you.

I daresay poor Uncle Melchior's death rather surprised you? it did us as he had written to Mama but a few days before asking her & Papa to his house— Three or four days after Mama received a letter from Aunt saying he was very ill & asking her to go to Jersey immediatly [sic] which she did but as the boat in which she crossed from Southampton to Jersey was delayed in the Channel by bad weather Mama did not arrive until after his death which took place on the evening of Sunday January 19*th* about 10 o'clock—he was buried on the following Wednesday & Mama returned home Thursday night—

Aunt of course had to come to London to see something about the will & as she was here over three weeks we saw a great deal of her & we all like her very much you see we could hardly judge before as we had only seen her twice & they were both very short visits—

What a strange thing it seems Uncle that you did not know poor Uncle Melchior had a wife when he has been married over nine years but as I was telling Mama none of you are very communicative— Now are you?

I suppose you remember the paintings of Uncle Anthony Grandpapa & Great Grandpa? Well a long time ago Uncle promised them to Mama—so Aunt has now sent them. I think Uncle, if all of you resembled Uncle Anthony you Must have been *very* handsome but Mama does not seem to think so & says she "always thought Alex & William the best".

With very best love from ALL to yourself—Aunt & all cousins (I don't know the number)

Believe me
Your affectionate niece
CHARLOTTE A. WILLIAMSON.

P.S. *Our* number is *ten* the same as Aunt Bessie.

A.H.W.'s children "were a loving family all held together we four girls", wrote Mollie, "did not separate none would marry to leave the others. The two older girls broke their engagements to remain at home, with the younger ones. All lived such nice happy lives together in contentment". This she contrasts with the troubles and disunion of the Williamson cousins, whose lives she could not understand, nor why they "all seemed to go down" (6 August 1930). When Uncle Mel's widow died (in 1905), Charlotte Antonia Williamson (Mrs. Moser) wished to run the administration of the legacies and suggested that Mollie should give her a power of attorney. O. H. Wagner (1843-1909). however, advised her against this and she did not reply.

Cousin Henry Wagner (1840-1926) had advised after Uncle Mel died and wrote her nice letters for many years. Mrs. Moser once told her he was very rich, "and when I wrote him I was very cautious not to let him know as he perhaps would have thought I was after his money" (6 Aug. 1930). Mollie's brother Eugene was the only one of her family to marry. He settled in Kansas City and left a son Chester Wagner, living there in 1942, subsequent fate unknown. Mollie had never seen him. She had cousins on her mother's side, however, who valued and cared for her. Mrs. Edwin J. (Geraldine Ouellette) Parrock of 4129 Roland Avenue, Baltimore, who went to see her in 1944 and wrote about it to O.H.W., was a granddaughter of her mother's sister.

The eldest son of Anthony Wagner (1770-1847) to marry and leave issue was

Thomas Jepson Wagner (1810–1864). Like his father and his brother Melchior he was an attorney, admitted in King's Bench Trinity 1831, in Chancery 14 May 1832, in Exchequer Easter 1832, and in Queen's Bench (again) Hilary 1842. He practised first at 6 New Inn, Wych Street, Strand, but in 1834 was of 1 Union Place, Pimlico. On 9 October 1834 he married Catherine Powell p. 151) at St. George's, Hanover Square and by 1837 had moved to Abingdon, Berkshire, where he was managing clerk to Messrs. Frankham, solicitors. On the 11th of April 1838 he addressed a letter to his elder brother Anthony Mitchell Wagner from Wellington Place, Northampton, evidently on receiving the news of his mother's death and revealing an unhappy situation.

"I received your letter this morning and altho' I was aware of the illness of my poor mother I was in no way prepared for this melancholy event but on the contrary expected to hear of her restoration to health. I cannot but feel that I might have had an opportunity afforded me of seeing her before her death, especially when I am told 'I have insisted on severing myself from my family and friends' in spite of your entreaties and the solicitation of others. You must really have forgotten your letter to me forbidding me seeing my father and mother when you wrote. This remark is called forth from me by the tenor of your letter. It is the last time I shall refer to anything that is past as is it now and always has been my wish to be on proper and friendly terms with my own family. I have done all in my power both by my own exertions and through the kind offices of Mr. Taylor to establish that good feeling and understanding which ought to exist among us /and which I am extremely sorry should ever have broken/ but on all occasions I have met with a repulse. The only alternative therefore left me was to withdraw myself to the place where your letter has found me. It is my particular wish that all that has passed should be forgiven and that for the future such a feeling as ought to exist between brothers may be established between us. I shall write to my father tonight altho' I really feel to [sic] ill for the task.

I remain your affecte brother

T. J. Wagner

must rely on your keeping my address secret.

This original letter was bought from a dealer, Edward Hall of 16, Old West Road, Gravesend, by A. R. Wagner in 1961 through the good offices of Mr. P. I. King, County Archivist of Northampton. It is addressed to A. M. Wagner Esq., 4 Bishop's Court Chancery Lane, London.

T.J.W.'s eldest son Albert Charles (d. 1911) was born at Abingdon and was baptised at St. Helen's Church there on 13 September 1838. A daughter Isabella Louisa was born at Abingdon in 1839 and a second son, Arthur George, in 1840, who died at Abingdon in April 1842. The next year Thomas moved to Oxford where he lived at 26 Pembroke Street, in St. Ebbe's parish, close to Pembroke College. He set up in practice on his own account and in 1922 his daughter Isabella (Mrs. Riddle) told her nephew O.H.W. that he had soon a flourishing business. Here in 1843 another son was born and was named Orlando Henry for a reason never explained by him to his own son, but divulged to that son many years later by his aunt Isabella (1839–1925). In 1844 a horse named Running

Rein won the Derby—or was thought to have done so until Lord George Bentinck satisfied the Stewards of the Jockey Club that Running Rein was in fact a four year old named Maccabaeus and so not qualified to run. The Epsom stewards thereupon declared the second horse to be the winner. This was Orlando, the property of General Jonathan Peel (1799-1879), brother of Sir Robert Peel.[7] Great was the joy of Orlando's backers, and among them T.J.W., whose son was named accordingly. By a coincidence not noticed for some time after, O.H.W.'s grandson A.R.W. married in 1953 Jonathan Peel's great-great-granddaughter Gillian Graham.

An attractive miniature, which passed to his eldest son Albert and thence to his son Charles of Brooklyn, shows T.J.W. against a background of Oxford spires. Charles sent it to O.H.W. in England about 1932. It was photographed and returned, but by 1939 Charles had removed himself and its whereabouts is not at present known. In 1845 another son, Montagu St. Clair, had been born at 26 Pembroke Street and was baptised at St. Ebbe's on the 20th of February 1846. This child died, however, in 1854 and this, according to Isabella Riddle, bowled over his father whose favourite he was. Thomas's grief "was such that he took to drink and his business steadily declined. With a view to making a fresh start he left Oxford for a partnership in a firm at Bristol. Unfortunately he had undermined his health and after a few months at Bristol he had a stroke which led to softening of the brain and complete inability to work". His younger daughter Ada (Mrs. Richardson) said in 1928 that the move to 4 Lower Ashley Road Bristol took place in 1859, but the stroke, which left him stone deaf, not till 1861. In 1863 his wife died. His younger daughter Ada, who looked after him at the end said that she remembered him before his stroke as a very nice, kind man, and her mother, who had gone through a great deal, as sympathetic and long suffering.

They left two sons and two daughters. The elder son Albert Charles (1837-1911), having run through his small inheritance, removed himself in 1865 to New York. He married at Brooklyn in 1868 Mary Elizabeth Wilkinson, a widow, who was a Roman Catholic, in which faith, accordingly, their children were brought up. They had three sons and a daughter; Alexander Frederick (b. 1870) who married and had a son; Charles Albert (b. 1872) who married but had no children; Orlando Henry (b. 1874) who married and had a son and daughter; and Ada Jane, who married. Albert Charles died at 363 18th Street, Brooklyn, on 23 Sep. 1911. Contact was maintained with Charles till about 1932, but was then lost and the present whereabouts of any living descendants of Albert Charles is unknown.

T.J.W.'s elder daughter Isabella Louisa (1839-1925) married in 1864 Francis Samuel Riddle, and had four daughters, two of whom married and left descendants. His younger daughter Ada Jane (1847-1935) was married twice, first in 1873 to William Jordan Peters (d. 1884), a solicitor's clerk, of Bristol and later of Fishponds, Gloucestershire; secondly in 1895 to George Richardson (d. 1914), a fishmonger of Cardiff. Of the first marriage there were three daughters, who all married and left issue.

The Wagner male line was continued by T.J.W.'s second son, Orlando Henry (1843-1909), to the reason for whose first name reference has been made above. He was educated at Christ's Hospital, worked for a short time in a shipbroker's office and then became an assistant master at the Christ's Hospital junior school at Hertford. It was here that he met his first wife Eliza (Cheek) (1846-1876), whom he married in 1866 at St. George's Hanover Square. Her father, Nathaniel Cheek (1819-1853), had been a butcher in Hertford and dying aged 30 had left a widow, Eliza (Green) (1815-1913) with a son aged four and two daughters of whom Eliza was the elder. He left his widow, however, tolerably well provided for and this and her strength of character made her the firm centre of the family when her daughter died and her son in law Wagner fell, as will be seen, on evil days. She lived to be 97 and is yet remembered well by her great-grandson A.R.W.

The Cheeks in the two previous generations were publicans and retail brewers in the town of Hatfield near Lord Salisbury's gates,[8] having come there from Little Berkhampstead, not far away, about 1790. John Cheek (1757-1812) had married Sarah (1755-1823) daughter of William Montague (1728-1788), a tailor of Aylesbury, whose ancestry can be traced back six generations on a yeoman line in neighbouring Waddesdon to a William Mountague living there about 1540. Their possible Norman origin and remote connection with the baronial Montagu family are discussed by A. R. Wagner in *English Genealogy* (3rd ed. 1983, p. 62). The son of John Cheek and Sarah, Nathaniel Cheek (1788-1832), publican and retail brewer of Hatfield, married Mary Anne (Pratchett) of a family who were Lord Salisbury's tenants at Birchwood Farm on the Hatfield Estate and publicans and gardeners in Hatfield. Eliza (Green) Cheek (1815-1913) was the daughter of George Green (1788-1875), a boot and shoe maker of Aylesbury, of Hertford and later of 87 High Street, Shoreditch.

As an assistant master at Christ's Hospital, Hertford, O. H. Wagner (1843-1909) was soon made Assistant Steward and was promised the reversion of the Stewardship; but in 1878, when the Steward retired, another man was appointed. "There is very little doubt", his son wrote, "that this treatment ruined my father's life as it deprived him of a position for which he was particularly fitted and led him into a situation which demanded qualities which he did not possess".

In 1864 Simpkin, Marshall published *A Chronological Key to ancient and Modern History Compiled from the Best Authorities by Orlando Henry Wagner (M.C.P.) (Assistant Master, Christ's Hospital, Hertford)*. A copy of this slim work was presented in September 1865 to the Rev. A. D. Wagner "with the compiler's comp[ts.]". A volume of his poems, *Lee-Side Musings*, is inscribed "Henry Wagner. From the Author. 1 April 1876." By Eliza (Cheek) O.H.W. had two sons (one of whom died in infancy) and three daughters. She died in 1876 and in 1877 he married secondly Louisa (d. 1916) daughter of William Heald of Sleaford, Lincolnshire, and had two more sons.

In 1878, failing to be appointed to the Stewardship of which he had long done the work and to which he believed he had a moral right, O.H.W. left Christ's Hospital. "He then started a first class Preparatory School in Cheriton Road, Folkestone. After struggling for some years the numbers began to increase and he moved into a house specially built for a School in Westbourne Gardens. Here the School continued to flourish and he soon had forty boys. In 1884 financial troubles began to press and though the School should have been a paying concern my poor father", his son and namesake wrote, "handicapped by lack of capital and a notable weakness for finance was unable to make both ends meet and after vainly

158

struggling was declared bankrupt in 1888. The foolish creditors disbanded the School—their only valuable asset and we moved to Rutland House—Upper Grosvenor Road Tunbridge Wells with a nucleus of ten pupils."

"After two years my father gave up entirely and retired with my stepmother and the two younger boys to Sleaford and henceforth I and my three sisters made our home with my dear Grandmother Mrs. Cheek of Hertford. My father continued at Sleaford for some years in very poor circumstances and then through the influence of my brother in law Alec Parkes he came to London to help and finally to manage the business of Adams & Parkes Clerical & Medical Agents. In 1902 this business also came to an unfortunate end, and my father retired to Baldock [Hertfordshire]. In March 1905 he had a stroke and he was practically never able to walk again. He died after a short illness on March 8th 1909 and was buried in Baldock cemetery."

His three daughters married husbands in comfortable circumstances. The second, Ida Mary (1872-1948), was the first to be married in 1892, to Septimus Alexander Parkes (d. 1903), youngest son of Charles Parkes, chairman of the Great Eastern Railway. The eldest, Leila Catherine Kellock (1869-1918), married in 1898, as his second wife, her first cousin once removed, Dr. John James Powell (1857-1905) of Weybridge, Surrey. The third, Ethel Adela (1874-1954), married in 1899 Dr. Lysander Maybury (d. 1957) in Southsea. All left children. The sons of the second marriage, Albert Charles Leonard Wagner (1878-1971) and Caspar Henry Granville Wagner (1880-1916) settled and married in Alberta, Canada, respectively at Calgary and Medicine Hat. Caspar returned to fight in the war of 1914 and was killed at Beaumont Hamel. Albert had a son and daughter who have both married and had issue.

The eldest son of O.H.W., his namesake Orlando Henry Wagner (1867-1956), was born at the home of his grandmother, Mrs. Cheek, Montagu House, Hertford. "At the age of six", he records, "I went to a small Dame's School kept by a Miss Kingston, at the age of seven I went to the Hertford Grammar School and on Dec[r] 8th 1875, the day after I was eight, I entered Christ's Hospital—Hertford. Here I remained for two years and in January 1878 I went to the London School [Christ's Hospital]: There I remained till Dec[r]. 1883. I was a Senior Deputy Grecian for some time but I unfortunately just missed becoming a Grecian.[9] We were of course living at Folkestone and my father rather unwisely—perhaps however for financial reasons—kept me at home for a year. Beyond reading for the Oxford Local exams which I passed with honours—(being among the first 20 in Greek), I did very little except enjoy myself but no doubt the year of idleness in the bracing air of Folkestone was good for me. In January 1885 I went to Sir Anthony Browne's School Brentwood Essex, of which the Head Master—The Rev. J. H. Newnum was an old friend and colleague of my father."

"While at Brentwood I tried several times for Scholarships at Oxford, but I was not successful although I only just missed one at Trinity. In October 1886 I went up as an undergraduate to Worcester College—Oxford.[10] I passed 'Smalls' & Mods in my first year and started to read Honour Theology—At the end of my second year in July 1888 financial troubles came on my father and I was unable to return to Oxford. I therefore acted as assistant master in the School at Tunbridge Wells till Dec[r] 1889 when my kind cousin Henry Wagner offered to send me back to Oxford for a year to finish my course. I therefore went back in

Jan^ry 1890 and passed the three necessary groups & took my B.A. degree in Decr 1890."

"I then took a mastership at St. Helens School Dublin where I remained two terms only as I found the distance too great. In Septr 1891 I went as a master to St. Leonards School where I remained till July 1894. After one term at an Army Crammers at the Oaks—Upper Deal I took a mastership at Arden House Henley in Arden which belonged to my dear friend Mrs. Bicknell. I remained here till Mrs. Bicknell's sudden death in April 1899. In the meantime I had met [the words are addressed to his son] your dear mother (whose father—The Rev. G. E. Bell was Vicar of Henley in Arden) and we had become engaged."

"In May 1894 I went as Scholarship Master to Windlesham House, Brighton which was owned by Mrs. Scott Malden. After a short time I became Head Master. In the meantime Mr. Henry Wagner had offered me the necessary capital to buy a School and after a rather weary search I decided to go into partnership with a man at St. Leonards and therefore resigned my post at Brighton in July 1900. The St. Leonards School proved a swindle, so I was glad to be able to go to act as Head Master of Arden House for a term owing to the illness of my friend Oswald Nelson."

Henry Wagner had taken an interest in his young second cousin once removed, the younger Orlando, since the days when he used to invite him as a Blue Coat boy at Christ's Hospital, London (1878-1883), to No. 13 Half Moon Street. Henry's doubts about the progeny of his great-uncle Anthony, cannot, however, have been lessened by the bankruptcy of the latter's grandson, the elder Orlando, in 1888 and his continued efforts to do what he could for this latter's son must be seen as a tribute to the boy's own qualities.

At this point one may interpolate this note which O.H.W. made later.
"Certain Obstacles encountered.
Owing to scarlet fever at a critical time I missed by one place becoming a Grecian and so left at 16 years of age. I then wasted over a year educationally at home, but I did pass the Oxford Local & so obtained exemption from Responsions. This was not realised by me, when I went to Oxford and my first Tutor, Mr. Pope was too idle to get the facts & I therefore did not take Honour Mods as I should have done, but for no earthly reason was booked for Hon. Theology. My father's financial troubles compelled me to miss my 3rd year and so all chance of an Honours degree and also the almost certain captaincy of College Soccer and Lawn Tennis. My mastership at St. Leonards School—a second rate affair was a mistake & so was my partnership at Ancaster House. On the other hand my year at Folkestone was very good for my health and helped me to form some valuable lifelong friendships. My time too at Arden House gave me valuable training in a first class School and also enabled me to meet my dear wife."

We now return to O.H.W.'s narrative. "In Jany 1901 I took a mastership at Pencarwick School Exmouth. Here I spent a very pleasant year with J. H. H. Copleston and in Jany 1902 I entered into partnership with the Rev. F. Burrows at Ancaster House Bexhill on Sea. There were about 20 boys and fine School buildings and there seemed no reason why the venture should not prove a success. I soon found however that Mr. B. was a most inefficient Schoolmaster and very lazy and the victim of a very serious failing[11] which absolutely prohibited success.

160

Moreover his wife, a well meaning and hard working woman, proved quite impossible to work with owing to her interfering ways, and after a miserable year during which I worked very hard with the unhappy consciousness that it was all in vain, I was fortunately able to dissolve the partnership and after long negotiations the natural honesty of Mr. Burrows triumphed over his wife's shiftiness and I was able to regain the bulk of my capital about Octr 1902."

"At the same time I accepted a private tutorship with Col. Robinson of Stanhill Court, Charlwood Sussex, Mrs. Robinson being a daughter of the great sugar manufacturer—Sir H. Tate the founder of the Tate gallery. Here I spent two very happy terms, my pupil Ted being a very nice boy, and the whole family kindness itself. In May 1903 I went for a term to my friend J. C. Thomson of Ickwell Bury, Biggleswade. I helped in the work there and at the same time did a certain amount of Inspection work for the Board of Education. I also did some private tuition for Mrs. Gribble of Henlow."

"While at Biggleswade I heard of a School for sale at 28 Alfred Place West[12] and after some negotiations with the owner W. Hatch I eventually bought it. The house was a most unsuitable one[13] but the connection though small seemed sound and we hoped that hard work would enable us to work it up into a flourishing concern. Your dear Mother and I were married on Septr 1st 1903 and after a short honeymoon in Paris we started our first term at Alfred Place West."

This was probably written soon after A.R.W.'s birth in 1908. A few years later O.H.W. added the following. "We began with thirteen boys and continued to increase slowly but steadily but in June 1906 when we had reached twenty-three we moved to a larger and more suitable house at 90 Queen's Gate. Here the numbers increased rapidly and we were soon quite full with forty five. On Septr 6th 1908 you [Anthony Richard Wagner] were born & your sister Rosalind on May 3rd 1911."

This narrative could be somewhat amplified and continued from a school diary which O. H. Wagner kept from September 1903 to April 1931, when he retired, and from "A Summary of Old Diaries" of a more personal nature running from 1893 to 1936. Among other matters he regularly notes the friends who entertained him, the places where he took holidays and the plays he saw; in earlier years also his football, cricket and lawn tennis activities and the private theatricals he took part in, for he had a natural aptitude for most games and for acting.

It was on the 28th of September 1895, when a master at Arden House, that he first met his future wife Monica (1878-1971) one of the daughters of the Rev. George Edward Bell (1833-1924), Vicar of Henley in Arden. The pedigree of this family is known back to Robert Bell of Adderstone Hill House, Bamburgh, Northumberland, whose son Robert (1673-1725) of Easington Grange in Belford, describes himself in his will as gentleman. Thomas Bell (1702-1790) succeeded his father, this Robert, at Easington Grange, a farm in a beautiful situation on Budle Bay opposite Holy Island. But his son Robert (1745-1821) established himself at 4 Albion Street, Hull as a sperm chandler, oilman and shipowner. He prospered and acquired a country house (Wincolmlee House) at Sutton in Holderness. His younger son Thomas (1786-1851) succeeded to his business and was father of the Vicar of Henley in Arden.[14]

The vicar's own life had been varied, for, his father dying when he himself was only seventeen, he joined a party of young men going out to Australia to dig gold in 1852. A letter dated in January 1853 from Richmond near Melbourne gives his impressions. He was "inclined to think that I have been foolish to leave England, & I shall be rejoiced when the day again comes that will see me deep in the study of Sophocles & Aeschylus and other friends now on the shelf". Accordingly he came home and took tutorships until he had raised enough money to go up to Oxford in 1860 to St. Alban's Hall. He took his B.A. degree in 1863 and then took orders. As curate at Princes Risborough, Buckinghamshire, he married a doctor's daughter there in 1865. He became Vicar of Henley in Arden in 1876 and so remained till 1914. Of his four sons and eight daughters, two daughters died young. Two of the sons had some success as authors. Robert Stanley Warren Bell (1871-1921) as "Warren Bell" wrote school stories and was editor of a boys' magazine *The Captain* and John Keble Bell (1875-1928) was a journalist, editor, playwright, dramatic critic and light novelist, writing as "Keble Howard".

In 1964 Monica (Bell) Wagner printed a book, *My Memories*, in which she tells a vivid story of her life. She tells how she first met Orlando Wagner, when he had come to teach at Arden House, at a dance at Beaudesert Park, Mr. H. R. Heatley's school. This was in 1895 when she was 17. He asked her to dance without having been introduced and she replied stiffly, "I am afraid I have no dances left." After that she met him intermittently and at a concert at Arden House she was requisitioned to accompany him when he sang comic songs. They went for occasional bicycle rides together (O.H.W. notes this in 1897) and he for walks with her and her younger sisters. One of these averred that an approach by Orlando to his future parents in law received the answer, "No, Monica can do better than marry a penniless schoolmaster."

In 1897-8 Monica Bell had a happy year in London at the Royal College of Music. In 1898 Orlando notes her return to Henley, "Many bike rides with M." and "Dance at Vicarage". Then she stays with Powell cousins at Weybridge for the Regatta, and "We are now really engaged except for parental acknowledgments." On her twenty first birthday the 13th of May 1899 "M & I are publicly engaged." But financial stringency delayed their marriage till the first of September 1903. In 1899 Monica had joined her brother Bob (R. S. Warren Bell) at a flat in London and in 1900 took on the running of competitions for *The Captain* which he edited. One of the winners she spotted was P. G. Wodehouse, who became a regular contributor.

Mention has been made already (p. 159) of Henry Wagner's offer to Orlando of capital to buy a school and his successive frustrating attempts to find the right one. He records receipt of "a preliminary cheque for £1,000" in 1901. Henry, however, thought Orlando's marriage improvident—as perhaps was to be expected of Orlando's father's son—and declined to meet his bride. But he did not even now sever all communication, as Monica thought he had, for in 1907 Orlando recorded "Call Cousin Henry at his request & explain Baldock situation [p. 158]. He will help but only through me", and again in 1909, when Orlando senior died, "Cousin H. very kind in helping". In this year also Henry proposed Orlando as a director of the French Hospital (p. 140) and made a present of £50 to Orlando's infant son, Anthony Richard (born 6 September 1908) "and A. calls to thank him". Later that year Henry gave Orlando the mourning ring which Melchior Wagner (1685-1764) had worn for his wife Mary Anne (Teulon) (1691-1742). In January 1910, moreover, Orlando had taken his half brother

Bertie (p. 158), over from Canada on a visit, to see Henry.

These, however, were but pale preliminaries to what occurred on the 4th of May, 1910, when, Orlando records, "Cousin Henry calls with James Michell and makes Monica's acquaintance & goes over house. This finally heals the breach which he caused by his mistaken attitude to my marriage. Monica received him very kindly & tactfully and he evidently appreciated it. We all owe much to the good offices of James Michell."

Monica too recorded this occasion. "Seven years had passed since our marriage, and the school was flourishing even beyond our hopes when one afternoon as I was sitting in the study and Anthony, aged two, was playing on the floor, the parlourmaid announced Mr. Henry Wagner and Mr. James Michell. The Rev. James was staying with his Cousin Henry at 13 Half Moon Street and had said to him: 'You know you have nothing against that young couple in Queen's Gate. They have made good and you ought to go and see them'."

"The parlourmaid's unexpected announcement was naturally a great surprise to me. I must admit that my feelings were not unmixed with resentment at the way Orlando had been ignored for so long by Cousin Henry, and I immediately mounted my high horse and became frigidly polite. I asked the maid to tell Mr. Wagner, who was occupied with his class upstairs, that Mr. Henry Wagner was here, and a most astonished Orlando appeared. I suggested that possibly his cousin and Mr. Michell would like to see the school, and when they came down from their inspection—Cousin Henry wreathed in smiles—there was coffee awaiting them (Cousin Henry never drank tea). This visit was the first of many, and he would frequently come to supper with us on Sunday nights, having first been to service at St. Augustine's Church, which was opposite Number 90. From that day on his interest in us increased with the years."

In 1911 Henry gave Orlando Melchior's inlaid box and in 1912 the Family Bible (p. 146). On the 1st of August 1912 Orlando and Monica "go to Switzerland to stay with Cousin H. at Grimentz and Zinal" and stay till the 24th. On the 4th of January 1913 Orlando goes with Henry to stay at Sierre & Vermala to see Henri Savioz,[15] returning on the 13th, staying the night at Dijon. In 1913 he records that "Cousin Henry forms habit of coming regularly to supper on Sunday evenings". On the 13th of May 1918 "Cousin H. gives M. jewelled watch". From the 30th of May to the 27th of June he allowed Orlando's children and their nurse to stay at 7 Belvedere Terrace, Brighton, when in quarantine for mumps. And on the 29th of July Cousin Henry signs his new will at Lloyd's". This was at Lloyd's Bank, St. James's Street, and by this will Henry made Orlando his residuary legatee. On the 1st of August Orlando went to Brighton with Henry and stayed till the 8th. In 1921 "Cousin Henry is taken ill at Brighton and never comes back to London again. I gradually have to take more charge of his affairs & go to Brighton to see him as frequently as possible."

On 28 April 1924 "Sir Charles Holmes & Mr Collins Baker come to 13 Half Moon Street and select a dozen pictures which Cousin Henry is presenting to the National Gallery, where they now hang [p. 143]. A grateful letter from Lord Curzon follows. June 12. Present five pictures to Alpine Club for Cousin Henry. 3 Elijah Waltons—1 E. J. Donne 1 Blampied."

" June 17th Cousin Henry having given me a power of attorney, has a small operation which is quite successful and his mental powers which have shown

163

periodical signs of weakness greatly improve. Cousin Henry presents all his Huguenot papers [p. 140] to the French Hospital in two cupboards specially made for the purpose.

"Nov. 9th. I take cheque for £200 to Rev. H. H. Jones St. Johns Carlton Hill from Cousin Henry for church schools." This is a sample of the kind of thing Orlando was constantly doing for Henry at this time. On the 26th of December "I go to Brighton. Cousin Henry decides that I am to dismantle 13 Half Moon St. and try to dispose of the lease."

In 1925 Henry allowed Orlando and Monica to present a picture and cross from his collection to Henley in Arden church in memory of Monica's father. In January 1926 "Anthony comes to Brighton for the night & Cousin H. tips him £5." In April "in response to a wire from Nurse Cameron I go off to Brighton and find Cousin Henry very ill. He passed away peacefully at 11.40 on April 24th. No words will express all I owe to the dear old man, but I did my best to acknowledge my debt and did all I could for him in the last ten years of his life. He left me his residuary legatee and many responsibilities which I have carried out to the best of my ability." "He was taken to St. Martin's Church on Ap. 26th. A Requiem Service was held at 6 o'c. On Ap. 29th he was buried in his father's grave in Brighton Cemetery at 3 o'c. after service at St. Martin's taken by the Bishop of Chichester, Archdeacon Hoskyns , Vicars of Brighton & St. Martin's & Rev. C. C. Inge. Thousands of people attended R.I.P."

From the first moment in 1903 Orlando Wagner's day school never looked back. He took boys from the age of six to ten, after which they would be sent to boarding preparatory schools, and for the special advantages it had to offer his school in South Kensington was ideally placed in these years when so many leading members of the professional classes lived within easy reach. His school diary summarizes each term's events and gives the school order. In 1903 there were three classes of 5, 4 and 4. At the end of 1932 there were seven, of 9, 10, 10, 11, 8 and 13. This last, the junior class, for once broke Orlando's rule of never having more than 12 boys in one class. This rule helped to make possible the close individual attention to each boy which he believed was ideally needed at this age. This and his great gifts as a teacher with minutely conscientious attention to detail gave him his phenomenal success as a schoolmaster.

Edward Boyle (later Lord Boyle of Handsworth), whom he thought almost if not quite the ablest boy he ever taught, wrote a tribute to him which he allowed Monica Wagner to print.[16] "Mr. Wagner", he wrote, "was such a charming and kindly man—he had just about the most winning smile of anyone I have ever known—that it was easy to overlook his sure skill and quality as a teacher. For he certainly was a great teacher . . . What was his secret? I think that above all it was his insistence on accuracy, and on his pupils gaining a real grasp of the concepts with which they were dealing . . . I come back to Mr. Wagner's charm and his humour. I have never known anyone get more pleasure out of an amusing situation . . . It is now nearly thirty years since I left Wagner's, but I am conscious that there is not one of my teachers to whom I have owed quite so much." In a foreword to the same book he wrote to Monica Wagner,[17] "You were an integral part of Wagner's and no headmaster's wife can ever have been more popular. How vividly I remember the singing class you took on Friday mornings—you would not allow us to join in unless we could sing audibly and *in tune*; you were insistent on this and how right you were. What I used to enjoy most of all was the way you harmonized the scales by ear—in fact, your playing was one of the first things that awakened my lifelong pleasure in music."

Monica wrote[18] that "Orlando worked for many hours after the boys left at 4 p.m. He was his own secretary and accountant, and sent out a weekly report on every boy." The move from Alfred Place West (now Thurloe Street) to 90 Queen's Gate in 1906 had been made possible by a legacy of £500 to Monica from her great aunt Eliza (Hester) widow of George Borwick. Till 1921 the Wagner family lived at 90 Queen's Gate over the school, but then moved to a flat near by at 4 Sussex Mansions, Sussex Place (now Old Brompton Road). In 1930 Orlando took a partner, J. W. Rowlands, and himself moved from South Kensington to Spencer House, Park Side, Wimbledon Common. He had kept on Henry Wagner's Brighton house, 7 Belvedere Terrace, till this time, but it was now let and so remained until it was sold in 1955. In 1933 Orlando retired from the school, which was taken over by Mr. Rowlands, and Mr. E. J. Lefroy. In 1934 he bought for Monica Spencer Cottage, Minchinhampton, Gloucestershire. In 1936 he left Spencer House and moved to 68 Trafalgar Square, Chelsea, the name of which was shortly afterwards changed to Chelsea Square. In 1955 this house was made over to his son Anthony and Orlando and Monica moved to a flat, 40 Melton Court, South Kensington, which was their home until his death in 1956 and hers in 1971.

Among Orlando's interests in retirement was the Incorporated Association of Preparatory Schools of which he was a Council member from 1924 to 1942 and chairman in 1930. He became a governor of his old schools Brentwood and Christ's Hospital and an Almoner and eventually Chairman of the Education Committee of the latter. He was chairman of the trustees of the French Protestant Church in Soho Square and, as has been mentioned already, a Director of the French Hospital. His Oxford College, Worcester, gave him especial pleasure by making him a member of Senior Common Room. As a chairman of committees he had the valuable gift of keeping proceedings short and to the point but offending nobody.

His son, Anthony Richard, entered the College of Arms as Portcullis Pursuivant in 1931 and was Garter King of Arms from 1961 to 1978. He has married and has a daughter and two sons. Orlando's daughter, Rosalind Monica, is married to the Right Honourable Sir Melford Stevenson, Justice of the High Court from 1957 to 1979 and a Privy Councillor since 1973. They have a daughter and son. A brief account of the family "The Wagners of Brighton and their connections", with a pedigree, was contributed by A. R. Wagner to the *Sussex Archaeological Collections* (Vol. 97), in 1960.

NOTES

Chapter 1. Wagners of Goldberg, Coburg and London (*Pages 1 to 13*)

1. *Ratsprotokolle*, Coburg, B.35, ff. 85 & 92.
2. W. A. Shaw, *Letters of Denization and Acts of Naturalization for Aliens in England and Ireland 1701–1800*, Huguenot Society Publications, Vol. XXVII, 1923, p. 93.
3. The diary of John Evelyn, ed. E. S. de Beer, Vol. IV, Oxford, 1955, pp. 548, 565, 568.
4. P.R.O., L.C. 3/63 p. 174.
5. This descended through Melchior's daughter Ann Paillet to her descendant Dr. Rooke, who gave it to Mary Ann Wagner (1791–1868), who gave it in 1868 to Henry Wagner.
6. Staatsarchiv Coburg, Bestand Altere Justizbehörden Nr. 146 fol. 1–2.
7. It was really in 1750, cf. T. D. Kendrick, *The Lisbon Earthquake*, 1956, 5, 11, 17, 20.
8. 1758.
9. Memoir of Melchior Seymour Teulon, *The Methodist Magazine*, June 1808.
10. Henry Wagner, "The Huguenot Refugee Family of Paillet", *Miscellanea Genealogica et Heraldica*, New Series, III, 321–3:*BN. 19–20. Emma Rooke was a daughter of High Chief Naea by Fanny Young Kekeloakalani, a daughter of John Young, a British sailor, and sister of Grace, wife of Dr. Rooke. Her only child, Albert Edward Kauikeaoule (1858–62) was a godson of Albert Edward, Prince of Wales. Milton Rubincam, "America's Only Royal Family. Genealogy of the former Hawaian Ruling House", *National Genealogical Society Quarterly*, June 1962, Vol. 50, pp. 79–92.
11. Anthony Wagner, *Pedigree and Progress*, 1975, pp. 242, 265.
12. Henry Wagner, "Jackson of London", *Miscellanea Genealogica et Heraldica*, New Series, Vol. IV, p. 74; and "Pedigree of Smith of Westminster and Dry Drayton, Co. Cambridge", ib. pp. 61–4. Dr. Smith's son and namesake was Dean of Christ Church 1824–31.
13. *Part One South of Piccadilly*, Vols. XXIX & XXX, 1960, pp. 322–426, Plates 50–1, 55, 204–228, Plan Pocket B. For 93 (later numbered 89) Pall Mall see p. 364, Pl. 204, Plan Pocket B.
14. P. 323.
15. P. 337.
16. A. M. W. Stirling, *The Ways of Yesterday*, 1930, p. 56.
17. *Memoirs of William Hickey*, ed. Alfred Spencer, Vol. II (1775–1782), 1918, p. 261.
18. Henry Wagner Collections, Catalogue, I. p. 2.
19. By Mr. Ralph Edwards and later by Mr. Michael Wynne of the National Gallery of Ireland, who inspected them in 1969.
20. Proved 30 Dec. 1796. P.C.C. 646 Harris.
21. Thomas Walley Partington, one of the Commissioners of the Lottery, sometime of Lincoln's Inn, died 8 March 1791 "at his house at Offcove [sic] in Sussex". (Gentleman's Magazine).
22. Henry Wagner, "Jackson of London", *Miscellanea Genealogica et Heraldica*, New Series, Vol. IV, page 74, and "Pedigree of Smith of Westminster and Dry Drayton, Co. Cambridge", Ibid. pp. 61–4. Samuel Smith's son and namesake was Dean of Christ Church 1824–31.
23. Charles James Feret, *Fulham Old and New*, 1900, Vol. II, p. 67.

Chapter II. London and Sussex: the Michells (*Pages 14 to 27*)

1. B.N. 115.
2. D.N.B.: John Nichols, *Illustrations of the Literary History of the Eighteenth Century*, Vol. IV. 1822, p. 867: *The Gentleman's Magazine*, Vol. LXIX, p. 1055: M. A. Lower, *The Worthies of Sussex*, 1865, pp. 229–30.
3. Nichols, loc. cit.
*BN = Henry Wagner's MS. "Book of Numbers".

4.   Letters in the possession of A. R. Wagner, dated 18 May 1835 from 8 North Parade, Bath. See also his sister's diary reference to this occasion p. 22 *supra*.

5.   V.C.H. Sussex, Vol. VII, p. 249.

6.   Henry Wagner, *Book of Numbers*, p. 103.

7.   J. G. Bishop, *Brighton in the Olden Time*, 1880, p. 112 n.

8.   *Thraliana, The Diary of Mrs. Hester Lynch Thrale*, ed. Katherine C. Balderston, Oxford, 1951, pp. 6, 414, 761. Sir Anthony Wagner has a letter from Mrs. Mostyn, daughter of Mrs. Thrale, to H. M. Wagner, which once enclosed an autograph of Dr. Johnson.

9.   BN. 116.

10.   GNQ. 120. GNQ = Henry Wagner's MS. "Genealogical Notes & Queries

11.   BN.

12.   GNQ. 118.

13.   GNQ. 118.

14.   BN. 31.

15.   GNQ. 98–9.

16.   GNQ. 125.

17.   BN. 117.

18.   GNQ. 124.

19.   His name came from his three godparents, Mrs. George Wagner, his grandmother, Henry Chicheley Michell, his uncle, and Mr. Neill Malcolm of Poltalloch.

20.   Henry Wagner's MS. *Genealogical "Notes and Queries"*, June 1862, pp. 87–8.

21.   *Burke's Landed Gentry*, Vernon-Wentworth of Wentworth Castle.

22.   GNQ. p. 88.

23.   BN. 37: GNQ. 129.

24.   GNQ. 120–1.

25.   BN. 37–8. Henry Wagner adds, "His grandson Malcolm W. it may be added, has now not only the taste, but is an accomplished musician." A.R.W. can confirm this, having heard Malcolm play in the late 1920's.

26   Henry Wagner (GNQ. p. 57) records "Shortly before Mr. Simpkinson, Dr. Heinrich Barth, the great African traveller, proposed to Emily. My Father used to know the Miss Griffins, when still spinsters, & living near de Rhams, at Winkfield—& Sir John Franklin also. Simpkinson, I think, left the Navy, because of some row with authorities abroad."

27.   "Pedigree of Majendie" [by Henry Wagner]. *Proc. Huguenot Soc.* Vol. IX. No. 3, 1912. "Pedigree of Guillemard" [by Henry Wagner]. *Miscellanea Genealogica et Heraldica*, New Series III, 388.
        Wesselowski, *The Genealogist*, New Series XII, 102.
        De Wesselow. The Marquis of Ruvigny, *The Plantagenet Roll of the Blood Royal*, Essex Volume, 1908, p. 275.
        The Rev. John Nassau Simpkinson (1817–1894), elder brother of Francis Guillemard Simpkinson, Curate of Hurstmonceux 1840–5, wrote the *Life of Rev. G. Wagner*, 1858.

28.   The Times, 24 Dec. 1906.

29.   Henry Wagner noted, GNQ. p. 122. "Had the Col. of the 5th retired, wh. the Duke wanted, in order that Lord Charles [Wellesley] might have the command, John Henry would not have left it." (?)

30.   Henry Wagner (GNQ. pp. 6–7) writes "Mr. Mossop, the elder of the brothers, who proposed to my aunt [Mary Ann Wagner or Ann Maria?] but never married, was Vicar of Cranbrook, near where Uncle Coombe was first Curate, & at whose house they used to meet. The younger brother had his fortune left him by a man, whose acquaintance he had made by accident, on a stagecoach, I think!" "Rev. John M[ossop] V. of Hothfield, got his fortune with his first wife, Miss Aynscombe, a connexion of P. S. Duval's."

31.   Clifford Musgrave, *Life in Brighton*. 1970, p. 282.

Chapter III.   The Rev. Henry Michell Wagner (*Pages 28 to 90*)

1.   Diary of Anne Elizabeth Wagner, 1815.

2.   Diary of Anne Elizabeth Wagner, 1816.

3.   22nd June 1819.

4. Letter of the 5th February 1821 from the Duchess of Wellington to H. M. Wagner.
5. Letter of the 17th November 1822.
6. Ibid.
7. Diary of H. M. Wagner, 13th August 1819.
8. Diary of H. M. Wagner, 29th April 1820.
9. Diary of H. M. Wagner, 19th July 1821.
10. Ibid.
11. Ibid.
12. 23rd November 1820.
13. Diary 5th July 1819.
14. Diary 6th July 1819.
15. Ibid.
16. Diary of H. M. Wagner, 4th March 1821.
17. 7th November 1821.
18. Diary of H. M. Wagner, 20th March 1823.
19. Ibid.
20. Letter to the Duchess of Wellington of the 21st October 1822.
21. Letter from the Duchess of Wellington to H. M. Wagner, 20th April 1823.
22. Letter from H. M. Wagner to the Duchess of Wellington, 26th January 1824.
23. Letter from H. W. Wagner to the Duchess of Wellington, 23rd January 1824.
24. Letter from H. M. Wagner to the Duchess of Wellington, the 23rd January 1824.
25. Letter to H. M. Wagner dated the 21st April and transcribed in his diary of the 4th May 1824.
26. Diary of the 1st June 1824.
27. Diary of H. M. Wagner, the 12th May 1824.
28. Diary of H. M. Wagner, 11th June 1824.
29. Diary of H. M. Wagner, 14th June 1824.
30. Diary of H. M. Wagner, 15th June 1824.
31. Letter of the 21st March 1825 from the Duke of Wellington to the Dean of Christ Church.
32. The Dean of Christ Church was H. M. Wagner's second cousin.
33. Letter (undated) from H. M. Wagner to the Duchess of Wellington.
34. Letter of the 18th October 1825 from the Duke of Wellington to H. M. Wagner.
35. Letter of the 12th December 1827 from the Duke of Wellington to H. M. Wagner.
36. T. W. Horsfield. The History, Antiquities and Topography of the County of Sussex.
37. J. A. Erredge. The History of Brighthelmston.
38. The chapel was rebuilt by Sir Arthur Blomfield in 1877–1882.
39. This bank defaulted in 1825.
40. St. Margaret's was demolished in 1959.
41. Whether this was J. S. M. Anderson or Robert Anderson it is difficult to say:
42. H. M. Wagner's Diary of the 28th November 1824.
43. Ibid. 29th November 1824.
44. Ibid. 30th November 1824.
45. Ibid. 1st December 1824.
46. Josiah Bateman. The Life of Henry Venn Elliott.
47. Letter of the 21st July 1824 from H. M. Wagner to the Duchess of Wellington.
48. Letter of the 8th December 1825 from the Duchess of Wellington to H. M. Wagner.
49. Diary of Ann Elizabeth Wagner, 14th December 1828.
50. Ibid. 17th September 1828.
51. Letter of the 28th November 1829 from Henry Wagner to the Duchess of Wellington.
52. Ibid. 28th Nov. 1829.
53. John Sawyer. The Churches of Brighton.
54. "The Churches of Brighton".
55. John Sawyer. The Churches of Brighton.
56. Quoted in John Sawyer's "The Churches of Brighton".
57. Ibid.
58. Brighton Herald. 20th October 1849.

59. Copy letter from H. M. Wagner to George Morgan in the Brighton Library.
60. Copy letter from H. M. Wagner to W. Clarke 1st Sept. 1858 in the Brighton Library.
61. Copy letter of 28th Jan. 1859 from H. M. Wagner to W. Clarke in the Brighton Library.
62. Letter of the 16th November 1855 from H. M. Wagner to the Marquess of Abergavenny. (Copy in Brighton Library).
63. H. M. Wagner to Dr. A. T. Gilbert 16th July 1856. Copy letter in Brighton Library.
64. H. M. Wagner to Sidney Gurney 17th January 1856. Copy letter in Brighton Library.
65. H. M. Wagner to Sidney Gurney, 17th Jan. 1856. Copy letter in Brighton Library.
66. Diary of Anne Elizabeth Wagner, 15th December 1835.
67. Diary of Anne Elizabeth Wagner, 16th December 1835.
68. Minutes of the Vestry, 17th December 1835.
69. Minutes of the Brighton Vestry of 23rd January 1840.
70. Minutes of the Brighton Vestry of the 22nd April 1841.
71. Minutes of the Brighton Vestry of the 26th October 1841.
72. Minutes of the Brighton Vestry of the 9th November 1841.
73. Stopford A. Brooke's Life and Letters of Frederick Robertson.
74. Diary of Anne Elizabeth Wagner, 14th May 1835.
75. Brighton Herald, 20th November 1841.
76. Brighton Herald, 27th November 1841.
77. Diary of Anne Elizabeth Wagner, 12th December 1832.
78. Brighton Gazette, the 27th January 1842.
79. Brighton Herald, 19th February 1842.
80. Brighton Gazette, 9th December 1847.
81. Minutes of the Brighton Vestry, 6th May 1847.
82. Ibid.
83. Minutes of the Brighton Vestry, 9th December 1847.
84. Brighton Gazette, 16th December 1847.
85. Minutes of the Brighton Vestry, 9th December 1847.
86. Minutes of the Brighton Vestry, 21st December 1847.
87. Minutes of the Brighton Vestry, 4th December 1851.
88. Minutes of the Brighton Vestry, 4th December 1851.
89. The Brighton Gazette, 11th December 1851
90. Ibid.
91. Brighton Gazette, 20th May 1852.
92. Brighton Gazette, 20th May 1852.
93. Brighton Gazette, 23rd September 1852.
94. Brighton Herald, 8th April 1854.
95. Letter of the 22nd June 1853, quoted in Stopford A. Brooke's Life and Letters of Frederick W. Robinson.
96. Letter of the 22nd June 1853, quoted in Stopford A. Brooke's Life and Letters of Frederick W. Robertson.
97. Frederick Arnold, Robertson of Brighton.
98. Ibid.
99. Sawyer. The Churches of Brighton.
100. Brighton Gazette, 25th October 1866.
101. Brighton Gazette, 25th October 1866.
102. Ibid.
103. Brighton Herald, 3rd November 1866.
104. Brighton Gazette, 25th October 1866.
105. Ibid.
106. Ibid.
107. Brighton Gazette, 25th October 1866.
108. Ibid.
109. Sawyer. The Churches of Brighton.
110. Sawyer. The Churches of Brighton.
111. Ibid.

112. Minutes of the Brighton Vestry, 14th November 1850.
113. Ibid.
114. Minutes of the Brighton Vestry, 14th November 1850.
115. Copy letter of the 13th February 1856 from H. A. Stattwood to H. M. Wagner in the Brighton Library.
116. Diary of H. M. Wagner, 16th December 1856.
117. Diary of H. M. Wagner, 26th November 1856.
118. Diary of H. M. Wagner, 1st December 1856.
119. Ibid. 2nd December 1856.
120. Ibid. 6th December 1856.
121. Ibid. 12th December 1856.
122. Diary of H. M. Wagner, 30th December 1856.
123. Ibid.
124. Frederick Arnold. "Robertson of Brighton".
125. Diary of Anne Elizabeth Wagner, 12th January 1834.
126. Brighton Gazette, 13th October 1870.
127. Copy letter of the 18th May from H. M. Wagner to Mrs. A. Harvey in the Brighton Library.
128. Ibid.
129. Will of H. M. Wagner.

Chapter IV. The Rev. George Wagner (*Pages 91 to 99*)

1. Augustus Hare, The Story of My Life.
2. Ibid.
3. J. N. Simpkinson. Memoir of the Rev. George Wagner.
4. Memoir of the Rev. George Wagner.
5. J. N. Simpkinson. Memoir of the Rev. George Wagner.
6. Ibid.
7. Ibid.
8. J. N. Simpkinson. Memoir of the Rev. George Wagner.
9. Ibid.
10. Ibid.
11. The Story of My Life.
12. Ibid.

Chapter V. The Rev. Arthur Douglas Wagner (*Pages 100 to 136*)

1. R. V. Ballard. The Sussex County Magazine, Vol. 13.
2. Yseult Bridges, "Saint with Red Hands?"
3. Brighton Gazette, 25th May 1865.
4. Brighton Gazette, 25th May 1865.
5. Brighton Gazette, 1st June 1865.
6. Brighton Gazette, 1st June 1865.
7. Brighton Gazette, 18th May 1865.
8. Brighton Gazette, 1st June 1865.
9. Ibid.
10. Letter of the 6th April 1890 from Lord Chief Justice Coleridge to W. E. Gladstone, quoted in "Saint with Red Hands?" by Yseult Bridges.
11. Yseult Bridges, "Saint with Red Hands?"
12. Ibid.
13. Letter on the 25th July 1865 from Gladstone to A. D. Wagner, Yseult Bridges "Saint with Red Hands?"
14. Letter of the 25th July from A. D. Wagner to Sir George Grey, Bernard Taylor "Cruelly Murdered".

15.   Letter of the 16th August 1865, A. D. Wagner to Gladstone, Yseult Bridges "Saint with Red Hands?"

16.   Ibid.

17.   Ibid.

18.   Letter of the 14th October 1880, Gladstone to Sir William Harcourt, Yseult Bridges "Saint with Red Hands?"

19.   Sawyer. "The Churches of Brighton".

20.   Sussex Daily News. !5th January 1902.

21.   Sussex Daily News, 15th January 1902.

22.   Ibid.

23.   Letter of the 7th September 1877 from Dr. R. Durnford to Dr. E. Pusey. Memoir of Richard Durnford by W. R. W. Stephens.

24.   Brighton Gazette, 11th December 1873.

25.   The Sussex Daily News, 15th January 1902.

26.   The Churches of Brighton.

27.   The Brighton Gazette, 10th September 1874.

28.   The Brighton Gazette, 10th September, 1874.

29.   Ibid.

30.   Letter of 7th September 1877 from Dr. R. Durnford to Dr. E. Pusey. Memoir of Richard Durnford by W. R. W. Stephens.

31.   Brighton Gazette, 6th May 1875.

32.   Ibid.

33.   Ibid.

34.   Letter of the 2nd September 1877 from Dr. E. Pusey to Dr. R. Durnford. Memoir of Richard Durnford by W. R. W. Stephens.

35.   Letter of the 7th September 1877 from Dr. R. Durnford to Dr. E. Pusey. Memoir of Richard Durnford by W. R. W. Stephens.

36.   Letter in the possession of the Vicar of St. Paul's church, Brighton.

37.   Ibid.

38.   Ibid.

39.   After his death, his half-brother, Henry Wagner, continued many of these contributions and in particular made himself responsible for completing the fittings of St. Bartholomew's and St. Martin's churches.

40.   He was also fond of presenting people with copies of a portrait of the Madonna Salus Populi Romani from the church of Santa Maria Maggiore in Rome.

41. A. D. Wagner. Parochial Sermons bearing on Subjects of the Day.

42.   Ibid.

Chapter VI. Henry Wagner (*Pages 137 to 145*)

1.   His cousins O. H. Wagner and A. R. Wagner followed this example.

2.   See p. 143.

3.   David Urquhart, 1805-1877. His son F. F. Urquhart Dean of Balliol, entertained at St. Gervais generations of Balliol men.

4.   BN. 61.

5.   Edna Healey, *Lady Unknown The Life of Angela Burdett-Coutts*, 1978.

Chapter VII.   The later Wagners (*Pages 146 to 165*)

1.   BN. 68.

2.   GNQ. pp. 99-100.

3.   BN. p. 68.

4.   A. R. Wagner, "The Powells of Devynock and Church Lawford", *Brycheiniog* (published by the Brecknock Society), Vol. X, 1964, pp. 29-37. The Glendower descent comes through Croft of Croft, Rudhall and Price of Brecon Priory.

5.   Inspired, perhaps, by that of Sir Watkyn Williams Wynn.

6.   Quoted by A. R. Wagner, *English Genealogy*, 2nd ed., 1972, pp. 209-10.

7. Recollections of Lady Georgiana Peel, 1920, pp. 210–11.
8. Their house, Greenaway, which had come down to O. H. Wagner, was sold by him in 1923 to the sitting tenant General Lindsay Lloyd.
9. As a Grecian, the equivalent of a Sixth Form boy, he would have remained at school till eighteen.
10. William Inge, then Provost of Worcester, was a cousin of Henry Wagner on the mother's side.
11. Drink.
12. South Kensington.
13. It Backed on to the Underground Railway, whose trains were then drawn by steam engines.
14. Some account of this family, "Papers of a middling family", by Anthony Wagner, was contributed to *Tribute to an antiquary*, ed. F. G. Emmison and R. Stephens, Essays presented to Marc Fitch, 1976. Robert Bell (1673–1735) married Elizabeth, daughter of George Wake, burgess of Berwick on Tweed, by Dorothy, daughter of Robert Clavering of Tilmouth, who brought royal and other interesting descents to his progeny.
15. Henry Wagner's former Swiss manservant, who became tubercular and was set up by Henry as a hotel keeper in the mountains.
16. *My Memories*, pp. 106–9.
17. Ib. p. 9.
18. Ib. p. 34.

INDEX

175

179